(CONSCA)

D1514708

La Nouvelle Agence
7, rue Corneille
75006 Paris

Consumer Capitalism

A volume in the series

Cornell Studies in Political Economy

edited by Peter J. Katzenstein

A full list of titles in the series appears at the end of the book.

Consumer Capitalism

Politics, Product Markets, and Firm Strategy in France and Germany

GUNNAR TRUMBULL

Cornell University Press

Ithaca and London

First published 2006 by Cornell University Press

Printed in the United States of America

Library of Congress Cataloging-in-Publication Data

Trumbull, Gunnar.
    Consumer capitalism : politics, product markets, and firm strategy in France and Germany / Gunnar Trumbull.
        p. cm. — (Cornell studies in political economy)
    Includes bibliographical references and index.
    ISBN-13: 978-0-8014-4382-4 (cloth : alk. paper)
    ISBN-10: 0-8014-4382-2 (cloth : alk. paper)
    1. Consumer protection—France.   2. Consumer protection—Germany.   3. Consumption (Economics)—France.   4. Consumption (Economics)—Germany.   5. Capitalism—France.   6. Capitalism—Germany.   7. Product management—France.   8. Product management—Germany.   I. Title.   II. Series.
    HC280.C63T78 2006
    381.3′40943—dc22   2005032280

Cornell University Press strives to use environmentally responsible suppliers and materials to the fullest extent possible in the publishing of its books. Such materials include vegetable-based, low-VOC inks and acid-free papers that are recycled, totally chlorine-free, or partly composed of nonwood fibers. For further information, visit our website at www.cornellpress.cornell.edu.

Cloth printing   10 9 8 7 6 5 4 3 2 1

CONTENTS

ACKNOWLEDGMENTS

Thankfully, books are not written alone, and I was fortunate to have extraordinary advisers. My greatest gratitude goes to Suzanne Berger, for her endless support, her thoughtful critiques, and her intellectual guidance. I also thank Peter Hall, Dick Samuels, and Nick Ziegler. They have been generous in their time and advice, and they have taught me what it means to be a citizen in an academic community.

Many other colleagues have taken time to comment on all or part of this manuscript. I would like to thank Rawi Abdelal, Regina Abrami, Steve Casper, Lars-Erik Cederman, Marie-Emmanuelle Chessel, Pepper Culpepper, Tom Cusack, Keith Darden, Orfeo Fioretos, Eugene Gholz, Michel Goyer, Bob Hancke, Matthew Hilton, Wade Jacoby, Peter Katzenstein, Jack Knight, Richard Locke, Isabela Mares, Jeremy Shapiro, David Soskice, Debora Spar, Sid Tarrow, Iselin Theien, David Vogel, Steve Vogel, and Lou Wells.

This book has received financial and research support from a number of organizations. Financial support has come from the Center for European Studies at Harvard University, the Industrial Performance Center at MIT, and the Harvard Business School. For their help in the field research portion of this project, I would like to thank David Soskice at the Wissenschaftszentrum für Sozialforschung in Berlin and Erhard Friedberg and Martha Zuber at the Centre de la sociologie des organisations in Paris. Additional support was provided by the American Institute for Contemporary German Studies, the German-American Center for Visiting Scholars, Harvard Business School's European Research Center, the Union fédérale des consommateurs, and the Institut national de la consommation.

Finally, I could not have finished this without the endless support and patience of my family. To my parents Betty and Jim, to my brothers Nat and Sam, and to my wife Seema.

Consumer Capitalism

CHAPTER ONE

The Rise of Consumer Capitalism

> New choices about consumption are not made at random. They
> conform to norms which guide behavior in every society. When the
> individual is uncertain about what choices are appropriate, he or she
> will look for guidance. . . . The real problem, therefore, is to explain the
> emergence, development, and elaboration of the various norms of
> consumption in society.
>
> —GIOVANNI SARTORI, 1991

Political science analysis of modern capitalism has focused on the institutions of national production and distribution. In the realm of production, researchers have argued that distinctive national configurations of supply-side institutions—labor, capital, supplier networks, corporate governance—induce producers to specialize in different product market strategies.[1] In the realm of distribution, scholars of the welfare state have drawn links between the degree and type of social transfer and the ways that labor and capital are deployed.[2] The goal of this

---

1. Andrew Shonfield, *Modern Capitalism: The Changing Balance of Public and Private Power* (Oxford: Oxford University Press, 1965); John Zysman, *Governments, Markets, and Growth* (Ithaca: Cornell University Press, 1983); David Soskice, *German Technology Policy, Innovation, and National Institutional Frameworks*, Discussion Paper FS I 96–319 (Berlin: Wissenschaftszentrum Berlin, 1996); Peter A. Hall and David Soskice, "An Introduction to Varieties of Capitalism," in *Varieties of Capitalism: The Institutional Foundations of Comparative Advantage*, ed. Peter A. Hall and David Soskice (Oxford: Oxford University Press, 2001); Wolfgang Streeck, "Lean Production in the German Automobile Industry? A Test for Convergence Theory," in *National Diversity and Global Capitalism*, ed. Suzanne Berger and Ronald Dore (Ithaca: Cornell University Press, 1996); and Michael Storper and Robert Salais, *Worlds of Production: The Action Frameworks of the Economy* (Cambridge, Mass.: Harvard University Press, 1997).

2. Gøsta Esping-Andersen, *The Three Worlds of Welfare Capitalism* (Princeton: Princeton University Press, 1991); Isabela Mares, *The Politics of Social Risk: Business and Welfare State Development* (Cambridge: Cambridge University Press, 2003); Jonas Pontusson, *The Limits of Social Democracy: Investment Politics in Sweden* (Ithaca: Cornell University Press, 1992); Margarita Estevez-Abe, Torben Iversen, and David Soskice, "Social Protection and the Formation of Skills: A

book is to introduce a third pillar—consumption—to the institutional analysis of modern capitalism. I argue that the institutions and regulations created in the post-war period to protect consumers exerted a systematic influence on the product strategies of consumers and producers through their impact on product information and product-related risk.

The unfettered marketplace, in which uncertainty rules and caveat emptor ("Let the buyer beware") dictates each consumer decision, has today virtually disappeared. Consumers have become the focus of intensive economic policymaking designed to protect them from the risks and disappointments of the market. The laws, regulations, and legal doctrines that swaddle today's consumer are relatively new. In most of the advanced industrialized countries, they trace their roots to a period of rapid new policy formation that started in the late 1960s and 1970s. In the context of growing consumer affluence that followed World War II, economic actors and policymakers came to reconceptualize the role of the consumer in society. Starting as an anonymous destination for manufactured goods, the consumer was reconceived as a coherent economic actor with a specific identity and rights. The transformation was rapid and dramatic. Today, arguably no other economic actor in the advanced industrial countries—not the investor, not the worker, not the welfare recipient—enjoys a more thorough set of legal and institutional protections than the modern consumer when he or she enters the corner store.

The institutions that make up the legal and regulatory framework of consumption today emerged from a broad reimagining of the very identity and status of the consumer in society. The transformation had three core elements. First, consumers came to be understood as a coherent social and economic interest group. The recognition of this group status was reflected in the rise of independent consumer associations, in the introduction of consumer advocacy bodies within the legislative and executive branches of government, and in the recognition of consumers as a legal class by the courts. Second, national governments dramatically reallocated the burden of product-related risk from consumers to producers. This shift emerged partly through regulatory policy, with the creation of robust product safety and recall standards, and partly through a revolution in legal doctrine of product liability law. Product externalities that had traditionally been borne by consumers suddenly became the responsibility of producers. Finally, public authorities intervened in the contractual relationship between producers and consumers. New laws, regulations, and legal standards forced producers to provide consumers with accurate and useful product information while monitoring contractual terms for product delivery, re-

Reinterpretation of the Welfare State," in *Varieties of Capitalism: The Institutional Foundations of Comparative Advantage,* ed. Peter Hall and David Soskice (Oxford: Oxford University Press, 2001); Peter Swenson, "Arranged Alliance: Business Interest in the New Deal," *Politics and Society* 25 (March 1997), 66–116; and Sigurt Vitols and Gregory Jackson, "Pension Regimes and Financial Systems: Between Financial Commitment, Market Liquidity, and Corporate Governance," in *The Varieties of Welfare Capitalism: Social Policy and Political Economy in Europe, Japan, and the USA,* ed. Bernhard Ebbinghaus and Philip Manow (London: Routledge, 2001).

pair, and replacement. Taken together, these three changes elevated the consumerist "value-for-money" agenda to a core government priority.[3]

These changes also initiated a shift in the orientation of modern capitalism. From the producer emphasis of government policies that had characterized the period of heavy industrialization, new sets of market rules emerged in the 1970s that looked to the consumer as the target and primary benefactor of both private industry and public policy. Private industry increasingly focused on consumer preferences as an input, both in new product design and in overall firm strategy. Public policy increasingly interpreted market regulation, ranging from competition policy to trade policy, in terms of its likely impact on consumers. The resulting set of economic institutions might be called "consumer capitalism": an organization of the political economy in which the institutionalized interests of consumers set the terms for government policy formation and for company-level product market strategies. This book traces the sources and impact of consumer capitalism as it emerged in France and Germany beginning in the late 1960s.

Market Failure and Product Choice

In order to understand the role of demand-side institutions in advanced capitalism, we must start by considering how supply-side institutions have been seen to influence producer strategies. The most thorough account of this impact has been elaborated by researchers studying national varieties of capitalism. At the heart of the "varieties of capitalism" framework lies a basic challenge facing all firms: to capture value from new investments. New investment in worker training may be lost if skilled workers are poached by other firms.[4] New long-term capital investments may be undervalued by stockholders interested in short-term returns.[5] In the varieties of capitalism approach, institutional constraints on labor and capital can help to overcome such impediments. Researchers working in the varieties of capitalism framework have tended to divide nations into one of two camps based on how they organize the supply side of the economy. Producers operating in coordinated production systems—including bank financing, formal worker training, collective bargaining, worker participation in management, dense cross-shareholding, and stable

3. The terms "consumerist" and "consumerism" are used in this text to describe an organized consumer movement acting to achieve new rights and protect interests, not merely a collection of individual consumers engaged in individual purchasing.

4. Labor poaching has been seen as a major obstacle both to technical training programs and to the promotion of company-specific skills. Pepper D. Culpepper, *Creating Cooperation: How States Develop Human Capital in Europe* (Ithaca: Cornell University Press, 2003); and Soskice, *German Technology Policy.*

5. John Zysman, *Governments, Markets, and Growth;* Sigurt Vitols, "Are German Banks Different?" *Small Business Economics* 10/2 (1998): 79–91; and Richard Deeg, *Financial Capitalism Unveiled: Banks and the German Political Economy* (Ann Arbor: University of Michigan Press, 1999).

supplier relations—enjoy a competitive advantage in products that are highly engineered and exhibit incremental innovation. Germany and Sweden are examples of coordinated production systems. Producers operating in liberal production systems—including equity finance, liquid labor markets, weak labor organization, liberal corporate governance, weak cross-shareholding, and shifting supplier relations—enjoy a competitive advantage in products that are highly innovative but of relatively low quality. Britain and the United States are paradigmatic liberal market economies.[6]

Implicit in the supply-side focus of the varieties of capitalism analysis is an assumption that consumers will purchase the kinds of products favored by national configurations of labor and capital. Yet 90 percent of all new products fail in their first two years on the market.[7] This suggests that consumer choices also play a role in determining producers' product strategies. In order to succeed, new investments must be recognized and valued by consumers. Successful investment in highly engineered goods—the sort of investment favored by coordinated market economies—requires that customers recognize and favor the higher quality that results. Successful investment in radically new kinds of products—the sort of investment favored by liberal production systems—requires that consumers be willing to take on the risks of being early adopters of new products. This means that institutions that mediate product risk and product information matter to consumer choice. National legal and regulatory institutions that indemnify consumer risk or subsidize access to useful product information can enable producers to capture the value of specific kinds of new investments. Attention to the management of product-related risk and information therefore offers a strategy for expanding the insights of vari-

6. David Soskice, "Divergent Production Regimes: Coordinated and Uncoordinated Market Economies in the 1980s and 1990s," in *Continuity and Change in Contemporary Capitalism,* ed. Herbert Kitschelt, Peter Lange, Gary Marks, and John D. Stephens (Cambridge: Cambridge University Press, 1999); Peter Hall and David Soskice, "Introduction," in *Varieties of Capitalism;* and Wolfgang Streeck, *Social Institutions and Economic Performance: Studies of Industrial Relations in Advanced Capitalist Economies* (London: Sage Publications, 1992). A broad range of studies focused on individual countries and industrial sectors has reinforced the view that these supply-side institutions have influenced the product strategies of domestic firms. See, for example, Wolfgang Streeck, "Lean Production in the German Automobile Industry? A Test for Convergence Theory," in *National Diversity and Global Capitalism,* ed. Suzanne Berger and Ronald Dore (Ithaca: Cornell University Press, 1996); Steven Casper, "National Institutional Frameworks and High-Technology Innovation in Germany: The Case of Biotechnology," in *Advancing Socio-Economics: An Institutional Perspective,* ed. J. Rogers Hollingsworth, Karl H. Müller, and Ellen Jane Hollingsworth (Oxford: Rowman and Littlefield, 2002); Culpepper, *Creating Cooperation;* Bob Hancké, *Large Firms and Institutional Change* (Oxford: Oxford University Press, 2002); Michael Storper and Robert Salais, *Worlds of Production: The Action Frameworks of the Economy* (Cambridge: Harvard University Press, 1997); Andrew Tylecote, "Corporate Governance and Product Innovation: A Critical Review of the Literature," research project conducted for the European Commission (May 1999); and Sigurt Vitols, "The Origins of Bank-Based and Market-Based Financial Systems: Germany, Japan, and the United States," in *The Origins of Nonliberal Capitalism: Germany and Japan,* ed. Wolfgang Streeck and Kozo Yamamura (Ithaca: Cornell University Press, 2001).

7. "New Product Launches: Nine out of 10 set to Fail," *ACNielsen News Release,* 23 May 2000 (http://www.acnielsen.com/news/european/uk/2000/20000523.htm).

Note: Solid arrows show causal links proposed by the varieties of capitalism literature; dashed arrows describe the impact of consumption institutions.

Figure 1.1   Supply-side and demand-side determinants of product choice

eties of capitalism research to incorporate the demand-side constraints of modern consumer capitalism. Figure 1.1 presents the hypothesized impact of supply-side and demand-side institutions on product choice.

Researchers of firm strategy have noted the role that consumer preferences play in influencing the product strategies of producers. In general, producers pay close attention to the exogenous demands of consumers.[8] Systematic differences in consumer demand can therefore form the basis for national competitiveness. "Across-country variation in demand characteristics . . . generates a parallel variation in product types," writes Bruce Kogut, professor of international management at INSEAD. "The cumulative capabilities of firms, developed in response to their home markets, provide the competitive basis for expansion overseas, yet at the same time, limit the feasible range of products."[9] Another close observer of business strategy, Michael Porter, reports similar findings: "A product's fundamental or core design nearly always reflects home market needs."[10] Most of Porter's examples are environmental: hilly terrain in Japan benefited the microwave communications sector, Finnish firms led in icebreakers, Swiss firms excelled in tunneling equipment. Nonetheless, both agree that systematic differences in national consumer preferences can drive domestic firms toward success in different product market segments.

How might the institutional context of consumption influence consumer preferences? Economist George Akerlof was among the first observers to point out the impact of market institutions on consumer choice. In his 1970 article "The Market for Lemons," Akerlof showed that price information alone does not provide adequate

8. Erik Von Hippel, "The Dominant Role of Users in the Scientific Instrument Innovation Process," *Research Policy* 5 (1976): 212–39; Ben-Åke Lundvall, "Innovation as an Interactive Process: From User-Producer Interaction to the National System of Innovation," in *Technical Change and Economic Theory*, ed. Giovanni Dosi (London: Pinter, 1988), 349–69; Paul L. Robertson and Tony F. Yu, "Firm Strategy, Innovation, and Consumer Demand: A Market Process Approach," *Managerial and Decision Economics* 22 (2001): 183–99; and Lars Bo Jeppesen and Måns J. Molin, "Consumers as Co-developers: Learning and Innovation outside the Firm," *Technology Analysis and Strategic Management* 15/3 (2003): 363–84.

9. Bruce Kogut, "Country Capabilities and the Permeability of Borders," *Strategic Management Journal* 12 (1991): 36.

10. Michael E. Porter, *The Competitive Advantage of Nations* (New York: The Free Press, 1990), 87.

information for a market to function efficiently.[11] He described the situation of a used car lot in which the consumer does not know the actual condition of the cars on sale and the salesman has no interest in providing the consumer with accurate information. In this used car setting, Akerlof argued, buyers have to assume that they are being cheated—that the cars they see have hidden flaws. In the absence of accurate information, even used cars *without* hidden flaws would nonetheless sell below their real value, since consumers would assume them to be flawed. Given this market context, car owners wishing to resell used cars are therefore likely to do so only if their cars are already damaged in some way. This situation of adverse selection generates a smaller used car market than would exist in the presence of better information. It also leads to a preponderance of hidden defects in the cars that are available in the market, the "market for lemons."[12]

More recently, scholars have noted that the dynamics identified by Akerlof in the second-hand market also characterize markets for new products. "When information is asymmetric about the nature and the quality of goods," writes political scientist Robert Boyer, "markets have a difficult task to perform."[13] Two sorts of difficulties in particular arise. First, accurate product information is necessary for making purchasing decisions regarding the hidden quality of new products.[14] For example, a producer may opt to invest in new research in order to achieve superior quality. But if this additional quality cannot be recognized by the consumer, he or she will resist paying the higher price for it, and the company's investment will have been lost. Alan Sykes, a researcher in economic law, summarizes the situation succinctly: "If purchasers do not know and cannot cheaply ascertain the quality of what they buy, willingness to pay will not adjust to improvements in quality."[15] This challenge was perceived not only by academics but also by practitioners at the time the new consumer protections were being introduced. Hans Friedrichs, Germany's economics minister during its period of consumer protection activism, wrote in 1974:

---

11. George Akerlof, "The Market for Lemons," *Quarterly Journal of Economics* 84 (1970): 488–500.

12. This kind of information asymmetry in the market for used cars helps to explain why new cars fall dramatically in value once they leave the dealership. It is the reputation of the manufacturer and their liability for the car, reinforced by warranties and lemon laws, that ensure that the price of a new car reflects its true value. Once the car has left the lot, the information and legal protection that accompany a new car are lost. The combined value of this information and legal protection is, in principle, exactly equal to the immediate drop in value of the newly purchased automobile.

13. Robert Boyer, "The Variety and Unequal Performance of Really Existing Markets: Farewell to Doctor Pangloss?" in *Contemporary Capitalism: The Embeddedness of Institutions*, ed. J. Rogers Hollingsworth and Robert Boyer (Cambridge: Cambridge University Press, 1997), 78.

14. Stefan Strassner, *Verbraucherinformationsrecht* (Saarbrücken, Germany: ÖR Verlag, 1992), 132–35; and Manfred Adams, "Ökonomische Analyse des Gesetzes zur Regelung des Rechts der Allgemeinen Geschäftsbedingungen (AGB-Gesetz)," in *Ansprüche, Eigentums- und Verfügungsrechte: Arbeitstagung des Vereins für Socialpolitik, Gesellschaft für Wirtschafts- und Sozialwissenschaften in Basel 1983*, ed. M. Neumann (Berlin: Duncker and Humblot, 1984), 664.

15. Alan O. Sykes, *Product Standards for Internationally Integrated Goods Markets* (Washington, D.C.: Brookings Institution Press, 1995), 37.

"When the consumer makes a purchasing decision without satisfactory market information, competition becomes practically meaningless. What is the benefit . . . of a better refrigerator, when the consumer cannot recognize it before the purchase?"

The second, related difficulty for consumers concerns the risks associated with radically new kinds of products. Consumers need credible assurances that radically innovative products will work and also not be overly dangerous.[16] If consumers are unable to assess the level of risk they will face from a new product, they are likely to avoid potentially risky kinds of innovation. As one observer noted about drug development: "Until a new product has established a reputation based on experience in using it, consumers are likely to balance the attractiveness of a potentially superior product against the risk of adverse characteristics not apparent when it is introduced."[17] For producers, this means that investment in certain kinds of radical innovation will remain unattractive until consumers believe that that such products are safe.

Traditionally, producers employed private means to manage consumer information and perceptions of risk. Strong brands, combined with product-specific advertising campaigns, helped to reassure consumers. Customers buying from a reputable producer would assume that new products could be trusted and that higher prices corresponded to higher levels of quality. This began to change in the 1970s, as the advanced industrialized states started managing consumer markets through new public policy initiatives. Product-related risk became a focus of government activism; innovations included new safety regulations, elaborate product standards, and lower burdens of product liability and recall. Product information was also increasingly managed by the state through product labeling, advertising restrictions, and state-funded comparative product testing. By the mid-1980s, the management of consumer concerns about product quality and safety—issues that had once been the sole concern of individual producers—had largely been taken over by public authorities.

With the state's assumption of responsibility for product risk and information came government control over the institutional context in which consumers made their purchases. How countries deployed these new institutions differed significantly. As the research presented below demonstrates, Germany responded by emphasizing product information as a means of consumer protection, on the grounds that this offered consumers a better basis for judging for themselves the qualities of products. France responded differently, implementing national policies that worked to insulate consumers from product-related risk. Their goal was not to inform consumers but rather to protect them from potential risks associated with new products. Both of these approaches offered an effective response to the challenges facing consumers. But they also created different market rules within which domestic consumers would learn to operate.

16. Horst Albach, *Culture and Technical Innovation: A Cross-Cultural Analysis and Policy Recommendations* (Berlin: Walter de Gruyter, 1994), 282.

17. Raymond A. Bauer, "Risk Handling in Drug Adoption: The Role of Company Preference," *Public Opinion Quarterly* 25/4 (Winter 1961): 546.

The impact of this difference has been to favor certain kinds of company investment over others in each country. The French approach allowed consumers to buy any product without concern about product-related loss, since government policies formally protected them against loss from any product. Hence even radical new products seemed attractive. Moreover, because French consumers did not need to rely on information about products to protect themselves—not that they tended to have ready access to such information in the first place—they were less discerning about incremental improvements in engineering or design. In this way, the French approach to consumer protection favored a product strategy that emphasized novelty and discouraged investment in incremental quality improvement. For Germany, the emphasis on consumer information as a means of protection had the opposite effect. Because German consumers relied heavily on product knowledge to ensure that they were buying safe and useful products, they also learned to discern incremental advances in design and engineering. By contrast, their reliance on information caused them to avoid radically new kinds of products for which reliable assessment remained difficult. This bias had implications for German producers, who disproportionately invested in the sorts of design and engineering improvements that German consumers favored. The result was to create two different dynamics of market competition in the two countries. Whereas German companies competed along dimensions of quality and engineering, French producers faced competition primarily in innovativeness and style.

The impact of the new consumerist discourse was not limited to policies specifically designed to address consumer protection. Under the influence of the growing public policy emphasis on consumer welfare, a new paradigm of government administration, one grounded on the idea of maximizing the consumer interest, came to dominate policy formation across a broad range of traditional government economic policies. Issues as diverse as the setting of industry standards, pricing, competition policy, and trade policy—all came to be reconceived during this period as matters of consumer protection. In each case, the final test of regulatory effectiveness was the impact, not on the producer, but on the consumer. Moreover, as the new areas of regulation came to be reinterpreted in terms of the consumer interest, they too espoused the particular consumer identity that had emerged during the consumer struggles that had taken place between the late 1960s and the early 1980s.

The Consumer as Citizen

Modern consumer protections emerged rapidly in France and Germany over roughly a ten-year period beginning in the early 1970s. One indication of the scale and speed of the change can be seen in the explosion of legislative projects designed to protect consumers. In Germany, 25 consumer-related laws were adopted between the end of the war and 1970; from 1970 to 1978, an additional 313 new laws were adopted.[18] In France, the number of consumer-related laws and ministerial decrees grew from a total of 37 in 1970 to 94 by 1978.[19] One observer of French consumer policy estimated that, by 1990, the country had adopted 300,000 product- and consumer-related legal and regulatory texts, with 1,000 new texts being added each year.[20]

Economists analyzing government regulation during this period proposed that new government regulations conform to the interests of industry.[21] Given the concentrated interests of business and the diffuse interests of the general public, business should be able to shape government regulation to suit its own interests. "As a rule," wrote George Stigler in 1971, "regulation is acquired by the industry and is designed and operated primarily for its benefit."[22] New consumer regulations should, in this view, reflect prior industry interests. The problem with this productionist view is that industry interests in France and Germany were virtually identical. In both countries, industry saw some benefits to greater consumer information and common standards but deeply feared government intervention as a means of achieving it. In fact, business in both France and Germany initially opposed nearly every regulatory and legal project that, taken together, would constitute the emerging national consumer protection regimes. Thus, from the productionist view, it is difficult to account for the rise of consumer protection at all, let alone the systematic differences that developed between France and Germany.

The postwar rise of national consumer protection policies needs to be understood instead as the political incorporation of consumers as a legitimate set of interests in society. Consumer protection in this view was not simply a regulatory issue but rather the formation of a new basic right of citizenship. In this sense, consumer protection can be seen as the most recent stage in the progressive accretion of citizenship rights. T. H. Marshall, in his historical analysis of the welfare state, argued that basic citizenship rights emerged in waves over time: civil rights such as free speech and contractual and property rights became incorporated in the eighteenth century; political rights to participate in selecting and running the government became incorporated in the nineteenth century; social rights to economic welfare became incorporated in the early twentieth century. Drawing on Marshall's approach, this analysis treats consumer protections as constituting a new extension of national cit-

18. Willi Laschet, "Verbraucher Sind Auch Kunden," in *Verbraucherpolitik Kontrovers*, ed. Hartwig Piepenbrock and Conrad Schröder (Cologne, Germany: Deutscher Instituts-Verlag, 1987), 60.

19. "La protection et l'information des consommateurs: des progrès décisifs," *Les Notes Bleues* (Paris: Service de l'information du ministre de l'économie et des finances, 1978), 14–20.

20. Alexandre Carnelutti, "Consommation et société," *Revue française d'administration publique* 56 (1990): 585.

21. George J. Stigler, *The Citizen and the State: Essays on Regulation* (Chicago: University of Chicago Press, 1975); and Sam Peltzman, "Toward a More General Theory of Regulation," *Journal of Law and Economics* 19 (August 1976): 211–40.

22. George Stigler, "The Theory of Economic Regulation," *Bell Journal of Economics and Management Science* (Spring 1971): 3.

izenship rights, one that emerged in the second half of the twentieth century and rapidly spread to all advanced industrial democracies.

The emerging consumer citizenship of the 1970s corresponded to Marshall's account in three respects. First, consumer protection had become, as Marshall defined citizenship, a "uniform collection of rights and duties with which all men—noble and common, free and serf—were endowed by virtue of their membership of the society."[23] Second, the new consumer protections were supported by a dedicated set of government institutions that served to uphold the associated rights. Third, the emerging citizenship was based on a model or idea of the perfect consumer citizen. Marshall writes, "societies in which citizenship is a developing institution create an image of an ideal citizenship against which achievement can be measured and towards which aspiration can be directed."[24] Politicians, consumer activists, and business leaders in the 1970s all came to see consumer protections as a new dimension of citizenship in Marshall's sense.[25] Their views were elaborated in a broad debate that reconceptualized the consumer's status in society, in a new set of institutions to protect the consumer in her new status and in an ideal vision of the modern consumer that emerged from a process of political contestation.

In France and Germany, the principle of consumer citizenship emerged first through a set of broadly written manifestos addressing consumers as a group with specific economic and political rights. In Germany, first in 1971 and then again in 1975, the government issued a "Report on Consumer Politics." In these, it advocated a menu of consumer rights, among them access to better information, more favorable contractual conditions for consumers, and the incorporation of consumer representatives into Germany industry's standardization board.[26] In France, the push for a general statement of consumer rights was initiated by the country's consumer groups. In 1975, eleven national consumer associations laid out a public charter of consumer rights that included, among others, access to information and training.[27] These were later taken up by the new secretary of state for consumption in 1976 as well as by the opposition Socialist Party.

Nor were such proposals limited to France and Germany. International organizations at this time were propounding similar consumer doctrines. In 1973 the Consultative Assembly of the Council of Europe adopted a "Consumer Protection Charter," which, while lacking any enforcement, would inform national debates on

23. T. H. Marshall, *Citizenship and Social Class* (London: Pluto Press, 1992), 8.

24. Marshall, *Citizenship*, 18.

25. Historian Matthew Hilton notes a similar Marshallian interpretation of consumer rights in Britain. Matthew Hilton, *Consumerism in Twentieth-Century Britain: The Search for a Historical Movement* (Cambridge: Cambridge University Press, 2003), 284.

26. *Verbraucherbericht*, BT-Drucksache 6/2724 (1971); *Verbraucherbericht*, BT-Drucksache 7/4181 (1975); Bernd Biervert, Wolf F. Fischer-Winkelmann, and Reinhard Rock, *Verbraucherpolitik in der Marktwirtschaft* (Hamburg: Rowohlt, 1978), 64; and Marianne Schatz-Bergfeld, *Verbraucherinteressen im Politischen Prozess: Das AGB-Gesetz* (Frankfurt am Main: Haag and Herchen, 1984), 62.

27. "Pour une loi-cadre de la consommation," propositions presented by the national consumer organizations, April 1975.

consumer protection.[28] The European Community's Council of Ministers approved a "First Preliminary Program for Consumer Protection" in April 1975 and a second in 1981.[29] These defined five consumer rights: protection of health and safety, protection of economic interests, redress, information and education, and representation in government decisions. Most of these initiatives traced their inspiration to the 1962 Consumers' Bill of Rights announced by U.S. President John F. Kennedy a decade earlier.

These political programs made consumers the focus of intensive institution-building. New groups, agencies, and committees were established both within the government and in civil society. Within governments, the new agencies worked with consumers to represent their interests in the legislative process. These bodies are far too numerous for a full accounting, but some of the early agencies are worth noting. In 1960, France created the National Consumption Committee (CNC) to give consumers input into regulatory issues and, in 1976, a secretariat of state for consumption. This position was transformed in 1981 under François Mitterrand into a full Ministry of Consumption.[30] Germany created a Consumer Advisory Board (Verbraucherbeirat) to the government in 1972. Any new legislation that might have an impact on consumers was referred to this board and was required to include a description of its probable impact.[31] While Germany did not create a full Ministry of Consumption, as France did, both the Economics Ministry and the Agriculture Ministry created their own consumer protection subcommittees. These different bodies and agencies each represented consumer interests to the government and distributed information about government projects to consumers.

Consumers also created and joined activist groups outside of government. In France, for example, funds given by the government to independent consumer groups grew from 3.7 million francs in 1970 to nearly 40 million francs in 1980.[32] In Germany, government funding to consumer groups grew nearly as rapidly, from 12 million DM in 1970 to 48 million DM in 1980.[33] Membership in these organizations also increased rapidly, as grass-roots mobilizations drew in an active rank and file. This period of consumer activism also saw a rapid growth in the popularity of consumer groups oriented to publishing the results of comparative product tests.

28. Ibid., 93–94.

29. Thierry M. Bourgoignie, "Consumer Law and the European Community: Issues and Prospects," in *Integration through Law: Europe and the American Federal Experience,* ed. Thierry Bourgoignie and David Trubek (Berlin: Walter de Gruyter, 1987), 103.

30. Maria Aubertin and Edmond Robin, *Les nouveaux rapports entre producteurs et consommateurs* (Paris: La mission à l'innovation, 1981).

31. "Zwei DGB-Vertreter im Verbraucherbeirat," *Informations Dienst,* Bundespressestelle des Deutschen Gewerkschaftsbundes (11 August 1982), 1–2.

32. Unless otherwise indicated, values are given in local currency. While exchange rates during the 1970s and 1980s fluctuated, one German deutschmark equaled approximately two French francs in the early 1970s and three French francs by the early 1980s. One dollar equaled approximately five French francs over most of this period.

33. Jürgen Bornecke, *Handbuch der Verbraucherinstitutionen* (Bonn: Verlag Information für die Wirtschaft, 1982), 230.

Germany's Stiftung Warentest was established in 1966, and France's two product testing publications *Que choisir?* and *50 millions de consommateurs* were first circulated in 1961 and 1970, respectively. Circulation of these magazines grew rapidly in the 1970s: from less than a hundred thousand subscribers in either France or Germany in 1970 to over six hundred thousand subscribers in each country by 1980. The U.S. publication, *Consumer Reports,* had earlier origins but still grew from a circulation of one million in 1966 to two million by 1976.[34] The rapid growth in subscriptions for these product information journals suggests that the new consumerism was not merely imposed from above but was also founded upon a genuine discontent among the consuming public.

The emergence of consumers as a coherent interest group in society led to a substantive policy shift in relation to consumers. Most importantly, it redefined the kinds of risks and costs that consumers should face in the marketplace. At its root, the new consumerism signaled a move away from the traditional legal principle of caveat emptor. In what amounted to a dramatic reallocation of property rights, the financial burden of negative product externalities, which for much of the age of industrialization had fallen on consumers themselves, was reassigned to the companies that designed, manufactured, and distributed dangerous goods. This reallocation marked a turnaround in national regulatory approaches to risk. The rise of the welfare state in advanced industrial countries had been grounded in the principle of social insurance. Its goal was to externalize the risks associated with the production process, spreading them across the entire society. By limiting the burden of liability that producers faced, social insurance served as a spur to industrial innovation.[35] The new consumerist agenda reversed that logic, forcing companies to internalize the risks emerging from the products they produced. This reversed responsibility signaled the beginning of an era of corporate accountability that was until then virtually unknown.

Legal reforms in the 1970s increased the liability of producers for product-related damage or loss. This transformation occurred through the reinterpretation of the principles of product liability law in the courts. At stake was the responsibility of producers whose products caused consumers harm—yet whose behavior could not be proved to be negligent. In the 1968 avian flu case (*Hühnerpestfall*), courts in Germany reversed the burden of proof on producers.[36] This meant that producers were henceforth required to prove that they had not acted negligently in producing a defective product. In France, the courts found for the first time in 1973 that the presence of a defective product implied producer negligence—even if the negligence itself could not be proven. In both cases, the findings gave consumers

34. Norman Isaac Silber, *Test and Protest: The Influence of Consumers Union* (New York: Holmes and Meier, 1983), 123.

35. David Moss, *Without Fail: Government as the Ultimate Risk Manager* (Cambridge: Harvard University Press, 2002); and Isabela Mares, *The Politics of Social Risk: Business and Welfare State Development* (Cambridge: Cambridge University Press, 2003).

36. In this case, a German chicken farmer successfully sued the manufacturer of the vaccine used by his veterinarian when a tainted dose killed his chickens.

reasonable legal recourse if they suffered losses due to design or manufacturing error.[37]

The recognition that consumers constituted a coherent interest in society with distinctive rights was also reflected in new laws granting consumer organizations the right to pursue collective legal action against producers or distributors. French consumer groups were granted the right to pursue collective lawsuits in 1973. German consumer associations were also permitted to pursue class action suits, although only in particular areas of law. The primary targets of the procedure in Germany were unfair advertising, for which group action suits were allowed in 1965 and the use of unfair contract terms, allowed in 1976.[38] In the United States, the consumer movement had largely financed itself through fees arising from successful consumer class action lawsuits. In France and Germany, consumer groups were unable to support themselves from class action lawsuits because of legal restrictions on punitive damages and group compensation, but these cases nevertheless offered a highly public forum in which consumer groups could promote themselves and their goals.

There is one final sense in which the emergence of consumer protections has paralleled past instances of citizenship expansion: despite the similar paths described above, systematic national policy differences also emerged. As with the extension of labor rights and welfare benefits in previous periods, the new rights of consumer citizenship diverged in ways that reflected the domestic politics of specific countries. If the citizenship model is correct, we should not be surprised to see systematic national differences. Historically, such divergences have characterized each stage of the expansion of national rights of citizenship.

For the sake of clarity, it is important to differentiate this approach to consumer citizenship from two other ways in which the idea of citizenship has been invoked with respect to consumers. First, consumption has often been perceived as a tool for extending existing citizenship rights to excluded segments of the population.[39] Liz-

37. Warren Freedman, *International Products Liability* (Buffalo, N.Y.: William S. Hein, 1995), 77; Roland N. McKean, "Product Liability: Implications of Some Changing Property Rights," in *The Economics of Legal Relationships*, ed. Henry G. Manne (St. Paul, Minn.: West Publishing Company, 1975), 261; Jules L. Coleman, *Risks and Wrongs* (Cambridge: Cambridge University Press, 1992), 412–13; Geneviève Viney, "The Civil Liability of Manufacturers in French Law," in *Comparative Product Liability*, ed. Christopher J. Miller (London: British Institute of International and Comparative Law, 1986), 77; and Agnès Chambraud, Patricia Foucher, and Anne Morin, "The Importance of Community Law for French Consumer Protection Legislation," in *European Consumer Policy after Maastricht*, ed. Norbert Reich and Geoffrey Woodroffe (Dordrecht, The Netherlands: Kluwer Academic Publishers, 1994), 218.

38. Comité européen de coopération juridique, *Réponses des gouvernements aux questionnaires relatifs aux systèmes judiciaires ou parajudiciaires pour la sauvegarde des droits des consommateurs et relatifs aux clauses de contrats abusifs en cas de vente, de location-vente et de location ayant pour objet des biens mobiliers corporels* (Strasbourg, France: Conseil d'Europe, 1974); and Bernard Seillier, *Rapport fait au nom de la commission des affaires sociales sur le projet de loi relatif à la pharmacie d'officine*, report 257, second ordinary session (Paris: Sénat, 1991).

39. David Vogel, "Tracing the American Roots of the Political Consumerism Movement," in *Politics, Products, and Markets*, ed. Andreas Føllesdal, Michele Micheletti, and Dietlind Stolle (New Brunswick, N.J.: Transaction Press, 2003), 87; and Lawrence Glickman, "Buy for the Sake

abeth Cohen, for example, has argued that women and African-American consumers in the United States used the power of organized consumption to pursue core components of political and social citizenship: "When African Americans launched the modern civil rights movement by demanding equal access to public sites of consumption in the 1940s and 1950s after being shut out during World War II, or when they protested their exclusion from the society's general prosperity . . . during the 1960s, the supposedly free markets of the Consumers' Republic helpfully provided a measure of their segregation, a justification for action, and a strategy of protest."[40] Organized consumer actions have helped excluded classes of citizens translate purchasing power into political power.

A second, related strand of research has focused on the duties that modern citizens bear in their roles as consumers. This approach has focused on responsible consuming, taking into account externalities of consumption, including environmental impact and labor rights. Socially conscious consumerism has deep roots, most notably in the carefully controlled consumerism of utopian socialism and in the consumer cooperative movements of the late nineteenth and early twentieth centuries.[41] Recent research on ethical consumption has focused on consumer boycotts, green consumption, fair trade movements, and consumer morality.[42] Some have also noted a darker side of socially conscious consumption: a desire to avoid what might be called "unethical" consumption, which singles out specific minority groups for economic discrimination.[43] This body of research reminds us that consumption decisions have real consequences and that modern consumerism embodies not just new rights but also broader responsibilities.

The research presented in this book casts its net more narrowly. It focuses specifically on affluent, or "value-for-money," consumerism. Leaving ethical issues aside, it is about government intervention in the contractual relationship between the consumer and the producer to ensure that the private interests of consumers are met. It seeks to understand the manner in which consumption became politicized, regu-

---

of the Slave," in *Au Nom du Consommateur,* ed. Alain Chatriot, Marie-Emmanuelle Chessel, and Matthew Hilton (Paris: Découverte, 2005).

40. Lizabeth Cohen, *A Consumer's Republic: The Politics of Mass Consumption in Postwar America* (New York: Knopf, 2003), 406.

41. Ellen Furlough, *Consumer Cooperation in France: The Politics of Consumption, 1834–1930* (Ithaca: Cornell University Press, 1991); and Noel Thompson, "Social Opulence, Private Asceticism: Ideas of Consumption in Early Socialist Thought," in *The Politics of Consumption: Material Culture and Citizenship in Europe and America,* ed. Martin J. Daunton and Matthew Hilton (Oxford: Berg, 2001).

42. Margaret Levi and April Linton, "Fair Trade: A Cup at a Time?" *Politics and Society* 31/3 (2003): 407–32; Michele Micheletti, *Political Virtue and Shopping: Individuals, Consumerism, and Collective Action* (New York: Palgrave Macmillan, 2003); Flore Trautman, "Pourquoi boycotter? Logique collective et expressions individuelles: Analyse de systèmes de représentations à partir du cas Danone," *Le mouvement social* 207 (2004); and Paulette Kurzer, *Markets and Moral Regulation: Cultural Change in the European Union* (Cambridge: Cambridge University Press, 2001).

43. Cheryl Greenberg, "Political Consumer Action: Some Cautionary Notes from African American History," in *Politics, Products, and Markets,* ed. Micheletti and Stolle, 67–74.

lated, and institutionalized. The contention is that an explicitly political account of national consumer protection as a right of citizenship can illuminate current issues and challenges of consumer capitalism. From a practical perspective, it should shed light on the nature of current policy conflicts over product safety standards and trade liberalization. From a theoretical perspective, it offers to broaden our understanding of modern capitalism by integrating the institutions of consumption into our current analysis of capitalist production.

Consumer Identity and Models of Protection

The political incorporation of the consumer in France and Germany took the form of a struggle in which the very identity and role of the consumer became the focus of political discourse and contestation. Was the consumer an economic actor, on a par with producers and suppliers? Was the consumer a social actor, to be insulated from the risks inherent in market transactions? Or was the consumer simply another societal interest group, capable of representing its own interests through mobilization and negotiation? Depending on how one answered such questions, different policy solutions appeared more or less attractive. The result was that struggles over individual regulatory policies in France and Germany were waged in the context of a broader debate over the social and economic status of the modern consumer. At the heart of the politics of consumer protection was a contest over ideas. The winners and losers of these struggles would set the terms on which the new consumer protections were selected and designed.

The central role that ideas played in consumer policymaking had important consequences. First, it meant that countries tended to adopt *systematic* approaches to consumer protection. Across a wide variety of policies—from truth in advertising to consumer contracts—specific regulatory responses in each country reflected a general underlying strategy of consumer protection. Functioning like ideal types, they provided a common framework that dictated how often disparate areas of regulatory policy should be addressed. Second, the different capabilities of consumer and producer groups to advocate their own preferred ideas about the consumer led to systematically *different* national strategies over regulating consumption, differences that would have implications on how consumers and producers made product choices.

France pursued an approach that focused on insulating consumers from product-related risk. In this *protection model*, consumers came to be viewed as an endangered group in society needing defense against dangerous or low-quality products. This conceptualization of the consumer drew in part on the experience of the United States, where consumer protection policies of the 1960s and 1970s had placed a high burden of responsibility on producers. In this model, the consumer was seen foremost as a political actor, a consumer citizen. Consumer protection in this view was understood as a basic societal right that the government itself had a mandate to ensure. Solutions therefore focused on creating and enforcing new consumer rights, on insulating consumers from market risk, and on mobilizing consumers to protect what they perceived to be their political rights. Regulatory approaches under this protection model therefore tended to focus on the end goal of consumer safety rather than on intermediate procedural goals. This *protection model* also tended to encourage private law approaches to enforcing individual consumer rights. A strict standard of product liability, for example, was a hallmark of this protection model.

Germany pursued a different approach that focused on providing consumers with adequate information. This *information model* viewed the consumer as an economic actor in society operating on a par with other economic actors, including manufacturers, employers, suppliers, and workers. This view of the consumer drew in part on the consumer protection policies developed by the Labour government in Britain in the 1960s that emphasized the need for better consumer information.[44] In this information model, the consumer was understood to have a purely economic status. Consumer problems were therefore interpreted in terms of market failure rather than as a breakdown in political rights. The rhetoric of the *information model* stressed consumer sovereignty (*Der Kunde ist König,* "the customer is king"), which meant that consumers always controlled the final purchasing decision. Solutions to consumer grievance therefore focused on overcoming information asymmetries between producers and consumers and on reinforcing the mechanisms of quality production in order to offer consumers a better set of market options. Regulatory responses under this model tended to focus on ensuring fair business procedures and on encouraging industry self-regulation.

The notion that ideas about group identity and causality can set the trajectory of policy formation is not new.[45] What is interesting in the case of French and German consumer policy is that these ideas became the focus of domestic political struggles over the best approach to consumer protection. Producers preferred to view consumers as economic actors—another part of the production chain that also included suppliers and retailers—since this implied that they might legitimately bear their share of product-related risk. Consumer groups preferred to view consumers in other ways: either as an organized interest group capable of negotiating directly with producers or as a special category of political citizenship deserving administrative relief. In this sense the contest to determine the direction of consumer protection in the two countries took the form of a struggle for the very identity of the consumer.

Ideas about the social identity of the consumer played a central role in shaping consumer protection policies in France and Germany in part because most of these areas of regulation were entirely novel. Product liability law, the regulation of con-

44. Matthew Hilton, *Consumerism in Twentieth-Century Britain: The Search for a Historical Movement* (New York: Cambridge University Press, 2003).

45. Luc Boltanski and Laurent Thévenot, *De la justification: Les économies de la grandeur* (Paris: Gallimard, 1991); Pierre Muller, "Les politiques publiques comme construction d'un rapport au monde," in *La construction du sens dans les politiques publiques: Débats autour de la notion de referential,* ed. Alain Faure, Gilles Pollet, and Philippe Warin (Paris: Éditions L'Harmattan, 1995); and Deborah Stone, "Causal Stories and the Formation of Policy Agendas," *Political Science Quarterly* 104 (1989).

sumer contracts, product labeling standards—all of these policies emerged as comprehensive consumer protections only in the 1970s. Without strong historical legacies or institutional path dependencies, the terms of these debates had to be elaborated without a defining ideological or cognitive context. As a result, the discussions that surrounded each of these specific policy areas formed a composite arena of discourse in which the broader issue of the consumer's role in modern society could be disputed and, eventually, resolved.

Not all consumer policies were new. Indeed, some were extremely old. But such was the strength of the consumerist debate that even longstanding economic policies tended to be reinterpreted in the 1970s in terms of the logic of consumer protection. The regulation of product price and quality, for example, had been employed by governments since the Middle Ages both to support producer guilds and to restrict hoarding and fraud during periods of scarcity. These were some of the earliest regulatory tools for organizing and policing producers. Beginning in the 1970s, however, policies concerning price and quality regulation evolved in ways that reflected the challenges and aspirations of affluent consumption. While the legal and institutional bases for the policies remained the same, they took on an entirely new social purpose. Quality standards that had once served to manage supplier relations and encourage compatibility were reconceived as tools of consumer protection. Prices, too, came to be regulated during this period, not in terms of their implications for producers and distributors but in terms of their meaning for consumers. In Germany, for example, prices came to be understood as a means of conveying useful information about the relative merits of products, and pricing policies attempted to make the meaning of prices clear to the consumer. Both areas of policy had deep historical roots. But both were reinterpreted in the 1970s in terms of an emerging national consensus concerning the new identity and status of the consumer in society.

The French and German experiences with consumer protection were also not isolated cases. Such changes either had already occurred or would soon occur in nearly all of the advanced industrialized countries. But France and Germany offer an analytically valuable comparison. These countries had experienced similar postwar economic trajectories, with similar demographic trends, and a similar emphasis on promoting industrial growth. Both were viewed as "coordinated" political economies with highly institutionalized labor and capital markets and strong welfare state commitments. Moreover, consumer protection issues arose in the two countries at almost exactly the same time. These similarities created the conditions for a valuable paired policy comparison—one in which similar initial conditions led to very different policy outcomes.

Consumption and Production

That consumption could be important to the organization of a capitalist economy is, in a sense, unsurprising. Classical economic theorists had long emphasized the central role of the consumer in economic growth.[46] Adam Smith wrote that "consumption is the sole end and purpose of all production."[47] And historians have increasingly noted the role of consumers in defining and constituting the modern marketplace.[48] In a fascinating account, historian Colin Campbell offers a demand-side reinterpretation of Max Weber's productionist *Protestant Ethic and the Spirit of Capitalism*.[49] Scholars of business management concur that companies make product and production decisions based on the demand conditions they face.[50] It would not be an exaggeration to say that consumerism has today become a core social and economic fact of modern society. Given this, why have political scientists continued to analyze the broad orientations of national economies solely in terms of the institutions of production?

Part of the reason is that social scientists have long embraced a supply-side account of modern consumption. In the years right after World War II—a period in which consumer durables were rapidly penetrating a growing middle-class market—both sociologists and economists argued that consumers were taking their purchasing cues from producers. Frankfurt School social theorists Max Horkheimer and Theodor Adorno saw producers as dictating the cultural conditions of consumption.[51] Economist John Kenneth Galbraith echoed their critique, emphasizing the role of marketing and advertising in setting the terms of consumer demand.[52] These early critics saw that the fixed investments of modern mass production required that producers generate a stable demand for the goods they pro-

46. According to David Hume, the luxury aspirations of feudal lords led them to rationalize their land holdings in order to generate greater rents through greater efficiency. David Hume, *Essays, Moral and Political* (1748); Thomas Malthus, *Principles of Political Economy* (1820); John Stuart Mill, *Principles of Political Economy* (1844); and Andrew Brewer, "Luxury and Economic Development: David Hume and Adam Smith," *Scottish Journal of Political Economy* 45/1 (February 1998): 82.

47. Adam Smith, *An Inquiry into the Nature and Causes of the Wealth of Nations* (1776), book IV.

48. Grant McKracken, *Culture and Consumption: New Approaches to the Symbolic Character of Consumer Goods and Activities* (Bloomington: Indiana University Press, 1988); Gary Cross, *Time and Money: The Making of Consumer Culture* (London: Routledge, 1993); Martyn J. Lee, *Consumer Culture Reborn: The Cultural Politics of Consumption* (London: Routledge, 1993); Robert H. Frank, *Luxury Fever: Money and Happiness in an Era of Excess* (Princeton: Princeton University Press, 2000); Martin Daunton and Matthew Hilton, *Material Politics: The State and Consumer Society* (Oxford: Berg, 2000); Matthew Hilton, *Consumerism in Twentieth-Century Britain: The Search for a Historical Movement* (Cambridge: Cambridge University Press, 2003); Lizabeth Cohen, *A Consumer's Republic;* Iselin Theien, *Affluence and Activism* (Oslo, Norway: Akademica, 2004); and Marie Chessel, Matthew Hilton, and Alain Chatriot, *Au Nom du Consommateur* (Paris: Découverte, 2005).

49. Colin Campbell, *The Romantic Ethic and the Spirit of Modern Consumerism* (Malden, Mass.: Blackwell, 1989).

50. Michael E. Porter, *The Competitive Advantage of Nations* (New York: The Free Press, 1990), 87–90; Horst Albach, *Culture and Technical Innovation,* 269–75; Bruce Kogut, "Country Capabilities," 36; and Paul L. Robertson and Tony F. Yu, "Firm Strategy, Innovation, and Consumer Demand: A Market Process Approach," *Managerial and Decision Economics* 22 (2001): 183–99.

51. Both were living in Los Angeles at the time they wrote this work, although they later returned to Germany. Max Horkheimer and Theodor Adorno, *The Dialectic of Enlightenment* (1944).

52. John Kenneth Galbraith, *The Affluent Society* (London: H. Hamilton, 1958).

duced.[53] The distinction that they drew between real needs and induced or unreal needs offered an alluring critique of modern capitalism, one that would remain a trope of social science research on consumerism for many decades.[54]

Beginning in the 1970s, the image of the purely passive consumer came under critical scrutiny. In the United States and Europe, consumers began to be reconceived as strategic players. Economist Gary Becker proposed that consumers as economic actors took into account their own reservoirs of time and money in making new purchasing decisions. His household "consumption function" was a direct analogy to the producers' production function.[55] In sociology, studies by Pierre Bourdieu and Jean Baudrillard argued that consumer choices reflected not just underlying needs but also—indeed more importantly—group and class aspirations.[56] Baudrillard writes, "The fundamental conceptual hypothesis for a sociological analysis of 'consumption' is *not* use value, the relation of needs, but *symbolic exchange* value, the value of social prestation, of rivalry and, at the limit, of class discriminants."[57] Others went further, theorizing consumption as a realm of personal freedom and new identity formation in which individual consumers could subvert the class logic of consumption through a creative (mis-)appropriation of mass products.[58] Taken together, these later theories helped to reconceptualize the consumer as active and strategic. But they never directly confronted the productionist orientation that had been built into the study of modern mass consumption. Although consumers were seen to enjoy a degree of individual agency—exactly how much was disputed—their aggregated choices were nonetheless understood to reflect the broader economic imperatives of mass production.

Within political science, new theories of mobilization emerging in the 1960s and 1970s reinforced this productionist bias by suggesting that consumers *could not* play a formative role in the political economy. Rational choice theories of collective action expounded by Mancur Olson and Russell Hardin implied that consumers would be too numerous, and their interests too diffuse, to be capable of representing their own interests effectively.[59] Sociological studies of new social movements

53. Jürgen Habermas, *The Structural Transformation of the Public Sphere: An Inquiry into a Category of Bourgeois Society,* translated by Thomas Burger (Cambridge, Mass.: MIT Press, 1991), 189. The original German edition, *Strukturwandel der Öffentlichkeit,* was published in 1962.

54. For more recent treatment of the same theme, see David Miller, *Market, State, and Community: Theoretical Foundations of Market Socialism* (Oxford: Clarendon Press, 1990), 129; and Juliet Schor, *The Overspent American: Why We Want What We Don't Need* (New York: Harper, 1999).

55. Gary S. Becker, *The Economic Approach to Human Behavior* (Chicago: University of Chicago Press, 1976).

56. Jean Baudrillard, *For a Critique of the Political Economy of the Sign* (St. Louis, Mo.: Telos Press, 1981); and Pierre Bourdieu, *Distinction: A Social Critique of the Judgement of Taste,* translated by Richard Nice (Cambridge: Harvard University Press, 1984).

57. Baudrillard, *Political Economy,* 30–31.

58. Michel de Certeau, *The Practice of Everyday Life,* translated by Steven Rendall (Berkeley: University of California Press, 1984); John Fiske, *Reading the Popular* (London: Routledge, 1989); and Celia Lury, *Consumer Culture* (New Brunswick, N.J.: Rutgers University Press, 1996).

59. Mancur Olson, *The Logic of Collective Action: Public Goods and the Theory of Groups* (Cam-

affirmed the possibility for broad citizen mobilization, but they tended to focus on movements with goals that were idealistic and socially progressive: the peace movement, the environmental movement, feminism. That they ignored the consumer movement—which emerged at the same time as these other movements—can be attributed in large part to the nature of its goals: explicitly material concerns that had little to do with the postindustrial values, cultural innovation, and lifestyle focus that characterized the other social movements.[60] The value-for-money ethos of the consumer movements also fit poorly with Ronald Inglehart's influential thesis concerning the rise of postmaterialist values in western society.[61] Political scientists ignored the emergence of powerful national consumer movements in part because their theories told them that such mobilization should not exist.[62] Yet it did exist, and the pressure consumers placed on both policymakers and producers would, over time, change the face of industrial capitalism.

Of course, producers also contributed to the project of regulating the consumer sphere. But their interests confronted an organized counterforce from mobilized consumers. The result was that national approaches to consumer protection emerged from a political struggle, one that focused on who would bear the risks inherent in new product development. In this contentious process, policies preferred by producers rarely coincided with policies preferred by organized consumers. Who won and lost in the resulting struggles depended critically on the ways in which producers and consumers organized to represent their group interests. In Germany, where producers were highly organized and consumers relatively weak, protections were designed in ways that favored producer interests. In France, by contrast, highly mobilized consumer groups faced relatively disorganized industry interests, so consumers were able to achieve policies that corresponded more closely with their own preferences. Thus, to understand the rise of national consumer protection regimes, we need to take seriously the organized interests of consumers themselves and the political contests that pitted them against the interests of business.

The empirical core of this study is a comparison of the emergence of eight central issues of consumer policy: product liability law, product safety standards and recall, misleading advertising, comparative product tests, product labeling, quality

---

bridge, Mass.: Harvard University Press, 1965); and Russell Hardin, *Collective Action* (Baltimore: Johns Hopkins University Press, 1982).

60. Alain Tourraine, *The Voice and the Eye: An Analysis of Social Movements*, translated by Alan Duff (Cambridge: Cambridge University Press, 1978), 85; and Alan Scott, *Ideology and the New Social Movements* (London: Unwin Hyman, 1990), 17.

61. Ronald Inglehart, *The Silent Revolution: Changing Values and Political Styles among Western Publics* (Princeton: Princeton University Press, 1977).

62. Path dependency may also have played a role. The modern study of political economy formed as a comprehensive political science discipline during a period, mainly in the 1960s, when few demand-side institutions existed. By the time these institutions were being created, in the 1970s, research projects in political economy were firmly focused on institutional configurations of capital and labor. See Jonathan Frenzen, Paul M. Hirsch, and Philip C. Zerrillo, "Consumption, Preferences, and Changing Lifestyles," in *The Handbook of Economic Sociology*, ed. Niel J. Smelser and Richard Swedberg (Princeton: Princeton University Press, 1994), 404.

standards, consumer contracts, and pricing. For each issue, the study traces the process of policy emergence and formation in each country. It tracks the role of organized consumer and producer groups in the policy process as well as the impact of the newly implemented policies on individual consumers and producers. Through a careful tracing of parallel policy processes in different national contexts, this approach allows us to track the sources of national consumer protection policies and their impact on product market strategies.

CHAPTER TWO

Consumption Contested

The Third Estate revolted in 1789, the Russian proletariat in 1917. Are
we at the dawn of an equally radical struggle? It's not impossible.

—*Le consommateur piégé*, 1973.

The emergence of consumer protection in France and Germany and
the divergent policies adopted in the two countries are best understood as the political incorporation of the consumer as a new category of citizenship. In each country, the elaboration of the status of the consumer citizen took the form of a contest
between producers and consumers over the very idea of the modern consumer. In
the resulting competition over the consumer ideal—and over the policies that would
flow from it—the interests and organizational capacity of producers and consumers
played a central role in determining which consumer ideal would dominate. At stake
was the extent of the burden that consumers and producers would bear for product-
related risks. If consumers were seen primarily as economic actors in society, with a
status similar to that of producers—the model that prevailed in Germany—it followed that they should bear their share of the market risk. If, on the other hand, consumers were seen primarily as political actors with a distinct social status from
producers—the model that prevailed in France—then there would be a strong case
for insulating them from market risk altogether. Each conception of the consumer
in turn entailed a distinctive and coherent set of policy prescriptions. Thus, when
producer and consumer groups addressed issues as varied as consumer contracts,
product advertising, door-to-door sales, or class action legal suits, they did so in the
shadow of a broader idea of the status and condition of the consumer.

This account of consumer protection as the political incorporation of the citizen
consumer places a particularly heavy burden on the role of ideas in policymaking.
First, the account of consumer protection as a right of citizenship implies a recon-
ceptualization of the very status of consumers as an economic group and a coherent
interpretation of their interests. In this uncertain context, the political stakes in the
formation of new policies were not initially clear. The resulting ambiguity was cap-

tured at the time by the French politician Michel Rocard who, writing in 1973, described the new consumer politics as "a novel confrontation, one that has not yet been translated into the conflicts that we understand. It is political in the profound sense of the term."[1] This was, in other words, a radically new area of policy. It was characterized by a high degree of uncertainty, in which policymakers took on the role of problem solvers. In this fluid context, ideas about the economic and social identity of the consumer became especially salient in policy formation.[2]

Second, entirely new institutions were being created to enforce the new rights of consumer citizenship. Successful ideas about policymaking both dictated and became embedded in these new institutions.[3] Of course, not all of the new institutions succeeded. Especially in France, institutions of consumer protection were characterized by a significant period of trial and error. If a large number of new institutions were perceived to have failed, the very idea of consumer protection that they embodied would have become discredited.[4] But to the extent that the new institutions were seen to be effective, they tended to persist, locking out alternative strategies of consumer protection. This meant that, once national consumer protection policies had been successfully elaborated, they were subject to strong path dependencies that constrained future solutions.[5]

Finally, treating consumer protection as an extension of citizenship rights implied the elaboration of an ideal consumer status to which policymakers aspired. The elaboration of this ideal of the citizen consumer served three purposes: it built consensus around the emerging policies; it set a benchmark by which success would be measured; and it determined how new areas of consumer policy that might emerge in the future would be managed. The consumer ideal thus served as a policy model, providing a conceptual framework and focal point for practical policy formation.[6]

1. Interview with Michel Rocard, *Le Figaro,* 14 February 1973.

2. Hugh Heclo, *Modern Social Politics in Britain and Sweden: from Relief to Income Maintenance* (New Haven: Yale University Press, 1974); Peter A. Hall, "Policy Paradigms, Social Learning, and the State: The Case of Economic Policymaking in Britain," *Comparative Politics* 25/3 (April 1993): 291; Ann Swidler, "Culture in Action: Symbols and Strategies," *American Sociological Review* 51 (April 1986): 277; and Pierre Muller, "Les politiques publiques comme construction d'un rapport au monde," in *La construction du sens dans les politiques publiques: Débats autour de la notion de referential,* ed. Alain Faure, Gilles Pollet, and Philippe Warin (Paris: Éditions L'Harmattan, 1995), 161.

3. Craig Parsons, *A Certain Idea of Europe* (Ithaca: Cornell University Press), 19–20.

4. Pepper Culpepper, "Institutional Change in Contemporary Capitalism: Coordination and Politics in Finance during the 1990s," forthcoming (http://ksghome.harvard.edu/~pculpepper/Finance.pdf).

5. Paul Pierson, "When Effect Becomes Cause: Policy Feedback and Political Change," *World Politics* 45/4 (July 1993).

6. See, for example, Deborah Stone, "Causal Stories and the Formation of Policy Agendas," *Political Science Quarterly* 104 (1989); Geoffrey Garrett and Barry Weingast, "Ideas, Interests, and Institutions: Constructing the European Community's Internal Market," in *Ideas and Foreign Policy: Beliefs, Institutions, and Political Change,* ed. Judith Goldstein and Robert Keohane (Ithaca: Cornell University Press, 1993); Erik Bleich, "From International Ideas to Domestic Policies: Educational Multiculturalism in England and France," *Comparative Politics* 31/1 (October 1998); and Randal Hansen and Desmond King, "Eugenic Ideas, Political Interests, and Policy

What was striking about the political incorporation of consumers in France and Germany was that three competing consumer ideals, or policy models, were in play. Each offered a distinct account of the status and rights of the new citizen consumer and of the policy solutions that they entailed.[7] Moreover, policymakers and economic actors were aware of the competing models and of the need to choose among them. The choice among these models, however, was not an obvious one. Conceptually, each model appeared to offer a viable approach to the challenges faced by consumers. Nor did any of the available models appear to be more or less economically efficient. So whatever the outcome, the conceptions of consumer citizenship that eventually emerged in France and Germany had their origins in a political struggle waged in the 1970s and early 1980s that was fundamentally about which of the available policy models to embrace. In this sense, specific domestic policy battles were part of a broader war over the identity and social status of the consumer.

It is this struggle over the broader meaning of consumption that makes the resulting confrontation between organized consumers and producers so interesting, particularly the process of policy formation in each country: the ways in which consumer and producer groups advocated their preferred policies, the ways in which the dominant policy model was institutionalized, and the mixture of successes and failures that either reinforced or undermined the prevailing model. That story, elaborated below, highlights the role of experimentation and contingency on the road from policy preferences to policy outcomes. The French case is striking in this respect, because the preferred policy models of both consumers *and* producers proved institutionally unworkable. After repeated trials and repeated failures, France managed to emerge in the mid-1980s with a policy that combined the lowest possible joint ranking, based on stated policy positions, of both consumer and producer preferences.[8]

Three Models of the Consumer

Amid the general move to incorporate consumers into politics in France and Germany, three policy models became the focus of intensive policy attention. These policy mod-

Variance: Immigration and Sterilization Policy in Britain and the U.S.," *World Politics* 53 / 2 (January 2001).

7. Mark Blyth, "The Transformation of the Swedish Model: Economic Ideas, Distributional Conflict, and Institutional Change," *World Politics* 54 / 1 (2001); Parsons, *A Certain Idea of Europe;* and Luc Boltanski and Laurent Thévenot, *De la justification: Les économies de la grandeur* (Paris: Gallimard, 1991).

8. Following traditional pluralist accounts, this study assumes that government officials chose policy configurations that offered the highest combined preference ranking for consumers and producers that were also compatible with providing adequate consumer protection. See Elmer E. Schattschneider, *Politics, Pressures, and the Tariff* (New York: 1935); Stephen K. Bailey, *Congress Makes a Law* (New York: Columbia University Press, 1950); David B. Truman, *The Government Process* (New York: Alfred Knopf, 1951); and Earl Latham, *The Group Basis of Politics* (Ithaca: Cornell University Press, 1952).

els—referred to here as the protection, information, and negotiation models—served as templates for designing a wide range of policy responses. Functioning as ideal types, they guided decisions about how particular policy concerns should be addressed. Moreover, because these models entailed specific policy prescriptions, they became the focus of a political struggle over the correct approach to consumer protection.

We have already encountered two of these models, which came to prevail in France and Germany. The approach that emerged in France, the *protection model*, stressed the political rights of the consumer to be protected from market-related risk. It emphasized the role of the government in insulating consumers from market externalities and the role of consumers in lobbying for new rights and protections. The approach that emerged in Germany, the *information model*, emphasized the economic rights of the consumer to participate in the marketplace on an equal footing with business. This approach stressed the challenges of market failure and the need to redress information asymmetries that worked to the disadvantage of consumers.

Yet it would be difficult to understand the outcomes that eventually emerged in France and Germany without also considering a third approach to consumer protection, called the *negotiation model*. This approach was in fact the preferred model for consumer groups in both countries. The negotiation model viewed consumers as a societal interest group capable of pursuing its interests directly with other interest groups. This approach was borrowed from the experience of the Swedish consumer movement in the 1960s and early 1970s, but it also drew inspiration from labor law. It assumed that consumers and producers shared many common goals and that through orderly and frequent negotiations the two groups could come to agreement on mutually satisfactory regulatory approaches to consumer protection. In this negotiation model, consumers were viewed primarily as a newly coherent interest group in society. Consumer problems were understood to derive from the organizational barriers that consumers faced and from the lack of discussion between consumer groups and producer groups. Appropriate solutions consequently emphasized state support to consumer groups, the creation of forums in which fair negotiations could take place, and the enforcement of the outcomes of such negotiations. This negotiation model tended to emphasize regulatory approaches that encourage mediation. A distinguishing characteristic of this approach was the consumer ombudsman. An administrative position first established in Sweden in 1971, the ombudsman enjoyed autonomy from the government and spearheaded the consumer interest in negotiations with industry. The negotiation model was particularly attractive for consumer groups because of the pivotal role it would give them in negotiation solutions with producers.

The salient features of all three models are summarized in table 2.1. The different strategies of consumer protection imposed different burdens on consumers and producers.[9] A strategy that emphasized information provision placed a high burden

9. Note that the chart does not describe the actual financial burden of regulation on producers and consumers. Because producers can pass on the costs associated with any regulation to consumers in the form of higher prices, it is difficult to generalize about where the financial burden—the incidence—of regulations fall.

Table 2.1   Three policy models for the consumer

	Protection	Negotiation	Information
Model country	United States	Sweden	Great Britain
Consumer identity	Political citizen	Interest group	Economic citizen
Analysis of problem	Inadequate rights	Need for negotiation	Market failure
Proposed solutions	Create new rights	Create forums for	Provide consumers with
	Insulate consumers from	negotiation	better information
	market risk	Make outcome of	Reinforce quality
	Mobilize consumers	negotiations binding	production
Regulatory emphasis	Focus on ends	Focus on fair discussions	Focus on procedure
	Encourage private law	Encourage mediation	Encourage industry
	enforcement		self-enforcement

of responsibility for product safety on consumers. This strategy corresponded to the information model that came to predominate in Germany and Britain. In this context, consumers enjoyed fewer protections against risk, but they were granted greater access to information that would allow them to make important consumption decisions. Conversely, a strategy that emphasized risk reduction would place a high burden of responsibility for product safety on producers. This strategy corresponded to the protection model that came to predominate in France and the United States.[10] In this context, consumers may not know much about the products they purchase, but they do so with the confidence that they are being protected against risks. In the negotiation strategy, the strategy of consumer protection adopted in the Scandinavian countries, consumers and producers negotiate a mutually acceptable combination of information and protection solutions. This approach serves to balance the burden of product safety between consumers and producers.

These three models of consumer protection were not conceptually arbitrary. In a sense, they represented a complete set of alternative solutions to the challenge of consumer protection. The policy space that they defined is depicted in figure 2.1. The vertical axis expresses the degree to which producers were required to take responsibility for product-related risk. In practice, this dimension corresponds to mandatory safety requirements, product liability standards, product recall programs, and so on. The horizontal axis expresses the degree to which information about products was provided to consumers. This dimension corresponds to standards of truth in advertising and labeling, comparative product testing, consumer education, and so on. The three models define a frontier of roughly equivalent protection. In other words, consumers may be equally safe when faced either with a reduced burden of risk and little product information or with a high burden of risk and a high level of information. In practice, of course, neither solution is entirely satisfactory. No matter how informed a consumer might be, certain risks necessarily remain unknown. Similarly, no matter how assiduously product risks are assigned

10. "Le droit européen de la consommation: L'unité communautaire dans la diversité des droits nationaux," *Revue de la concurrence et de la consommation* 102 (1998): 22.

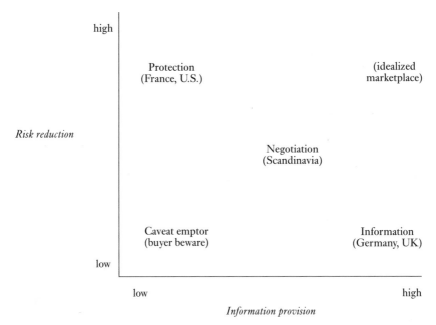

Figure 2.1   The policy space of consumer protection

to producers, certain kinds of losses, especially those to consumer health, can never be adequately avoided or remunerated.

Although business and consumers had different preferences over the information, negotiation, and protection strategies, they shared a common perception that these policy models represented conceptually coherent, mutually exclusive alternatives. These three models are probably not universal categories. They nonetheless were perceived to cover the entire range of policy options available to French and German policymakers at the time.

French and German policymakers were conscious of these three different options because they conducted detailed studies of the regulatory approaches adopted by other countries. The United States, Britain, and Sweden were all acting to protect consumers at the same time that French and German policymakers were deciding what to do. They therefore offered obvious models from which to draw. In France, these studies took place either in the context of the Consumer Committee for the French Plan or were initiated by consumer groups themselves.[11] French consumer groups undertook detailed surveys of the consumer policies developed in other countries, reporting on them in their own publications. Ralph Nader was invited twice to France in the early 1970s, for example, to introduce the U.S. model of the citizen consumer. The Swedish consumer ombudsman also visited. In Germany, the

11. Michel Génin and Bernard Suzanne, "Les rapports de l'industrie de consommation en Suède et aux États-Unis," *Les cahiers de l'ILEC* 7 (1963).

Commission for Economic and Social Change undertook a five-year survey of the entire German economy that included several studies of foreign approaches to product market regulation.[12] German consumer groups also participated. In 1964, when Germany was developing its own public product testing organization, they sent a group of product testing experts to England, Sweden, Denmark, and Norway to study their testing approaches.[13] German consumer groups, who were particularly interested in the negotiation model employed in Sweden, cosponsored with the Swedish embassy in 1967 a forum on consumer protection that brought together industry and consumer groups from both Sweden and Germany.[14]

At the same time, multilateral organizations were forming consumer advocacy bodies that provided forums for national representatives to meet. French and German policymakers met frequently in the context of European efforts to establish common standards for product market regulations within Europe. Debates occurred both within the Council of Europe and in the context of drafting directives within the European Economic Community.[15] Although none of the EEC directives proved effective at the time, they did generate debate on consumer issues among European policymakers. Further, in 1972 a new committee on consumer policy in the Organization for Economic Cooperation and Development began publishing annual comparative studies on national approaches to consumer policy.[16] Starting in 1977, the *Journal of Consumer Policy* explicitly compared national approaches to consumer policy. As a consequence of the growing interest in consumer policy, French and German policymakers became extremely well informed about the policy alternatives they faced.

Two additional features of the policy space depicted in figure 2.1 are worth noting. First, the three models being considered by France and Germany all differed from the low level of protection offered by the traditional legal standard of caveat emptor. Located in the lower left corner of the policy space, this traditional approach corresponded to a deregulated market, in which consumers enjoyed neither protections against product risk nor objective product information. In the past, this low standard of protection had been the norm rather than the exception. It characterized consumer society from the beginning of industrialization until the rise of postwar consumer protection movements. Indeed, it still characterizes many countries today. Second, figure 2.1 shows no policy model combining a high level of informa-

---

12. Kommission für wirtschaftlichen und sozialen Wandel, *Wirtschaftlicher und sozialer Wandel in der Bundesrepublik Deutschland: Gutachten der Kommission* (Göttingen, Germany: Verlag Otto Schwartz, 1977), ch. 9.

13. "Warentests in Europa," *Verbraucherpolitische Korrespondenz* 35/15 (December 1964): 11.

14. Wolfgang Hoffmann, "Die Anwälte der Konsumenten: Viele Verbraucherverbände—wenig Erfolg," *Die Zeit,* 26 March 1971, 29.

15. Thierry M. Bourgoignie, "Consumer Law and the European Community: Issues and Prospects," in *Integration through Law: Europe and the American Federal Experience,* ed. Thierry Bourgoignie and David Trubek (Berlin: Walter de Gruyter, 1987), 95; and *Protection du consommateur* (Strasbourg, France: Conseil de l'Europe, 1979).

16. Organization for Economic Cooperation and Development, *Consumer Policy during the Past Ten Years: Main Developments and Prospects* (Paris: OECD, 1983).

tion provision with a high level of risk reduction. This gap reflects in part the real lack of examples of this policy combination in the advanced industrial nations (pharmaceuticals are perhaps the most prominent exception). It also accurately reflects the nature of the policy negotiations that emerged around the consumer interest.

Policy Preferences of Consumers

Consumer interests are potentially diverse. The policy preference rankings of French and German consumer groups therefore tended to emphasize those consumer interests that also reflected the organizational strategies of consumer movements in the two countries. In France, where the consumer movement was founded in grassroots mobilization and political engagement, consumer groups favored approaches that built on mobilizing. Hence French consumer groups favored negotiating with industry and lobbying the government for legal protections. Both of these activities emphasized their organizational strengths. They were less enthusiastic about an information strategy, since that approach tended to treat the consumer as an individual rather than as a political or group actor. Thus, in general, French consumer groups preferred first the negotiation model, then the protection model, and finally the information model.

In regulatory fields as diverse as product labeling, consumer contracts, advertising, and product quality standards, French consumer groups gave their strongest endorsement to negotiated solutions. In 1975, the eleven major French consumer groups proposed a general framework law ("*loi cadre*") that would permit them to negotiate binding contracts with industry on a broad range of policy issues.[17] They proposed the formation of a "High Council on Innovation and Safety" that would give equal representation to consumers, professionals, and government officials. Its goal was to advocate safety and design standards for manufacturers and to identify "false innovations" that were expensive for society and burdensome to consumers.[18] The consumer group ORGECO, which was allied with the major French trade unions, strongly supported direct consumer group negotiations with individual companies as a productive approach to consumer protection.[19]

The second most-favored option of French consumer groups was the strategy of protection through the creation of special consumer rights. From an organizational logic, the protection approach was less satisfying for consumer groups than the negotiation model, as it did not rely as heavily on the vast organizational abilities of French consumer groups. Consumer groups nonetheless lobbied hard for higher safety standards, better contractual terms, and greater industry responsibility, all hallmarks of this approach. While they did not object to improvements in the avail-

17. Comité national de la consommation, *Un monde en mouvement: Les organisations de consommation* (Paris: Ministère de l'économie, 1980).

18. *Le Monde*, 30 April 1975.

19. Jacques Dubois, "Du mépris à la concertation," *Information consommation OR-GE-CO* 20 (1977): 2.

Table 2.2   Policy preference rankings of consumer and producer groups

Ranking	French consumer groups	German consumer groups	Producer interests (French and German)
1st	Negotiation	Negotiation	Information
2nd	Protection	Information	Negotiation
3rd	Information	Protection	Protection

ability of consumer information, especially when it resulted from negotiated agreements with industry, French consumer groups were skeptical that information alone could adequately help consumers. Truth in advertising, for example, was not an important policy issue for French consumer groups. When the government proposed a set of negotiated quality labels in 1976, the Federal Consumers' Union (Union Fédérale des Consommateurs, UFC) objected on the grounds that this should not substitute for real product quality.[20] As summarized in table 2.2, the French consumer preference ranking for strategies of consumer protection was negotiation, then protection, and then information.

German consumer groups pursued an organizational strategy different from that of their French counterparts, and this led to different policy preferences. German consumer groups had few individual members. They measured their success not in terms of their weight as a political force, but instead in terms of their expertise and their access to government and business decision-making. This organizational strategy led German consumer group to emphasize technical skills over mobilization. They thus tended to favor both negotiation and information models, since both strategies emphasize their organizational strengths. The protection model was the least-favored approach of the German consumer movement because, by making consumer issues political, it risked undermining the consumer movement's own privileged access to policymaking.

Like their French counterparts, German consumer groups placed the greatest emphasis on the negotiation approach to consumer protection. But if French consumer groups saw their role in negotiation as one of aggregating broad consumer interests, German consumer groups quickly perceived that they simply did not have the political power or popular legitimacy to negotiate on an equal political footing with business. In the early 1960s, for example, Germany's leading consumer association, the Association of Consumer Groups (Arbeitsgemeinschaft der Verbraucherverbände, AgV), had been pushing for the creation of a consumption ministry within the government. This would have given the AgV the authority to speak on an equal footing with other ministries. But by the early 1970s the AgV had changed its position, opposing a separate consumption ministry and pushing instead for access to consumer policy committees within the economics and agriculture ministries. Cornel Bock, a founding member of the AgV and its honorary president, explained the

20. Comité national de la consommation, *Un monde en mouvement*, 3.

group's approach: "The natural role of a modern consumer organization, that has already passed through its childhood and has become clever through experience, consists not in advocating exclusively self-help or exclusively government support, but instead far more in seeing itself and to prove its value as a partner 'on the side' of the economy."[21] Otto Blume, the founder and leading intellectual force behind the AgV, even proposed that consumers be admitted under revised codetermination laws onto company advisory boards.

With low membership and no independent basis of political power, German consumer groups were dependent for their policy access on the good will of the government. The Social Democratic Party–dominated coalition of the 1970s proved enthusiastic in integrating consumer groups into policy circles. In 1973, consumer groups were granted access to the multiparty Concerted Action negotiations of wage and money supply levels. In 1974, they were given access to technical committees within the German Institute for Standardization (Deutsches Institut für Normung, DIN), the national organization that oversees the establishment of technical standards. In 1976, they were given an important role in monitoring standard consumer contracts.

In exchange for this access to government policy, German consumer groups tended to avoid confrontations with industry. This aversion embodied consumer group opposition to the protection model. When the German trademark association criticized the AgV for conducting comparative product tests, for example, the AgV simply stopped conducting such tests. When the president of the Federal Cartel Office (Bundeskartellamt) called for the creation of a single office for consumer and competition policy, the president of the AgV opposed the idea out of concern that the new body would undermine the status of the AgV as an equal partner with industry.[22] Indeed, the AgV generally opposed any state-regulated consumer politics and strongly opposed a state-run consumer protection bureau.[23] Most of the major consumer legislative initiatives in Germany were initiated not by consumer groups but by Germany's political parties.[24] The conceptual essence of the protection strategy was consumer confrontation with industry, to which German consumer groups were strongly opposed.

The information model of consumer protection was the second-favorite option for German consumer groups. Over time, consumer information became the foundational activity of consumer protection in Germany, especially for regional consumer associations (Verbraucherverbände). The AgV also participated. In 1973, for example, they sent two buses on a tour through Germany under the slogan "To-

21. Cornel J. Bock, "Verbraucherbewegung am Wendepunkt," *Verbraucherpolitische Korrespondenz* 1 (January 1965): 4.

22. Günther Eberhard, "Verbraucherpolitik, Ziele, Mittel und Träger," *Marktwirtschaft* 2 (1973): 39.

23. *Wirtschaft und Wettbewerb* (October 1973): 665–66.

24. Heribert Schatz, "Consumer Interests in the Process of Political Decision-Making: A Study of Some Consumer Policy Decisions in the Federal Republic of Germany," *Journal of Consumer Policy* 6 (1983): 338.

gether for Reasonable Prices" ("*Gemeinsam für vernünftige Preise*"). They handed out brochures, showed educational movies, and offered computerized tests of consumers' knowledge of product prices.[25] If the primary focus of French consumer groups was to collect consumer complaints and present them to industry, one of the main focuses of German consumer groups was to gather technical product information and present it to consumers.

Policy Preferences of Producers

As opposed to the divergent views of French and German consumer groups, French and German industry had similar ideas about consumer policy. In both countries, the primary concern of business was to avoid government or consumer intervention in production decisions. Hence businesses evaluated the three policy models in terms of the level of regulatory intervention they were likely to generate. It is difficult to recapture the degree of concern felt by producers about the new consumer movement. Among the three, the information model appeared the least restrictive to business. Businesses in general recognized that better-informed consumers could be more responsive consumers. For Germany's leading industry association, the Federation of German Industries (Bundesverband der Deutschen Industrie, BDI), the greatest goal of the government was to help the consumer work through the enormous volume of information on products. Industry groups generally favored product labeling and consumer education, so long as these were objective, neutral, and voluntary. They especially favored school education on consumer issues and government support of regional consumer advisory centers. France's leading industry association, the National Council of French Employers (Conseil national du patronat français, CNPF), emphasized the emancipatory potential of consumer information: "Consumer information is the condition of a true freedom of choice: a poorly or insufficiently informed consumer has no real freedom of decision."[26]

After the information model, the second preference of business interests in France and Germany was the negotiation model of consumer protection. While this approach put them face to face with consumers, it had the benefit of avoiding direct government intervention in business decisions. Germany's standardization board, DIN, for example, accepted the creation of a consumer advisory board within its administration in exchange for a high degree of autonomy and freedom from government intervention. In France, the CNPF, when faced with the threat of direct government intervention, became an enthusiastic proponent of the negotiation approach. Indeed, the CNPF created a special committee, the Committee on Industry, Trade, and Consumption (Comité industrie commerce consommation, CICC), to negotiate with consumer groups. In the case of consumer terms of sale, for in-

25. Wolfgang H. Glöckner, "Aktion 'Gelber Punkt'—Ins Rote verfälscht," *Vorwärts* (1973).
26. *CNPF Patronat* (June 1976): 15.

stance, the CICC negotiated with consumer groups for two years before their efforts were brought to a halt by direct regulatory intervention by the government.[27]

The least desirable approach to consumer policy for producers was the protection model. This model implied a high level of government intervention to enforce a new strong set of consumer rights. In France, industry was critical of the Consumer Safety Commission (Commission de la sécurité des consommateurs, CSC) that was put in place in 1983 to regulate products directly in the interest of consumer safety. They worried that any of several ministries could bring cases, that even trade unions could apply for product reviews, and that the new commission's powers to investigate producers were too far-reaching.[28] Both French and German industry opposed product recall actions, for example, because of concern that they could be politically motivated and disruptive to industry.[29] Indeed, it was often the prospect of direct intervention that led producers to attempt direct negotiations with consumers. In sum, producers' preference ranking for models of consumer protection in both countries was first information, then negotiation, and then protection.

Consumer Policy in Germany

In Germany, consumers and producers agreed in liking the protection model least of the three options. Conflict therefore emerged only over which interest group would achieve its top preference. In this conflict the weak organization of the consumer movement placed limits on its ability to achieve its preferred policy, the negotiation approach. Moreover, the strong organizational capacities of industry in Germany permitted industry to make the information strategy an effective policy tool for consumer protection. German policy therefore came to favor producer over consumer policy preferences.

German consumer protection policy began with an emphasis on the information model of consumer protection, which it has maintained. As early as 1964, Economics Minister Kurt Schmücker became a strong advocate for consumer protection. His efforts focused on providing consumers with better information, including an improved legal treatment of weights and measures, a law on the labeling of wool products, and a government-supported body to undertake comparative product tests. He also foresaw a role for consumers in providing more accurate information. He pushed for the right for consumer groups to sue collectively in the context of misleading advertising, and he proposed public support for consumer representa-

27. *Information consommation OR-GE-CO* (May–June 1976), 6.

28. Marcel Garrigou, *L'assaut des consommateurs: Pour changer les rapports producteurs vendeurs consommateurs* (Paris: Editions Aubier-Montaigne, 1981), 11.

29. Hans-Wolfgang Micklitz, "Comparative Analysis of the National Country Reports on Post Market Control and Perspectives for a European Setting of Post Market Control," in *Post Market Control of Consumer Goods,* ed. Hans-Wolfgang Micklitz (Baden-Baden, Germany: Nomos, 1990), 418.

tion in Germany's technical standardization board, the DNA (precursor to the DIN).[30] Germany's consumer groups were strong supporters of these information goals. With state and federal support, they expanded Germany's network of consumer information centers. They also under took media-focused information campaigns. In 1965, German television and radio broadcast some sixty different consumer-oriented shows, including "Shopping Tips for Housewives," "My Money, Your Money," and "Women's Radio Advisor."[31]

Germany's leading consumer association, the AgV, supported the goal of informing consumers, but it also saw a special role for itself in negotiating directly with industry. Early negotiations focused on improving product label standards. The AgV worked closely with industry groups to develop standardized labels for products such as shoes, wine, detergents, and sausages. One of the first of these, a quality label for pantyhose that indicated the number and size flaws (which were common even in new pantyhose at the time), was negotiated among consumers, producers, and retailers in 1963.[32] In general, however, German industry was reluctant to sign such agreements. Negotiations often required many years, and the results were typically modest. The 1966 standard for labeling shoes, for example, resulted in an arrangement to label shoes with leather soles with the word *leather*.[33]

It seems surprising that industry was so hesitant to participate in negotiations with consumer groups over quality labeling. For starters, informative labels could potentially help producers as well as consumers. In the case of a wine labeling initiative in 1967, for example, the AgV argued that a label indicating alcohol content and whether or not sugar had been added could help prevent a "race to the bottom" in the overall quality of German wine.[34] Second, the AgV repeatedly emphasized that such labels should be voluntary. Indeed, it expressed strong apprehension about government intervention in negotiations with producers. With respect to these early quality label projects, the AgV stressed: "In the view of the consumer, all voluntary labeling projects are considered to be positive."[35] More generally, the AgV evinced deep concerns about government interventions to protect the consumer. When, in 1974, the economics minister of the state of North Rhine–Westphalia called producer and consumer representatives together to discuss consumer protection, the AgV praised the move as an alternative to direct government intervention, noting,

30. "Schmücker fördert die Verbraucherpolitik," *Verbraucherpolitische Korrespondenz* 6 (25 February 1964), 2–3.
31. "Verbraucherinformationen in Rundfunk und Fernsehen," *Verbraucherpolitische Korrespondenz* 12 (25 April 1965), 8–11.
32. "Endlich Licht im Strumpf-Dschungel," *Verbraucherpolitische Korrespondenz* 6 (25 February 1964), 8.
33. "Freiwillige Schuhkennzeichnung ab 1966," *Verbraucherpolitische Korrespondenz* 21 (25 July 1965), 8.
34. "Klare Kennzeichnung und freier Wettbewerb," *Verbraucherpolitische Korrespondenz* 35/6–7 (15–25 December 1967), 2–4.
35. "Endlich freiwillige Schuhkennzeichnung," *Verbraucherpolitische Korrespondenz* 41 (12 October 1971).

"No one desires a state managed consumer; any bureaucratization of consumer protection should be rejected."[36]

When, in the early 1970s, the German government nonetheless began to contemplate an extensive program of legislative initiatives to protect the consumer, it seemed only natural to bring Germany's consumer groups to the policy table. In 1973, for example, the German Ministry of Justice convened a discussion group to decide on a course of action for regulating consumer contracts. Nearly 150 of the most prominent production and labor associations attended. Consumer groups were also invited, and half a dozen representatives attended. But strong pressure from industry simply overwhelmed the consumer advocates, so that consumer interests did not figure strongly in the final proposed legislation. In the end, the resulting law on standard contract terms (Gesetz zur Regelung des Rechts der Allgemeinen Geschäftsbedingungen, or AGB-Gesetz) closely reflected industry interests.[37] As Germany's consumer groups had decided against a strategy of mass organization and protest, they were left with little recourse to apply pressure for their own views.

The political weakness of the AgV also limited its ability to fight for policies that might have given them greater latitude to negotiate with industry. Consumer groups were, for example, blocked from organizing class action suits that would group consumer claims for remuneration.[38] The primary concern, stated explicitly by the Free Democratic Party (Freie Demokratische Partei, FDP), Germany's pro-business liberal party, was that such claims would be unacceptably profitable for consumer groups and would thus risk putting them in a stronger bargaining position in relation to industry.[39] A similar dynamic emerged in the area of minimum product standards. In 1974, Germany's labeling organization (Deutsches Institut für Gütesicherung und Kennzeichnung, formerly known as Reichsausschuß für Lieferbedingungen or RAL) proposed that minimum acceptable safety standards for products be negotiated outside of the industry standardization board, DIN, by a committee composed of equal members from consumer and producer groups. While industry favored labeling, they objected to the influence that this arrangement would give consumers in setting product standards.[40] Under pressure from industry, the Economics Ministry refused to support the project. They embraced instead a new *Produktinformation* (PI) system created by the Federation of German Industries (BDI), which effectively removed government and consumer influence from labeling decisions.[41] In sum, industry accepted collaboration with consumer groups in the interest of pursuing an information strat-

36. "Hearing zu NRW-Verbraucherprogramm," *Verbraucherpolitische Korrespondenz* 30 (23 July 1974), 8.

37. Heribert Schatz, *Verbraucherinteressen im politischen Entscheidungsprozess* (Frankfurt: Campus Verlag, 1984), 68.

38. Alex Stein, "Die Verbraucheransprüche und ihre Geltenmachung durch Verbraucherverbände nach der UWG-Novelle," *Journal of Consumer Policy* 2 (1979).

39. *Frankfurter Rundschau*, 28 January 1982.

40. *Bundesanzeiger*, 23 March 1974.

41. Annemarie Bopp-Schmehl, Uwe Heibült, and Ulrich Kypke, *Technische Normung und Verbraucherinteressen im gesellschaftlichen Wandel* (Frankfurt: Haag and Herchen Verlag, 1984), 86.

egy of product market regulation but stopped short of acceding to equitable negotiations with consumers in this or any other policy area.

The failure of efforts to pursue negotiated solutions to consumer grievance left Germany to embrace the information model. If consumers were going to protect themselves through informed choices, then they needed to know that there were indeed safe products on the market to choose. Thus an important dimension of the information approach focused on giving producers incentives to pursue high-quality production. One focus of this effort was product standards. Germany's Equipment Safety Law (Gerätesicherheitsgesetz, GSG), for example, did not itself specify minimum safety standards. Instead, it made standards established by industry, in the context of DIN, mandatory for all producers.[42] Formally, consumers also participated in this process. In 1974, the economics ministry compelled DIN to accept consumer representatives on technical standards committees relating to consumer products. But these representatives acted in a technical rather than in a representative capacity. They were outnumbered by representatives from industry and had no formal veto power on standards decisions.[43] In this way, minimum product safety standards came to be set by industry's own standardization board rather than by the state. This approach was in turn reinforced by German judicial treatment of product liability, which granted companies grounds for exculpation if they could show that they had followed generally accepted manufacturing practices.[44]

By the late 1970s, Germany's approach to consumer protection was set, and it placed a strong focus on consumer information. Government funds supported the educational function of consumer groups. Strict regulations, enforced through monitoring by consumer groups, ensured accurate advertising and labeling, as well as reasonable contract terms. The German approach also supported legal and regulatory procedures that made industry-set standards of product design and manufacturing mandatory on all producers. Product standards in this approach would not be subjected to negotiations between producer and consumer groups, as the negotiation model advocated, but determined by industry itself. This combination of interventionist government treatment of information and a hands-off approach to product standards was the core of the German information model.

Consumer Policy in France

In France, the first preference of producers—the information model—was the last preference of consumers. The process of policy formation was therefore more dynamic. Early consumer protection initiatives favored industry by adopting the in-

---

42. Ibid., 101.

43. Christian Joerges, Joseph Falke, and Hans-Wolfgang Micklitz, *Die Sicherheit von Konsumgütern und die Entwicklung der Europäischen Gemeinschaft* (Baden-Baden, Germany: Nomos, 1988), 186.

44. Henricus Duintjer Tebbens, *International Product Liability: A Study of Comparative and International Aspects of Product Liability* (The Hague: Asser Institute, 1979), 74–75.

formation model. As consumer mobilization increased, the political influence of consumers also increased, and the information model became contested. The dominant policy model then shifted to negotiation. The negotiation model, representing the first preference of consumers and the second preference of producers, was the socially optimal policy in that it offered the greatest combined ranking. Yet this strategy also failed, primarily because of the inability of French industry associations to impose negotiated solutions on individual companies. As a consequence, France shifted to the only remaining position, the protection model. Because it was the second preference of consumers and the third preference of producers, this policy can be seen as a victory for the consumer movement. Interestingly, however, the protection model also represented the worst social outcome (that is, the worst joint ranking) for producers and consumers combined.

In a first policy stage from 1970 to 1978, France's early initiatives in consumer protection focused on providing consumers with accurate information. This policy approach was pushed most strongly by France's first secretary of consumption, Christiane Scrivener, appointed to the position in 1976 under the second government of Raymond Barre. Scrivener, who had just returned from the Harvard Business School with a mid-career MBA degree, was focused on the economic role that consumers should play in the economy.[45] "Their information," she wrote, "determines the very orientation of our economy."[46] Her formal program for consumer protection included four "axes of action" that embodied this information model: (1) incorporate durability into the design of products; (2) give consumers more information regarding durability, which manufacturers collect; (3) require improved documentation and construction, which would allow consumers to keep their products longer; and (4) create regulations to help the second-hand market function properly.[47] The agenda reflected the logic of consumer information that she had first outlined upon taking office in 1976:

> A more enlightened consumption, consumers who are better informed and able to make themselves heard—these are a means of reinforcing competition among producers and among distributors, a contribution to a more economical use of our resources that is also better adapted to our real needs, and an inducement to greater product quality and consequently greater exports.[48]

Some of Scrivener's specific policy initiatives for improving consumer information relied on market mechanisms. She pushed to legalize comparative advertising

45. Margaret de Miraval, "France's Consumer Minister," *Christian Science Monitor,* 14 February 1977.

46. Christiane Scrivener, "Le droit des consommateurs à l'information," *Allocutions ministérielles: Secrétariat d'État à la consommation* (1976): 2.

47. Christiane Scrivener, "La durabilité des produits, une exigence dont les industriels doivent davantage tenir compte," *Les Échos,* 6 March 1978.

48. French Ministry of Economics and Finance, "Conférence de Presse tenue par Madame Christiane Scrivener," 26 May 1976.

in France, on the grounds that this could provide consumers with valuable information, and proposed that producers be required to advertise negative features of their products as well as the positive ones.[49] She called for French companies to create their own consumer relations offices that could communicate individually with consumers.[50] However, Scrivener also felt that in many cases achieving an adequate level of consumer information required direct state intervention. She pushed policies that targeted both information and education. Information policies included a new standard for quality certificates, with the Ministry of Industry imposing a minimum standard of quality for all products.[51] In 1977, Scrivener introduced consumer education into the elementary school curriculum.[52] The *réforme Haby* called for consumer education in technical schools. The new curriculum had a strong commercial content, including instructions on how to distinguish real from fake Camembert.[53]

Yet this information strategy that Scrivener came to represent was increasingly challenged by the conception of consumers as an interest group. Writing in 1977, Michel Wieviorka noted that French consumerism at the time seemed to have two modes: "On the one hand, scandals that by their high social visibility give a sudden importance to general consumer themes and to groups dedicated to consumers; on the other hand, a sustained effort, much less popular, tending towards informing middle-class consumers."[54] The emerging conception of consumers as having a collective interest was latent in society. Indeed, business had shown itself to be quite open to negotiating directly with consumer groups on issues that related to consumer information.[55] As early as 1970 the CNPF was collaborating with the state-run National Consumption Institute (Institut national de la consommation, INC) to negotiate standard product labels. In 1973, the *loi Royer* granted consumer groups the right to file group lawsuits, a move that empowered consumer groups in relation to industry, although this law was later diluted through court interpretation.[56] In 1976, the Consumption Committee of the French Seventh Plan proposed the creation of an ongoing dialogue between consumers and producers, including representation of consumer groups in the administrative bodies overseeing technical product information (France's standardization board AFNOR, the labeling group

49. Gisèle Lévy, "La fin d'une époque. . . ." *Points de vente* 157 (December 1976): 34.

50. Christiane Scrivener, "Pour un 'service consommateurs' dans les entreprises," *Les notes bleues* (1977).

51. Gisèle Prevost, "Qualification des produits industriels," *Les Échos*, 27 September 1979.

52. Garrigou, *L'assaut des consommateurs*, 93.

53. Claudie Bert, "La consommation et les enfants," *J'informe*, 18 November 1977.

54. ". . . d'une part, des scandales qui par leur forte visibilité sociale donnent une importance soudaine aux thèmes généraux du consumerism et aux organisations qui s'y consacrent; d'autre part, un effort soutenu, nettement moins populaire, axé sur un effort d'information sur la consommation de couches petites-bourgeoises." Michel Wieviorka, *L'état, le patronat, et les consommateurs* (Paris: Presses universitaires de France, 1977), 245.

55. "Opinions sur la fonction consommation et la libre entreprise," *Humanisme et entreprise* (April 1977): 13–19.

56. *La croix*, 29 June 1974.

AFEI, and so on). The Consumption Committee also suggested that this negotiation approach might be employed to eliminate abusive consumer contract clauses and to simplify consumer litigation.[57]

The negotiation approach to consumer protection became the orthodoxy of the third Barre government, inaugurated in 1978, and was especially championed by the new economics minister, René Monory.[58] Monory's tenure marked the beginning of the second stage of French consumer protection, which lasted from 1978 to 1983. Monory was an economist by training, and he believed that the best approach to consumer protection was not through greater government regulation but rather through empowering consumers to represent their interests directly to business. To symbolize this view, he eliminated the position of secretary of consumption. Instead, he publicly referred to himself as the "Minister of Consumption" and advocated that government financial support to consumer groups be increased by a factor of four in his first two years in office.[59] "We need to make producers and distributors realize," Monory wrote, "that the consumer should become a partner in all things, and who participates at all levels: from product manufacturing to price setting."[60] Monory felt in particular that inflation might be held down if the two million current members of consumer groups in France were encouraged to join a single centralized organization.[61]

The negotiation model, first proposed by consumer groups in 1975, was also increasingly accepted by business as a useful alternative to direct government intervention.[62] Ambroise Roux, head of the CNPF, felt that consumer groups "should be encouraged and developed."[63] Raymond Eberhardt, also of the CNPF, described the potential advantages of interacting with consumer groups: "It is in trying to communicate, any time we can, and as objectively as we can, that we will come to understand each other, to find and perfect flexible means of contact that are better adapted to the problems we face."[64] From November 1979 to 1981, the CNPF met monthly with consumer groups to discuss consumer issues as diverse as advertising, automobile sales, and post-sale service.[65] Between 1980 and 1983, the newly created Conseil national de la publicité (CNP) negotiated with consumer associations to set standards for advertising. The CNP contained representatives of eleven con-

57. Jacques Dubois, "Les consommateurs dans le 7ème plan," *Information consommation OR-GE-CO* 15 (1976): 1–2.

58. *Ecodis* 351 (11 February 1980).

59. "René Monory: davantage de moyens pour informer les consommateurs," *Démocratie moderne*, 22 November 1979.

60. "Il faut faire comprendre aux producteurs et distributeurs, explique M. Monory, que le consommateur doit devenir un partenaire à part entière, qui participe à tous les niveaux: la fabrication des produits comme la formation des prix." Jean Marchand, "Des moyens accrus au service des consommateurs," *La croix*, 21 March 1979.

61. *Le nouveau journal*, 28 September 1979.

62. Dubois, "Du mépris à la concertation," 2.

63. Ambroise Roux, "La réforme de l'entreprise," *CNPF Patronat* (1976): 29.

64. Isabelle Musnik, "La croisade de C. Lalumière," *La vie française*, 8 February 1982, 20.

65. Gérard Lavergne, "Eux, les clients," *CNPF Patronat* (1981): 22.

sumer organizations and as many representatives of the media.[66] Similar efforts to have consumer and professional interests negotiate agreements were being undertaken at the regional and local level throughout France.

By the beginning of 1980, however, French consumer associations had become concerned that industry was not abiding by negotiated standards. In a letter of January 1980, the eleven major national consumer associations renounced participation in all collective agreements with business until an enforcement mechanism was put in place.[67] Their response came with the 1980 Socialist victory of François Mitterrand. In his campaign platform, the "110 Propositions" for France, Mitterrand asserted that "consumer associations must be supported."[68] Emphasizing the importance of the consumer, Mitterrand created a minister-level position dedicated to the consumer interest with the explicit goal of promoting negotiations between consumer groups and professional interests.[69] In September 1981, the newly appointed minister of consumption, Catherine Lalumière, said in an interview: "I believe that we can do nothing with individual consumers in the state of nature, nor if all effort is concentrated at the state level."[70]

The Mitterrand government proposed that consumer groups be treated in the same manner that emerging labor unions had been treated in the past. By this analogy, industry should be given the responsibility of making agreements with consumer groups. Consumer advocates also felt that the interests of consumers deserved a legal status similar to that of labor interests.[71] To this end, Lalumière appointed lawyer and consumer advocate Jean Calais-Auloy to head a committee to rewrite French consumer law.[72] While the new commission was given free reign to consolidate and rethink consumer protection laws, Calais-Auloy declared that it would focus quickly on "collective conventions," even suggesting that an approach might be considered to make the results of such conventions mandatory for businesses.[73]

Employers agreed to participate in these collective conventions as long as the resulting agreements were not made mandatory by the government. Maurice Simonet, head of the CICC, wrote in a letter to Catherine Lalumière that the concertation[74] meetings would "have a greater chance of arriving at a consensus if they bring to the table two parties rather than three. . . . The third party [the state], in such a case,

---

66. *CNPF Patronat* (July 1983): 71.

67. Didier Ferrier, *La protection des consommateurs* (Paris: Dalloz, 1996), 80.

68. "Il faut renforcer les associations de consommateurs. C'est une des priorités de mon action car je crois que l'on ne peut rien faire avec des consommateurs atomisés dans la nature et qu'on ne peut rien faire si tout est concentré au niveau de l'état." Alain Poirée, *Les discours consuméristes et leur perception par les Français* (Paris: ICC-CNPF, 1984), 36.

69. *Consommateurs actualités* (4 September 1981), 5–6.

70. "Je crois qu'on ne peut rien faire avec des consommateurs atomisés dans la nature et qu'on ne peut rein faire si tout est concentré au niveau de l'état." Josée Doyère, "Un entretien avec le ministre de la consommation," *Le Monde,* 17 September 1981.

71. *Que savoir* (June–July 1982): 53.

72. Josée Doyère, "Des 'conventions collectives' de la consommation rendront obligatoires les engagements des professionnels," *Le Monde,* 5 December 1981.

73. *Le Monde,* 21 December 1981.

74. The term "concertation" in the French language refers to a social dialogue or deliberative process involving multiple parties and intended to achieve common goals.

becomes more or less an arbitrator and its presence is more of an obstacle to concessions without which an agreement is difficult." He argued that concertation should be regional and sectoral in scope and not take place within state-sponsored regulatory bodies.[75] Jean Levy, who would become Simonet's successor, saw such conventions as attractive insofar as they could help industry to avoid greater state intervention: "A good experiment is better than bad regulation."[76]

But as consumer and producer groups gathered again to negotiate collective conventions, both sides quickly became disgruntled. For business, the participation of union-based consumer groups was of particular concern. The CNPF's vice president, Guy Brana, wrote of the union-based consumer groups: "The dialogue with consumers would certainly be cleared of ambiguity if certain associations [i.e., the union-based groups] would not deviate from their roles—for example if they were not also trying to change the broader structures of our society."[77] One industrialist was quite blunt about the situation in which labor-related consumer groups negotiated with producers: "We truly find ourselves in a sandwich."[78] For their part, consumer groups felt that industry was again not complying with negotiated agreements. Laurent Denis, head of the INC, wrote: "The only question that remains is whether [the results of collective conventions] should be made mandatory. Our answer is no, if professionals and owners respect their agreements. But that is not the case. . . . The *patronat* accuse consumer groups for not being representative. Is it not rather them who fail to respect their agreements?"[79]

Meanwhile Calais-Auloy, reporting back to the economics ministry on the commission's work, advocated greater government intervention:

> Individually, consumers find themselves in an inferior position that makes all negotiation with producers illusory. But this inferiority disappears if the consumers form groups to negotiate collectively: the negotiations can result in accords that oblige each economic partner to respect the interests of the other. . . . This system will only work if the law requires professionals to accept the accords signed by [consumer] organizations. This is what the "Commission de refonte" proposes. The commission has been inspired by the texts of the "Code de travail" concerning collective conventions.

What the commission specifically proposed was to "extend" voluntary accords by decree of the minister of consumption. "The collectively negotiated accords that are extended [would] take the place of law for all producers whether or not they are members of the negotiating group." Such a provision, borrowed directly from labor law, would allow consumers to take companies to court over convention breaches.[80]

75. "Reforme de l'INC et du CNC," *Économie et consommation* 114 (19 October 1981).

76. *Les Échos*, 13 July 1982, 6.

77. *Libération*, 20–21 February 1982.

78. Isabelle Musnik, "Bien Consommer, l'autre revolution," *La vie française*, 25 April 1983, 28.

79. Elisabeth Rochard, "Les consommateurs en désaccord avec le CNPF," *Le Matin*, 25 February 1982.

80. Calais-Auloy reported the preliminary conclusions of his committee to Lalumière in 1982. The final report was published two years later. Jean Calais-Auloy, *Vers un nouveau droit de la consommation*, rapport de la commission de refonte du droit de la consommation au secrétaire d'État

This corporatist solution was applauded by consumers but strongly opposed by industry. The Paris Chamber of Commerce and Industry (Chambre de commerce et de l'industrie Paris, CCIP) criticized the committee for its lack of industry representatives.[81] They argued that French business was simply not sufficiently organized to negotiate on an equal footing with consumer groups and foresaw that the diversity of business interests would put them at a disadvantage to France's politically active consumer groups.[82] The CNPF was also not happy with the analogy equating consumers and workers.[83] They argued that professional associations could not sign binding agreements with consumers because consumer groups were not truly representative and because consumer groups did not have the necessary technical training to consider the issues that would be involved in such negotiations.[84] The Ministry of Justice sided with industry, arguing that the analogy between consumers and labor unions was not legally valid.[85] In the end, however, it was the financial crisis of 1983 that largely put an end to Lalumière's corporatist aspirations.

This policy collapse signaled the move to the third stage of French consumer policy that endured for the next twenty years, in which consumers were protected through state intervention designed to shift the burden of product-related risk entirely onto producers. This policy was embodied in the 1983 law for consumer protection that created the CSC, which was modeled on the U.S. Food and Drug Administration.[86] Government ministries were granted extraordinary rights to survey the consumer market and to call for products to be withdrawn. In 1985, France endorsed a state-sponsored consumer defense by joining the functions of consumer protection and competition in the new General Direction of Competition, Consumption and the Elimination of Fraud (Direction générale de la concurrence, de la consommation et de la répression des fraudes, DGCCRF).[87] This protection model remains the dominant strategy of consumer protection in France today.

---

aupres du minister de l'Économie, des Finances et du Budget chargé de la consommation (Paris: Documentation française, 1984), 71–75.

81. Chambre de commerce et d'industrie de Paris, *La politique de la consommation* (Paris: CCIP, 1982), 16.

82. Chambre de commerce et d'industrie de Paris, *La creation du Conseil national de la consommation* (Paris: CCIP, 1983), 10.

83. Elisabeth Rochard, "Le CNPF ne veut pas de conventions collectives de la consommation," *Le Matin,* 19 February 1982.

84. Maria Aubertin and Edmond Robin, *Les nouveaux rapports entre producteurs et consommateurs* (Paris: La mission a l'innovation, 1981).

85. Ministère de la Justice, "Observations sur l'eventualité de conventions collectives entre les organisations de consommateurs et les professionnels," Paris, correspondence of 14 March 1980.

86. Françoise Vaysse, "Les anges gardiens de la sécurité," *Le Monde,* 14 April 1992.

87. Anne Fily and Philippe Guillermin, "Les politiques de la consommation dans les États membres de la CEE," *Revue de la concurrence et de la consommation* 70 (1992).

Contested Ideas and Policy Formation

France and Germany considered a broad set of regulatory options before pursuing divergent policy programs. Government officials in both countries commissioned reports on the strategies adopted in foreign countries, funded research on the potential impact of different strategies at home, and convened discussion groups in which domestic interest groups could present their ideas and concerns. Far from being constrained by an overarching policy paradigm, as the cultural interpretation would suggest, French and German policymakers appear to have been consciously seeking a useful new paradigm for the consumerist agenda. The role of ideas in the case of consumer policy is thus closer to the role that Anne Swidler attributes to culture. In times of policy innovation, ideas like culture act as a toolbox from which policymakers select based on other considerations.[88] In the case of product market regulation, the selection emerged from conscious political struggle between consumer and producer interests.

The case of consumer protection suggests that the tools of institutional analysis that have been deployed in comparative politics to explain periods of policy continuity can also be applied to understand periods of radical policy innovation. In radically new areas of public policy, alternative ideas about how the new policy should be addressed become the focus of political contestation. These different ideas have the status of policy models, in that they imply comprehensive but exclusive conceptual frameworks for regulation. The policy model that came to dominate policymaking in each country depended on the interests and the institutional form of the important economic actors in each society.

This "contested ideas" approach offers a hypothesis about how different countries will regulate consumer markets. In general, when consumers are mobilized and industry is disorganized, as in France, we should expect a protection approach to consumer policy to emerge. This model also appears to represent the approaches adopted in the United States and in Canada. By contrast, when consumers are not mobilized and industry is organized, as in Germany, we should expect an information approach to emerge. This model appears to represent the approaches adopted in Spain and in Austria. Finally, when consumers are mobilized and businesses are organized, a situation emerges in which a negotiation strategy may prevail. This model appears to describe the consumer policy setting in Sweden and, indeed, all of Scandinavia. In these countries, strong consumer cooperative movements formed the basis of a strong consumer mobilization, and producers were also highly organized.

This approach does not address the origins of consumer and producer organizational strategies. French and German industrial organizations have roots in their nineteenth-century experience of industrialization. Those roots precede the debate on consumer protection by nearly a century. The different organizational strategies

88. Ann Swidler, "Culture in Action: Symbols and Strategies," *American Sociological Review* 51 (1986).

of French and German consumer groups had a more recent origin, emerging only in the late 1960s and early 1970s. The contested ideas approach artificially separates the question of consumer group organization from the broader question of product market regulation. It therefore rests on the assumption that consumer organization is causally independent of producer interests. The following chapter takes up this point, showing that French and German consumer groups mobilized in response to a variety of exogenous factors, including existing government institutions, historical legacies, intellectual traditions, and alliances with labor and retailers.

CHAPTER THREE

The Organized Consumer

If important private consumption experiences . . . leave behind them
a trail of disappointment and frustration and if . . . political action is
available to the disappointed consumer, is it likely that this pursuit will
be taken up at some favorable occasion?

—ALBERT HIRSCHMAN, *Shifting Involvements*

The puzzle of modern consumer protection is the weakness of the political interests it protects. Consumers are by their nature disorganized: their goals are potentially diverse, the benefits of consumer protection measures are necessarily diffuse, so the costs of organizing such a large group must be high.[1] Moreover, the specific nature of consumer interests aggravates the challenges of organization. First, the interests of consumers often conflict directly with the interests of well-organized producers and organized labor.[2] Indeed, consumers are themselves commonly also members of these groups, and group actions such as product boycotts can hurt businesses and workers.[3] Second, the mundane nature of many consumer concerns—high prices, low quality, misleading advertising—provide a weak ideological basis for organizational solidarity compared, for example, to protests for human rights or the environment.[4] The technical complexity of consumer protec-

1. Mancur Olson, *The Logic of Collective Action: Public Goods and the Theory of Groups* (Cambridge, Mass.: Harvard University Press, 1965); Mark V. Nadel, *The Politics of Consumer Protection* (Indianapolis: Bobbs-Merrill, 1971); and Russell Hardin, *Collective Action* (Baltimore: Johns Hopkins University Press, 1982).

2. Claus Offe, "Ausdifferenzierung oder Integration: Bemerkungen über strategische Alternativen der Verbraucherpolitik," *Zeitschrift für Verbraucherpolitik* 5/1–2 (1981): 122.

3. Monroe Friedman, "Using Consumer Boycotts to Stimulate Corporate Policy Change," in *Politics, Products, and Markets*, ed. Michelle Micheletti, Andreas Follesdal, and Dietland Stolle (New Brunswick, N.J.: Transaction Publishers, 2004), 60.

4. Patricia L. MacLaughlan, *Consumer Politics in Postwar Japan: The Institutional Boundaries of Citizen Activism* (New York: Columbia University Press, 2002), 17.

tion issues can raise obstacles to citizen engagement. For all of these reasons, the obstacles to consumer mobilization should have been high.

Yet consumers nonetheless organized. In both France and Germany, organized consumer groups were able to play a critical balancing role in the political struggle with producers over the future economic and social identity of the consumer. Through this political process, the nature of each country's consumer organization became an important determinant of national policy outcomes. To understand the consumer policies that emerged in France and Germany, we must look more closely at the groups that represented consumers in the policymaking process.

French and German consumer mobilization strategies lay at opposite ends of a spectrum running from assimilation to confrontation.[5] At the confrontation end, France in the 1970s saw the rise of a particularly active and popular consumer movement. French consumer groups adopted a strategy of mass mobilization and radical opposition to industry. Individual consumers participated in extensive price surveys, political rallies, and product boycotts. The French consumer movement took on a political valence. Each of the major labor unions created its own consumer group, as did some political parties. These groups were given policy access at the ministerial level, so that consumerism quickly became a new arena for political struggle. The French groups took on the status of a watchdog to industry, looking out for transgressions, mobilizing against high prices and dangerous products, and filing frequent lawsuits. By the late 1970s, French consumer groups had become numerous, dynamic, and increasingly well funded. French producers complained that the "strong and imperative language" employed by consumer groups reflected a tendency to exaggerate problems in a way that undermined the integrity of the consumer movement as a whole.[6] But such exaggeration was a useful tool for consumer groups focused on cultivating interest among consumers in order to pursue the consumer interest.[7]

In Germany, by contrast, the consumer movement eschewed grass-roots mobilization and instead cultivated a strong technical competency that permitted it to sit as an informed participant in policy and technical forums. German consumer groups avoided politically polarized issues and party affiliations. Their contribution to debates occurred within individual ministries rather than at the ministerial level and was normally technical rather than political in substance. German consumer groups consulted with industry, participated on technical committees, helped to enforce competition and cartel regulations, and disseminated technical product information to consumers. From these different strategies of organization emerged different sets of goals, actions, and priorities for consumer policy.

The patterns of mobilization we observe in the two countries fit uncomfortably

5. Herbert P. Kitschelt, "Political Opportunity Structure and Political Protest: Anti-Nuclear Movements in Four Democracies," *British Journal of Political Science* 16 (1986): 66.

6. Alain Poirée, *Les discours consuméristes et leur perception par les Français* (Paris: I.C.C.-C.N.P.F., 1984), 45–46.

7. Harvey M. Sapolsky, "The Politics of Product Controversies," in *Consuming Fears: The Politics of Product Risk,* ed. Harvey Sapolsky (New York: Basic Books, 1987), 183.

within the French and German traditions of associational activism. The French have conventionally been viewed as skeptical of the political and economic influence of intermediate associations.[8] As Peter Hall writes of French policymaking: "Aggregations of individuals and formal organizations outside the state cannot pretend to speak for the general interest. Their political status is suspect."[9] This aversion to independent societal groups, compounded by the inherent challenges in organizing consumers, would appear to make France an unpromising context for consumer mobilization. In Germany, by contrast, the tradition of citizen mobilization has strong roots. Beginning in the 1970s—precisely when consumer issues were becoming politically salient—new and dynamic associations emerged to organize citizens on issues such as the environment, women's rights, and peace. Unlike the German consumer movement, these new citizens groups embraced grass-roots mobilization and activism.[10] How do we account for this difference?

This chapter traces the organizational strategies of the consumer movements in France and Germany and their relation to the institutional environment in which the consumer groups emerged. The consumer groups based their strategies in part on financial and political resources made available by their governments, in part on their interactions with potential allies among trade unions and retailers, and in part on national traditions of protest, organization, and representation. Critically, for the account of consumer policy presented above, consumers appear to have organized in ways that were largely independent of the interests of business. Had consumer organizations simply reflected business interests—had they emerged from similar institutional roots, had they embraced consumer concerns that had been molded by producers, or had they themselves been co-opted by business interests—then the role of consumer groups in negotiations with producers could not be interpreted as exogenous. Yet this was not the case. The dynamics of consumer mobilization in France and Germany were complex—with ample room for agency—and largely free of causal links to business.

The Organization of Consumers: Two Approaches

The French and German consumer movements were both structured in three tiers. At the top, single peak-level associations represented general consumer interests in

8. Michel Crozier, *The Bureaucratic Phenomenon* (Chicago: University of Chicago Press, 1964), 316–17; and Jonah D. Levy, *Tocqueville's Revenge: State, Society, and Economy in Contemporary France* (Cambridge, Mass.: Harvard University Press, 1999), 13.

9. Peter A. Hall, *Governing the Economy: the Politics of State Intervention in Britain and France* (New York: Oxford University Pres, 1986), 165.

10. This difference in organizational culture between France and Germany has been reinforced by researchers of social capital, who have found a far lower associational tendency in France than in Germany. See, for example, Jean-Pierre Worms, "Old and New Civic Ties in France," in *Democracies in Flux: The Evolution of Social Capital in Contemporary Society*, ed. Robert Putnam (London: Oxford University Press, 2002), 141; and Francis Fukuyama, *Trust: The Social Virtues and the Creation of Prosperity* (New York: Free Press, 1996), 10.

each country. Germany's Association of Consumer Groups (Arbeitsgemeinschaft der Verbraucherverbände, AgV), formed in 1953, had a dual goal of coordinating the interests of its member consumer organizations and of representing the general consumer interest to the government. France's National Consumption Institute (Institut national de la consommation, INC), created in 1968, was formally independent of other consumer groups, although at times it became embroiled in political debates. It acted as a technical resource on consumer questions, providing a sort of information clearinghouse for independent consumer groups, government, and business. It also published the results of comparative product tests in its in-house magazine, *50 millions de consommateurs*. Both groups received the majority of their funding from the government.

Below these peak associations operated a layer of national consumer groups. In Germany, these groups were organized by technical function. The Stiftung Warentest, created in 1964, conducted comparative product testing. The Verbraucherschutzverein, created in 1966, brought legal suits in cases of misleading advertising and unfair contract terms. The Stiftung Verbraucherinstitut, created in 1978, promoted consumer education and professional training. Other national groups focused on specific classes of consumers, including welfare recipients, housewives, farmers, and veterans. In France, national-level consumer groups were less differentiated, tending to offer an eclectic combination of services to consumers, including advice, legal support, price tracking, and lobbying. By the late 1970s, France had a dozen such groups, which often competed directly with one another for consumer recognition, membership, and public influence. Indeed, consumer advocates commonly criticized these national groups for their lack of coordination, which they perceived as a source of weakness for the French consumer movement. Josée Doyère, a journalist and longtime observer of France's consumer movement, wrote in 1975: "The eleven [national consumer] organizations continue to exhaust themselves in sterile quarrels. . . . The desire of each to be original leads them to trust no one, and certainly not other consumer groups."[11]

Finally, a third layer of regional and local consumer groups undertook intensive interactions with individual consumers. In France, these local unions were affiliated with the national consumer groups and grew rapidly in number during the 1970s. By 1984, one survey found that France had 860 local consumer unions affiliated with nineteen national consumer associations.[12] While their functions were diverse, they generally undertook similar activities: price surveys, public awareness campaigns, and the occasional product boycott and political rally. In 1976, for example, local consumer groups in the south of France organized under the name "Operation Vacation" hosted 248 consultation sites to assist tourists with grievances.[13] In an-

11. Josée Doyère, *Le combat des consommateurs* (Paris: Le Cerf, 1975), 206.

12. These included 149 local unions affiliated with the UFC, 87 with the labor-affiliated group AFOC, 70 with the family group UFCS, 68 with the FFF, and 63 with the CSCV. "Elements statistique sur la vie associative locale des organizations de consommateurs en 1985," *Bulletin intérieur de documentation de la répression des fraudes (BID)* 8 (August 1985): 64.

13. *Un monde en mouvement: les organisations de consommation* (Paris: Ministère de l'économie–Comité national de la consommation, 1980), 79.

other typical episode, in 1979, local unions affiliated with the Federal Consumption Union (Union fédérale des consommateurs, UFC) surveyed thousands of stores across France to assess compliance with price labeling laws.[14] They also undertook a number of government-sanctioned activities, including assisting in settling consumer disputes and participating on committees to evaluate permits for large store openings.

In Germany, the core activity of most state-level consumer groups was the funding and management of local consumer advice centers (*Verbraucherberatungsstellen*). These centers, open free to the public, provided technical information to consumers considering new purchases. A consumer interested in purchasing a new camera or vacuum could receive from the center both general advice on the technology involved as well as detailed information in the form of product test results and product data sheets. Germany had sixty-four such centers in 1972, almost twice that by 1982.[15] The services provided by the consumer advice centers were viewed favorably both by consumers and by business. In a 1984 evaluation of consumer centers in Hamburg, 90 percent of center users said they would go back for future purchases.[16] Producers also approved of the work of the consumer advice centers. Albrecht Schultz, former member of the board of directors at Braun, explained that brand name manufacturers had a strong interest in consumer advising because accurate information helped keep consumers from being disappointed, thereby encouraging repeat purchases.[17] Critically, content analysis of advice given at these centers showed that it focused primarily on aspects of product quality, with only rare mentions of price or of where the products might be purchased more cheaply.[18]

Consumer Mobilization

The similar structures of the French and German consumer movements disguised radically different organizing principles. One reflection of this difference was their record of individual membership. A Eurobarometer survey conducted in 1978 asked consumers whether they were members of organizations with "no links with manufacturers or traders and whose specific aim is to inform and defend the consumer." Three percent of the French respondents identified themselves as members of such

14. "Une enquête de l'Union fédérale des consommateurs," *Le Monde*, 12 December 1979; and Jürgen Bornecke, *Handbuch der Verbraucherinstitutionen* (Bonn: Verlag Information für die Wirtschaft, 1982), 138.

15. Wolfgang Hoffmann, "Wie aufgeklärt ist der Konsument?" *Die Zeit*, 11 August 1972, 37.

16. Lothar Maier, "Zur Wirksamkeit der Produktberatung in Verbraucherzentralen: Ergebnisse einer Umfrage," in *Die Qualität von Beratungen für Verbraucher*, ed. Volkmar Lübke and Ingo Schoenheit (Frankfurt: Campus Verlag, 1985), 189.

17. Albrecht Schultz, "Das Interesse der Industrie an adäquater Beratung des Verbrauchers durch Handel und Verbraucherberatungsstellen," in *Die Qualität von Beratungen*, ed. Lübke and Schoenheit.

18. Udo Beier, "Schwachstellen einer mit vergleichenden Warentestberichten arbeitenden Produktberatung: Eine Übersicht über empirische Untersuchungsergebnisse," in *Die Qualität von Beratungen*, ed. Lübke and Schoenheit, 189.

groups, compared to a statistically insignificant number of Germans.[19] Further-more, while 27 percent of French people reported the desire to join such a group, only 8 percent of Germans felt that way. This apparently low level of consumerist enthusiasm in Germany was not a product of ignorance. Fifty-five percent of Germans reported knowing of such consumer organizations, compared to only 44 percent of French citizens.[20] Rather, these different levels of citizen participation reflected the priorities of the consumer movements in the two countries. In France, consumer groups worked hard to cultivate a grass-roots membership; in Germany, consumer groups actively discouraged individual membership.

Most of Germany's consumer groups either discouraged individual membership or banned it outright. The AgV had fewer than one hundred individual members, and these were limited to prominent academics, lawyers and politicians who were "particularly suited to the goals of the organization."[21] Since the AgV represented Germany's other consumer associations, they might reasonably have shunned individual participants. But most of Germany's state-level consumer centers also discouraged individual membership. Of the eleven state-level consumer centers in West Germany, only five permitted individual membership in their by-laws, and these did so only in limited numbers. The consumer center in Hesse, for example, provided openings for six individual members. City states like Berlin and Hamburg allowed unlimited individual membership, but they too generally experienced only low levels of citizen participation.[22]

Germany's consumer groups actively opposed expanding their membership. They argued that admitting individual members into consumer organizations could bias their representation towards the interests of the middle class, since activists were likely to be of a relatively high socioeconomic level.[23] A publication of the consumer center of North Rhine–Westphalia explained the opposition to broader citi-

19. The level of national consumer participation in such groups has often been a source of mis-understanding in comparative studies of consumer mobilization. In a 1978 analysis of the consumer movement, Jacqueline Poelmans estimated that 45 percent of German families and 25 percent of French families were affiliated with consumer groups. Estimates by consumer groups themselves found that French consumer groups had a total of two million members in the late 1970s, and that German consumer groups had as many as eight million members in the mid-1980s. These impressive numbers typically include individuals and families that simply subscribe to the publications of consumer-oriented associations. Also, many groups that are members of Germany's AgV are not perceived by their own members as being consumer groups. See Jacqueline Poelmans, *L'Europe et les consommateurs* (Brussels: Editions Labor, 1978), 140; "Un hypersyndicat?" *Le nouveau journal*, 28 September 1979; and Hartwig Piepenbrock, "Die Legitimation der Verbraucherverbände zur Wahrnehmung von Verbraucherinteressen," in *Verbraucherpolitik kontrovers*, ed. Hartwig Piepenbrock and Conrad Schroeder (Cologne: Deutscher Instituts-Verlag, 1987), 102.

20. George H. Gallup, *The International Gallup Polls: Public Opinion 1978* (Wilmington, Del.: Scholarly Resources, 1979), 365.

21. By-laws of the AgV, Section 4, Paragraph 1.

22. Piepenbrock, "Die Legitimation der Verbraucherverbände," in *Verbraucherpolitik kontrovers*, ed. Piepenbrock and Schroeder, 101–7.

23. Christine Czerwonka, Günter Schoppe, and Stefan Weckbach, *Der aktive Konsument: Kommunikation und Kooperation* (Göttingen: Verlag Otto Schwartz, 1976), 193.

zen participation: "In the context of socially oriented consumer work we must consider the problems and information needs of specific minorities that are possibly not represented, or even opposed, by the majority or average citizen."[24] The low membership in the German consumer movement was a target for critics of the system. Some felt that these groups had insulated themselves from the real interests of working-class consumers, had discouraged creative strategies of defending consumer interests, and had failed to develop the necessary legitimacy to negotiate directly with industry.[25] But Germany's business and political leaders disagreed. Industry worried that a politically powerful consumer movement would lead to greater regulation. Moreover, *both* the Christian Democratic Union (CDU) and the Social Democratic Party (SPD) opposed the enlargement of individual consumer membership out of concern for the direction in which a politicized consumerist agenda would take such groups. Indeed, the lone political voice advocating expanded popular participation in Germany's consumer movement was the centrist liberal party, the Free Democratic Party (FDP).[26]

In France, by contrast, grass-roots mobilization lay at the heart of the consumer movement. This approach may have reflected, in part, a greater interest in consumer issues on the part of the French public. As early as 1972, a survey conducted by the National Consumption Institute (INC) found that 20 percent of French citizens over fifteen years of age said they were "ready to belong" to a consumer organization.[27] By 1979, an estimated two million French citizens described themselves as actually belonging to such a group.[28] While many of these were relatively passive members, paying their dues for the monthly magazine, a growing number of French citizens were becoming grass-roots activists.

The formation of these local consumer unions began as an explicit strategy of the consumer movement in the early 1970s. One of the largest mobilizers was the Federal Consumers' Union (UFC). The UFC, created initially as an umbrella consumer organization in 1951, became independent and began publishing the results of comparative product tests in its monthly journal *Que choisir?* in 1960. In 1973, the UFC began inviting its local readers to meetings hosted all over France. Where interest was sufficiently high, the UFC sponsored local consumer unions. These local unions blossomed over the course of the decade, with 40 registered in 1976, 100 in 1977, and 161 in 1979. By 1980 the UFC had 170 local unions with a total of fifty thou-

---

24. *Die Verbraucherberatung in Nordrhein-Westfalen aus Sicht der Bevölkerung 1984/5* (Bielefeld, Germany: VZ Nordrhein-Westfalen, 1985), 1.

25. Reinhard Rock, Bernd Biervert, and Wolf F. Fischer-Winkelmann, "A Critique of Some Fundamental Theoretical and Practical Tenets of Present Consumer Policy," *Zeitschrift für Verbraucherpolitik* 4/2 (1980): 98; and Roberta Sassetilli, *Power Balance in the Consumption Sphere: Reconsidering Consumer Protection Organisations* (Florence: European University Institute Working Paper, 1995).

26. Christine Czerwonka and Günter Shöppe, "Verbraucherpolitische Konzeptionen und Programme in der Bundesrepublik Deutschland," *Zeitschrift für Verbraucherpolitik* 1/3 (1977): 286–87.

27. Dominique Pons, *Consomme et tais-toi* (Paris: Epi, 1972), 97.

28. *Le nouveau journal*, 28 September 1979.

sand members.[29] Most were relatively small, with less than 200 members; some grew to have over 500 members. By 1980, the local unions were handling 35,000–40,000 consumer complaints each year, as well as participating in price surveys, mobilizations, and regional consumer assemblies (unions régionales des organisations de consommateurs, UROCs).[30]

While the UFC was focused on consumer issues from its inception, France's consumer movement also drew in a diverse set of related associations. One large set of groups had their origins as family associations, founded mainly in the immediate post–World War II period, with the goal of promoting family life and values. These groups initially had a large but passive membership. They published monthly magazines that tended in their early years to focus on the private challenges of the French family or of rural life.[31] By the 1970s, many of these groups refashioned themselves as consumer protection organizations, so that by 1984, these family associations accounted for over a third of all of France's local consumer unions.[32] Although often less militant than the UFC, these groups nonetheless managed consumer complaints, negotiated with producers, and sat on other government bodies dealing with consumer protection.

A third source of new consumer mobilization came from the labor union movement. The Organisation générale des consommateurs (ORGECO) was the first such group, created in 1959 to represent all consumers who were also union members. However, France had three major private sector trade unions, and by the mid-1970s they began breaking away from ORGECO to create their own affiliated consumer groups. The first was Force ouvrière (FO), which broke from ORGECO in 1974 to form l'Association force ouvrière consommateurs (AFOC). By 1988, AFOC alone had 60,000 members, distributed 15,000 copies of its publication *Les Cahiers de l'AFOC,* and handled 40,000 to 50,000 legal cases per year.[33] It was followed in 1979 by the communist trade union, the Confédération générale du travail (CGT), which created its own consumer group, Association pour l'information et défense des consommateurs salariés (Indecosa CGT). Jean-Louis Moynot, secretary of the CGT,

29. Jean-Marc Biais, "L'état se dépense pour les consommateurs," *La vie française,* 30 January 1978; Josée Doyère, "Les associations de consommateurs," *Le monde dimanche,* 16 November 1980.

30. François Daujam, *Information et pouvoir des consommateurs: Le rôle de l'Union fédérale des consommateurs,* thesis, department of economic and social sciences, University of Toulouse, 29 April 1980, 54–63.

31. These groups included: l'Union féminine civique et sociale (UFCS), founded in 1925; la Confédération nationale de la famille rurale (CNFR), founded in 1944; l'Union nationale des associations familiales (UNAF), founded in 1945; la Confédération syndicale des familles (CSF), founded in 1946; la Fédération des familles de France (FFF), founded in 1948; and la Confédération nationale des associations populaires familiales (CNAPF), founded in 1952. CNAPF was renamed the Confédération syndicale du cadre de vie (CSCV) in 1975. Claude Romec, "Organisations de consommateurs," *Réforme,* 15 December 1975; Jean Marchand, "Des moyens accrus au service des consommateurs," *La croix,* 21 March 1979.

32. "Elements statistique sur la vie associative locale des organisations de consommateurs en 1985," *Bulletin intérieur de documentation de la répression des fraudes (BID)* 8 (August 1985): 64.

33. Maurice Lecroel, "Force ouvrière et les consommateurs," in *Force ouvrière, les consommateurs et l'écologie,* ed. René Mauriaux (Paris: FNSP-CEVIPOF, 1994), 19–20.

explained that their goal was to "introduce a class dimension that is most often absent from the ideology of consumer defense."[34] Indecosa-CGT created twenty-nine affiliated local groups by 1981, and 240 by 1989.[35] Finally, in 1981, the Confédération française démocratique du travail (CFDT) trade union broke away to form l'Association études et consommation (ASSECO-CFDT). These union-affiliated groups applied organizing skills developed in the context of labor mobilization to attract and motivate their own activist consumer memberships.

One of the surprises of the French consumer movement was the relative weakness of France's consumer cooperatives. Their representative group, the Fédération nationale des coopératives de consommateurs (FNCC), had a vast membership. Like the UFC, it created its own product testing lab, the Laboratoire coopératif d'analyses et de recherches (LaboCoop), to provide consumers with an early source of product testing results. Yet, unlike in the Scandinavian countries, France's cooperative movement had a difficult time adapting to the value-for-money consumer movement that emerged in the 1970s. Because of its ties with producers, it was unwilling to take a confrontational stance. Even in its product tests, it did not reveal the specific brands it was testing (labeling them instead "product A" and "product B") out of concern that it would hurt the interests of cooperative producers. Of all the segments of the French consumer movement, the stance of the cooperatives perhaps most closely resemble its German counterpart. The LaboCoop was eventually closed in 1985.[36]

The high degree of mobilization of the French consumer groups allowed them to undertake public efforts unimaginable in the German context. High prices were a major concern, so it became the focus of periodic consumer actions. In 1976, roughly 800 local "consumer clubs" affiliated with the Popular Association of Families (Associations populaires familiales, APF) sponsored a "3–6–9 boycott." In response to recent price increases, they called on consumers to stop buying meat for three days, then fruit for six days, and then mineral water for nine days.[37] They emphasized that it was not only a shopping boycott but also a consuming boycott. "We refuse not simply to buy, but also to consume," wrote the APF. "Which means: no stocking up, no supplementary purchases before operation 3–6–9."[38] In 1980, the family group Confédération syndicale du cadre de vie (CSCV) organized hundreds of consumer members in Moselle to visit a local supermarket called Radar that the CSCV felt was overcharging customers. Carts full, the activists met at the registers at 4:30 in the afternoon and demanded a 10 percent reduction in price. Having blocked the checkout lines, CSCV members distributed pamphlets outside. When the police arrived,

34. *Les Echos,* 21 December 1979.

35. INC Archive, folder Indecosa CGT: "Extrait de l'allocution prononcée par Lydia Borelli lors du 10ème anniversaire d'Indicosa CGT," *Montreuil,* 29 November 1989.

36. "L'intérêt des consommateurs et l'ouverture des magasins le dimanche." *Informations indecosa-CGT* 9 (October 1985): 2.

37. Roger-Xavier Lanteri, "Prix: Que peuvent faire les consommateurs?" *L'Express,* 20 September 1976.

38. *Combat familial* 99 (n.d.).

the consumer activists reported on product labeling infractions they had noted in the store. The store's director commented: "If we start to discuss price, where will it go? Asking for a 10 percent reduction! They are completely shameless."[39] Such mobilizations became central to the identity of France's consumer movement. They helped to galvanize their membership and to boost the prestige of the national associations to which these local groups belonged.

France's trade union–affiliated consumer groups were active participants in such activities, but they often faced difficult conflicts of interest. Consumer boycotts could hurt the interests of labor; producer or labor actions could, in turn, leave consumers without access to products and services. Indeed, consumer boycotts were periodically organized in retaliation for work stoppages. On 15 November 1973, fruit and vegetable retailers closed their shops in protest over narrowing sales margins. On 19 November, French consumer groups called for a four-day consumer boycott of these retailers.[40]

Another source of tension concerned retail zoning. The 1973 *loi Royer* created departmental commissions for commercial town planning (Commission départementale d'urbanisme commercial, CDUC) to evaluate large new retail projects. Consumer groups, including union-affiliated groups, were invited to sit on these commissions.[41] In this context, they often found themselves advocating the opening of new large stores—because of the convenience and price advantage they offered to consumers—even when this threatened union jobs at traditional downtown retailers.[42] These sorts of tensions were never fully resolved and in the late 1980s the UFC called for discussions with organized labor "to think together about better means to not inconvenience the public, without undermining the right to strike."[43]

The French consumer movement also found common cause with France's growing large retail sector. Price surveys, conducted frequently by French consumer groups, consistently found that large-surface-area stores offered lower prices than traditional retailers.[44] In part for this reason, consumer groups came to the aid of large retailers in their efforts to secure business licenses for new stores. In 1970, consumers marched on the chamber of commerce in Dunkerque to apply pressure

39. Elisabeth Rochard, "Opération marchandage en Moselle," *Le Matin,* 20 June 1980.

40. *Combat,* 13 November 1973.

41. Small retailers opposed the idea of consumer participation in the CDUC. The UFC lobbied in the Sénat for the consumer to be integrated into these consultative groups, and they were eventually given two positions on each CDUC under the *loi Royer.* Daujam, *Information et pouvoir des consommateurs,* 41.

42. Interview with Pierre Marleix, Paris, June 2003.

43. *Libération,* 3–4 December 1988, 4.

44. A price survey conducted in 1973 by the local UFC union of France's Alpes-Maritimes department, for example, found that the small shops were on average 12 percent more expensive than the large surface stores. The survey was conducted during July and August by 200 members of the local union, who surveyed prices in 2,000 different stores. "La naissance de l'U.F.C.," *Bulletin d'information de l'UFC* (September–October 1973): 6–7; see also Pierre Combris, J. Hossenlopp, and Elise Zitt, "Evolution des associations de consommateurs et leurs impact sur les industriels," *Problèmes économiques* (11 January 1978), 10.

for the licensing of a new Centre Lemaire shopping center in the suburb of Synthe.[45] Similarly, Eduard Leclerc, founder of the Centre Leclerc chain of discount stores, describes collaborating with consumer groups to station 2,500 consumers in buses in the woods thirty kilometers away from the mayor's office in Rochefort— they were ready to protest if the zoning license for a new Leclerc store was not approved.[46]

In return, many of France's large retailers supported the goals of the consumer movement. FNAC, a large music and book cooperative, twice invited Ralph Nader to speak in France. FNAC also volunteered the building for its new Montparnasse store as the site of the first "Consumer Salon" in 1972, which an estimated 200,000 people visited.[47] A new Printemps 2000 store that opened in Rennes in 1973 made room for a Maurice column[48] at the center of the store on which consumer groups were encouraged to post product information and warnings.[49] In 1976, the Darty chain stirred controversy among France's consumer groups by offering one-third of their print advertising space for consumer group messages. Some groups took the opportunity; others criticized the initiative on the grounds that it would tarnish their reputation for independence.[50] In 1978, the retailer Intermarché announced that it would provide indications of the comparative qualities of products in its stores. It also provided facilities for consumers to test new products themselves and compiled information on comparative pricing.[51] Retailers also become some of the first businesses to negotiate protection standards with consumers.

The German Consumer Movement

Germany's consumer groups were less activist than their French counterparts, but they were far from inactive. In 1967, Germany's consumer groups hosted the first biannual "Week of the Consumer and Housewife." In cities around the country, state consumer associations hosted lectures and forums with titles like "Power and Powerlessness of the Consumer" and "Is the Consumer Really Manipulated?"[52]

45. Dominique Pons, *Consomme et tais-toi* (Paris: Epi, 1972), 98.

46. Éduard Leclerc, *Ma vie pour un combat* (Paris: Pierre Belfond, 1974), 103–4.

47. Michel Wieviorka, *L'état, le patronat, et les consommateurs: Étude des mouvements de consommateurs* (Paris: Presses universitaires de France, 1977), 131.

48. Maurice columns, named for a nineteenth-century Paris printer, were originally commissioned by the Baron Haussmann to display theater posters. They continue to be used for posting notices in public.

49. In Lorraine, the cooperative store Geric de Thionville placed a permanent information board in its store, where consumers and consumer groups are allowed to post information. No advertising or politics are allowed. Jean-Louis Bonnot, "Oui aux clients, non aux consommatisme," *Points de vente* 166 (October 1977): 45; Wieviorka, *L'état, le patronat, et les consommateurs*, 53–54.

50. "Quelques questions à Bernard Darty à propos de sa publicité au service des consommateurs," *Points de vente* 155 (October 1976), 12; for an example, see *Le Monde*, 26 June 1976.

51. *Le Figaro*, 17–18 June 1978.

52. *Verbraucherpolitische Korrespondenz* 30 (25 October 1967), 19.

They also periodically published informational brochures with titles like "The Elderly as Customer and Consumer" and "Laundry Damage: Evidence and Prevention." Over the next decade, Germany's consumer groups would undertake a wide variety of experimental activities aimed at better informing the consumer. Some focused on education through entertainment. The consumer center of North Rhine–Westphalia hosted a play to show how much time a woman could save through the use of modern household equipment and careful management of time.[53] The national Consumer Protection Union (Verbraucherschutzverein, VSV) sponsored a play by students from the Berlin Kreuzberg and Neuköln districts to spread the word about consumer contract abuses.[54] Beginning in 1971, the AgV even sponsored a highly successful international consumer film festival based in Berlin.[55]

Other actions represented more serious efforts to disseminate useful information. The Bonn consumer center, for example, conducted an independent test of freezers and found that most did not cool below the required −18 degrees Celsius.[56] The consumer center in Hamburg, working in collaboration with the German Nutrition Association (Deutsche Gesellschaft für Ernährung, DGE), offered a telephone service to inform consumers where they could find the best retail sales.[57] In 1973, the AgV itself sent two double-decker buses around Germany, visiting sixty cities over the course of two months. This "Bus-Aktion," which coincided with Germany's fourth Consumer Week, provided talks and exhibits that emphasized price comparison, knowledge of legal rights, and new efforts at consumer protection.[58] The Bus-Aktion was such a success that one AgV bus continued to circulate through Germany for most of the spring and fall of 1974.[59]

While the AgV and its member organizations did not rely on grass-roots activism, they did aggressively confront groups that they felt opposed the interests of consumers. From the early 1960s, they met regularly with professional associations for producers of consumer goods to advocate and negotiate informational product labels. Although industry initially balked at these efforts, they did eventually succeed in developing labels indicating such details as the percentage of wool in textiles and the fat content of sausages.[60] Occasionally their information campaigns led to consumer boycotts. In 1970, for example, the consumer center of Baden-Württemberg published a report on "The Practices of Real Estate Agents" that stimulated a boy-

53. "Verbraucherinformation auf neue Art," *Verbraucherpolitische Korrespondenz* 38 (16 December 1969).

54. "Jetzt wird 'Kleingedrucktes' der Verwaltung überprüft," *Der Tagesspiegel,* 13 September 1977.

55. *Verbraucherpolitische Korrespondenz* 3 (19 January 1971).

56. "Minuspunkte für Tiefkühlkette," *Verbraucherpolitische Korrespondenz* 23 (7 June 1977).

57. "Markttips per Telefon sollen den Einkauf erleichtern," *Verbraucherpolitische Korrespondenz* 37 (14 September 1971), 5.

58. "Busse rollen für die Verbraucher," *Verbraucherpolitische Korrespondenz* 38 (18 September 1973), 2.

59. *Verbraucherpolitische Korrespondenz* 17 (23 April 1974).

60. "Wollkennzeichnungsgesetz noch 1964 im Bundestag," *Verbraucherpolitische Korrespondenz* 2 (15 January 1964), 2.

cott against several agents in Stuttgart for excessive fees.[61] Germany's farmers were also a regular target for invective from consumer groups. From the late 1960s, the AgV reported monthly on changes in the price of a basket of about thirty consumer food products. They regularly attacked egg and milk producers and grain and vegetable growers for raising their prices unnecessarily.[62] They argued that farm lobbying had hurt consumers—adding an estimated 400 DM per year to the grocery bill of the average consumer—and created inflationary pressure in the German economy. Farmers responded in 1968 with mass protests and with calls to have the AgV's budget reduced.[63] In a statement that was revealing of the consumer movement's approach to organization, the AgV criticized the farmer activism: "Those responsible for Germany's agriculture should understand clearly, that a polemic of radicalization helps nobody."[64]

Another target of consumer attention was German retailers. The AgV was particularly critical of Germany's Store Closing Law (Ladenschlußgesetz)—what they dubbed "the worst law of all time"—which required that stores close at 6:30 p.m. on weekdays, 2 p.m. on Saturdays, and not open on Sundays. They complained of the inconvenience for working women, noting in particular that shorter shopping hours gave consumers less time for comparison shopping.[65] But retail opposition was strong. The Association of German Retailers (Hauptverband des Deutschen Einzelhandels, HDE) strongly opposed liberalization, arguing that longer store hours would increase prices for consumers who would, in the end, bear the costs of additional operating expenses. They also argued that liberalization would hurt single-family stores, which would be forced to stay open longer to remain competitive.[66] The Association of Middle and Large Retailers (Bundesarbeitsgemeinschaft der Mittel- und Grossbetriebe des Einzelhandels, BAG) also opposed liberalization on the grounds that increased wage costs would be likely to push a number of shops out of business.[67] Without sufficient grass-roots mobilization, the AgV probably had little chance of changing the policy. But the ongoing struggle did sour relations between consumers and retailers, blocking the kind of consumer/retailer collaboration that emerged in France in the 1970s.

German consumer groups never developed a fruitful working relation with Ger-

---

61. Verbraucherzentrale Baden-Württemberg e.V. *25 Jahre, 1958–1983*, 1982.

62. "Agrarpolitik gegen Preisestabilität," *Verbraucherpolitische Korrespondenz* 40 (6 October 1970), 4.

63. "Bauern will AgV mundtot machen," *Verbraucherpolitische Korrespondenz* 41 (13 October 1970).

64. "Bundesregierung als Prügelknabe der Bauernverbände," *Verbraucherpolitische Korrespondenz* 7 (5 March 1968), 2–3.

65. "Warum das 'schlechteste Gesetz aller Zeitem' eines Tages verschwinden wird," *Verbraucherpolitische Korrespondenz* 8 (15 March 1964), 2–3; and "Ladenschluss," *Verbraucherpolitische Korrespondenz* 5 (15 February 1968).

66. "Das Ladenschlussgesetz: Die Argumente des Einzelhandels," press release, Hauptgemeinschaft des Deutschen Einzelhandels, 3–4 November 1983.

67. "BAG für sachliche Argumentation in der Ladenschlussdiskussion," *Press-Information* (Bundesarbeitsgemeinschaft der Mittel- und Grossbetriebe des Einzelhandels, 22 May 1984).

many's labor unions. The Store Closing Law was one source of tension. German retail employees belonged to the large white-collar union, the Deutsche Angestellten Gewerkschaft (DAG), which also included both banking and insurance employees.[68] Taking on retailers meant taking on one of Germany's most powerful labor organizations. But the AgV criticized even Germany's largest union, the Deutscher Gewerkschaftsbund (DGB), for taking too little interest in the consumer movement.[69] The two groups did occasionally work together. For example, the DGB supported the AgV's initiative to create a new consumer academy.[70] But in general, the view of organized labor was that trade unions *were* consumer organizations and were sufficient to protect consumers.[71] In 1976, the DGB explained: "Consumer politics is an extension of wage politics. . . . We are not members of the AgV, since we see ourselves as an independent consumer organization, but we work for the same goal. Only our means and capabilities are different."[72] It may also be that German trade unions saw the consumer movement as unwelcome competition. Whatever the cause, German labor never engaged in the consumer movement in the way that labor did in France.

It is interesting to consider how German consumers might have responded to a more activist consumer movement. Was this ever a possibility? Evidence from consumer surveys in the early 1970s suggests that the German public might have welcomed more radicalism in this arena. A 1973 survey found that fully 81 percent of German consumers thought that consumer boycotts could be helpful.[73] In a 1974 survey of German consumers in Hesse, two-thirds indicated that they favored consumer boycotts, and fully half said that they were ready to join a consumer association, even if they had to pay dues to do so.[74] (By 1978 that number had fallen considerably.)

One consumer group in Germany that did pursue a more activist approach was the German Consumer League (Deutscher Verbraucherbund), created in 1965 by Hugo Schui. Described by one observer as the "pike in the carp pond of [German] consumer associations," Schui's group was financially independent of the government and regularly attacked both Parliament and the federal ministries.[75] In 1967, for example, he launched a nationwide consumer boycott of butter in an effort to

68. "DAG nennt Verbraucherzentrale Verbraucherunfreundlich," *Der Tagesspiegel*, 22 May 1980.

69. "Verbraucherorganisationen sehen Notwendigkeit zur Zusammenarbeit," *Der Tagesspiegel*, 6 September 1979.

70. Christine Czerwonka and Günter Shöppe, "Verbraucherpolitische Konzeptionen und Programme in der Bundesrepublik Deutschland," *Zeitschrift für Verbraucherpolitik* 1/3 (1977): 286.

71. Klaus Tonner, "Verbraucherpolitik als gewerkschaftliche Aufgabe," *Zeitschrift für Verbraucherpolitik* 3/3–4 (1979): 254.

72. "Arbeitnehmer- und Verbraucherorganisation," *Verbraucherpolitische Korrespondenz* 23 (8 June 1976), 7–8.

73. "Mehrzahl der Verbraucher befürwortet Käuferstreiks," *Verbraucherpolitische Korrespondenz* 38 (18 September 1973), 5.

74. "Zwei Drittel sind für Kaufboykotts," *Frankfurter Rundschau*, 23 October 1974.

75. Wolfgang Hoffmann, "Die Anwälte der Consumenten: Viele Verbraucherverbände— wenig Erfolg," *Die Zeit*, 26 March 1971, 29.

change government regulations that permitted reconstituted butter to be sold as fresh butter. Schui's group also went after retailers. In one action, he lodged complaints against 500 retailers that were not complying with price labeling requirements. He also established a chain of fifty "pilot stores" that agreed to undercut by 33 percent the markup that producers provided in their contracts with retailers.[76] By 1970, Schui's group had attracted 50,000 members, each of whom paid an annual fee of 6 DM. In return, they received the group's magazine, *Der Wecker* ("The Alarm Clock"), legal support against producers and distributors, and 500 DM of legal insurance to help them pursue consumer legal cases.[77] Schui also offered members discount flights to New York that significantly undercut conventional charter flights.[78]

Schui's early success suggests that a grass-roots consumer movement of the kind that emerged in France might have been possible in Germany. Yet Schui himself remained skeptical of the potential for German consumers to mobilize. Asked in 1972 about the possibility that recent consumer protests in Sweden might be reproduced in Germany, Schui responded: "It is a matter of the German mindset. Germans fear that such a [consumer] strike would be taken into the political debate. This is why so many resist [consumer] boycott actions."[79]

Institutional Context

One of the surprises of consumer mobilization in France and Germany is the considerable financial support that both governments gave to domestic consumer groups. In France, government funding to consumer groups grew from the equivalent of $675,000 in 1970 to $9 million in 1980. More than half of this support went to the government-sponsored National Consumption Institute (INC). Independent consumer groups were also big recipients. Between 1974 and 1983, inflation-adjusted transfers to these groups grew sevenfold. Financial support for union-affiliated consumer groups increased from 35,000 francs in 1974 to 1.6 million francs in 1983; family association support increased from 125,000 francs in 1974 to 1.5 million francs in 1983.[80] It is likely that the prospect of receiving these funds helped to induce family and labor groups to move into the field of consumer advocacy. Public funding for France's consumer movement was also popular with the general public. A 1974 study found that 75 percent of the French population felt that the govern-

76. "Verbände: Asoziale im Frack," *Der Spiegel*, 21 September 1970, 60–61.

77. Hoffmann, "Die Anwälte der Konsumenten," 29.

78. "Verbände: Asoziale im Frack," 60–61.

79. "Fragen an Hugo Schui zum Käufer-Boykott," *Die Zeit*, October 1972.

80. Marie-Elisabeth Bordes and Sylvie George, *Politique de la consommation dans la communauté Européene* (Paris: Université de Droit, d'Économie et de Sciences Sociales de Paris, 1982), 101; Noëlle Marotte, *Bilan et perspectives de la politique française a l'égard des consommateurs* (Paris: Conseil économique et social, 1984), 20; and Michel Bernard and Jacqueline Quentin, *L'avant-garde des consommateurs: Luttes et organisations en France et à l'étranger* (Paris: Editions ouvrières, 1975), 87–91.

$ millions

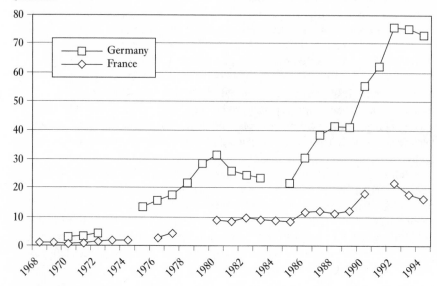

Source: Data compiled by author.

Figure 3.1   Government support to consumer organizations, 1968–1994

ment should support consumer organizations and give them input into government policy making.[81]

Consumer groups in Germany consistently received between three and four times the amount of government support as did French consumer groups. Including both state and federal supports, German transfers to consumer groups increased from $3.3 million in 1970 to $32 million in 1980. Rather than energizing the consumer movement, it appears that this high level of government funding actually discouraged these groups from mobilization to raise support from individual members. This was a concern held by many French consumer activists, who worried that increasing state support could keep the French consumer movement from achieving its full organizational capacity.[82] This phenomenon, what the French called "compensated weakness" (*faiblesse compensée*), may explain some, but not all, of the organizational strategy of German consumer groups. A large portion of German spending on consumer associations came from state-level governments. Different states placed different emphasis on consumer protection. In 1980, Bavaria spent only 0.19 DM per person on consumer groups, for example, compared to 1.28 DM per person in Bremen.[83] Yet there was no sign that consumer groups in the less generous states pursued more aggressive grass-roots organizational strategies.

81. Gérard Cas, *La défense du consommateur* (Paris: Presses universitaires de France, 1975), 82.

82. Alexandre Carnelutti, "Consommation et société," *Revue française d'administration publique* 56 (October–December 1990): 584.

83. *Handbuch der Verbraucherinstitutionen.*

In both France and Germany, government funds came with the expectation that consumer groups would support the consumer interest. In Germany, the government relied on consumer groups to perform narrowly circumscribed technical tasks. In testing products, enforcing specific laws, and informing consumers, these groups took on quasi-governmental functions. Moreover, to perform these functions well, Germany's consumer groups cultivated their reputation for technical competency. In the context of setting product standards, the AgV emphasized the need for "well-informed, experienced and confident consumer representatives in the technical committees."[84] The role of consumer representation in government reflected this technical orientation. Although prior to 1969, the AgV had pushed for its own consumer ministry, by the early 1970s it favored a technical advisory role within existing ministries.[85] The Economics Ministry created the consumer advisory council (Verbraucherbeirat) in 1972.[86] The Ministry of Food, Land, and Forest (Bundesministerium für Ernährung, Landwirtschaft und Forsten) created its own consumer committee (Verbraucherausschuss) in 1975.[87] In 1973 the AgV was even invited to participate in the "concerted action" negotiations at which Germany's wage and money supply levels were set.[88] Germany's consumer groups displayed a marked reticence to engage in politics. While they helped to police laws that were already written, they rarely advocated new kinds of consumer protections.[89] Instead, most moves for reform came from a combination of business interests, political parties, government bodies, and experts in the field. The SPD and CDU both created their own working groups on consumer politics to consider new initiatives.[90]

In contrast with its German counterpart, the French consumer movement was actively engaged with the government in new policy initiatives starting in the 1960s. The first move in this direction was the creation of the National Consumption Council (Conseil national de la consommation, CNC) in 1960, at the instigation of Jean Fontanet.[91] It was created to pursue three goals: to create a meeting place for consumers and a forum for them to interact directly with the government, to con-

84. "Verbraucher-Seminar des DNA," *Verbraucherpolitische Korrespondenz* 13 (5 May 1967), 8.

85. Klaus Wieken, *Die Organisation der Verbraucherinteressen im internationalen Vergleich* (Göttingen, Germany: Verlag Otto Schwartz, 1976), 27.

86. This consumer council included six members of consumer associations, three government representatives, three academics, three union representatives, and one member of the press. "Zwei DGB-Vertreter im Verbraucherbeirat," *Informations Dienst* (Düsseldorf: Bundespressestelle des Deutschen Gewerkschaftsbundes, 11 August 1982), 1–2.

87. Katherina Focke, "Verbraucherpolitik in der Marktwirtschaft," *Bulletin des Presse- und Informationsamtes der Bundesregierung* 65 (30 May 1973): 645.

88. Hanna Gieskes, "Gesucht wird der mündige, nicht der bevormundete Verbraucher," *Die Welt*, 25 October 1978.

89. Heribert Schatz, "Consumer Interests in the Process of Political Decision-Making: A Study of Some Consumer Policy Decisions in the Federal Republic of Germany," *Journal of Consumer Policy* 6 (1983): 388.

90. The SPD group was led by Anke Riedel-Martiny, the CDU group was led by Walter Picard. Wolfgang H. Glöckner, "Aktion 'Gelber Punkt': Ins Rote verfälscht," *Vorwärts*, 18 October 1973.

91. Jacques Dubois, *Les structures administratives de la consommation*, doctoral thesis (Paris: Université Paris II, 1984), 216.

tribute to the growing cohesion of consumer groups, and to bring together ministries whose work involved consumption. Composed of fourteen ministerial members and fourteen consumer representatives, the CNC met every six weeks.[92] Based on the experience of the CNC, consumer groups were later invited to participate in the Consumption Committee of the Sixth French Plan.[93]

France's consumer groups also coordinated their efforts in order to have a direct impact on policy formation. In May 1972, eleven of France's national consumer associations created the Coordination Committee for Consumer Organizations (Comité de coordination des organisations de consommateurs, CCOC). The group did not last long, but it did push for consumer protection legislation—permitting a seven-day grace period for door-to-door sales and allowing advertisements to include company names—that was eventually enacted.[94] On 29 April 1975, the same eleven consumer groups published a comprehensive proposal for a new package of consumer legislation.[95] In a thirty-page charter, they called for the abolition of the National Consumption Institute (INC) and the creation in its place of a technical organization dominated by consumer representatives and oriented towards serving consumer associations. They also proposed the creation of a high council on innovation and safety (conseil supérieur de l'innovation et de la sécurité) where consumers, professionals, and government officials could meet on an equal footing in order to give consumer input into product materials and production, to detect "false innovations," and to avoid the waste that resulted from them. A special tax on industry would finance commissions to promote consumer education and competition policy.[96] These initiatives were not in the end successful, but the effort did give consumer groups an introduction to high politics, an experience that set the precedent for continued communication in the political arena.

Like their German counterparts, French consumer groups undertook projects that required technical expertise. Beginning in September 1970, for example, the CNPF collaborated with the INC to create the Association française pour l'étiquetage d'information (AFEI), a nonprofit organization in the public interest to design model product labels.[97] In 1973, consumer associations also gained access to the

---

92. The fact that the newly created CNC incorporated family groups is generally thought to have made it more difficult for consumer groups to consolidate and become professional, contributing to the later fragmentation of the French consumer movement. Marcel Garrigou, *L'assaut des consommateurs pour changer les rapports producteurs–vendeurs–consommateurs* (Paris: Aubier-Montaigne, 1981), 32–33; and Jacques Dubois, *Les structures administratives de la consommation*, doctoral thesis (Paris: Université Paris II, 1984), 274.

93. Claude Romec, "Organisations de consommateurs," *Réforme*, 15 December 1975.

94. "Onze associations nationales créent un conseil de coordination des organisations de consummateurs," *Le Monde*, 16 May 1972.

95. Garrigou, *L'assaut des consommateurs*, 238.

96. "Onze organisations d'usagers proposent une charte nationale," *Le Monde*, 30 April 1975.

97. AFEI was eliminated in 1984. Pierre Frybourg, "L'étiquetage d'information," *Revue de la concurrence et de la consommation* 12 (1980): 14–16; "L'étiquetage informatif vous aide dans vos achats," *Information consommation OR-GE-CO* 27 (March–April 1978): 3–4; Jacques Dubois, "L'affichage des prix . . . ne doit être qu'un premier pas," *Information consommateur* 72/1: 3–4.

board of directors of AFNOR, France's product standardization board. Beginning in 1977, consumers were invited to participate in a government-sponsored program for consumer dispute settlement. Called Boîte Postale 5000, after the mail address to which complaints were sent, the system relied on consumer associations to negotiate settlements between consumers and local traders. But these more technical activities never constituted the core function of the French consumer movement. Indeed, several consumers were apprehensive about participating in these activities on the grounds that they tended to depoliticize the consumer cause.[98] Jean-Claude Jacquet, a consumer representative to France's National Consumption Council, warned that efforts to increase the technical capacities of France's consumer movements should "be grounded in a dense associational life, at the risk of failing to translate the real hopes and needs of consumers."[99]

The Legal Framework

As consumers organized, they confronted fundamental legal questions. What was the legal status of a consumer association? What claims could they make against a producer? What responsibility did they bear if their activities hurt the reputation of a producer? How the French and German legal systems answered these questions had implications for the emerging consumer movements. In neither country was the law particularly friendly to the consumer interest, but the impact was different. German law worked to contain and structure the kinds of opposition that consumer groups could raise against industry; French law became a sort of constructive impediment, forming a contested arena in which consumer groups could prove their autonomy and mettle. The factors that generated these two responses were not major points of legal doctrine but rather smaller differences bearing on implementation.

Courts in both France and Germany recognized the legal status of consumer groups, but neither country permitted the broad consumer class actions allowed in the United States. Each instead granted limited rights to consumer groups to protect consumers. In Germany, collective suits (*Verbraucherverbandsklagen*) were limited to two areas of law in which consumer group legal actions had been explicitly permitted. The 1965 amendment to the Law on Unfair Competition (Gesetz gegen den unlauteren Wettbewerb, UWG) established a strict standard for misleading advertising and empowered consumer groups to help enforce that standard. Approximately 1,000 UWG cases were brought by consumer groups between 1965 and 1977; 516 were brought in 1979 alone.[100] The 1976 law on standard terms of sale (Gesetz zur Regelung des Rechts der Allgemeinen Geschäftsbedingungen, AGB-Gesetz)

98. *Le Monde*, 26 November 1976.

99. "Le financement des organisations de consommateurs," *Inc Hebdo* 583 (26 February 1988), 5.

100. European Consumer Law Group, *Reports and Opinions: September 1977–March 1984* (Louvain-la-Neuve, Belgium: Cabay, 1984), 278–79.

also granted consumer groups the right to file suits against companies employing unfair terms of sale. Consumer groups brought a smaller but still significant number of AGB cases.

These laws, while drawing on the institutional capacities of consumer groups to enforce certain consumer policies, did little to extend the legal action of consumer groups in general. First, the collective legal suit was not extended to other kinds of legal action. Hence, consumer groups could not weigh in on liability suits, warranty disputes, or other kinds of consumer grievances. This restriction was unusual from a legal perspective in the German context since Germany, unlike France, had a long tradition of recognizing group legal suits (*Verbandsklage*), at least as they applied to labor and producer associations. Moreover, consumer group legal actions were restricted to blocking illegal activity, but did not extend to compensating consumers for losses except under extraordinary circumstances.[101] Together, these two restrictions limited legal dynamism within the consumer movement.

Moreover, it is interesting to note that until 1980, consumer advisory centers faced a statutory limitation on the legal advice they could offer consumers. While they were allowed to broach matters bearing on contract law, Germany's Law on Legal Consultation (Rechtsberatungsgesetz) did not permit them to give free advice on tort law. As product liability in Germany fell primarily under tort law, advisory centers often could not discuss legal recourse for product damage. (In one case, the bar association of West Berlin sued the radio producer RIAS for airing a twice-monthly show called "Consumer Studio" in which an economist offered legal advice to viewers who called in. Faced with a fine of 300,000 DM and huge legal fees, RIAS canceled the show.)[102] Even those consumer associations charged explicitly with pursuing legal action against companies that contravened consumer laws, such as the Consumer Protection Union (Verbraucherschutzverein, VSV), were not allowed to give legal advice to consumers, since such free legal advice was prohibited.[103] A 1980 change in the statutory lawyer fee scale (Rechtsanwaltsgebührenordnung, BGB I, 1507) made possible a more liberal treatment of consumer advisory centers under the Rechtsberatungsgesetz.[104]

In France, the 1973 *loi Royer* granted consumer groups the right to represent consumer interests in the courts.[105] But this right was quickly curtailed by a restriction

101. Individuals received compensation only if it could be shown that they would not have purchased the product if the company had acted lawfully—a burden of proof that was in practice rarely met.

102. "Juristische Klimmzüge an einem Nazi-Gesetz," *Frankfurter Rundschau*, 13 February 1975.

103. Armin Schoreit, "Zur Rechtsberatung des Verbrauchers in der Bundesrepublik Deutschland," *Journal of Consumer Policy* 1/2 (1977): 118.

104. Norbert Reich, "Rechtsberatung im Verbraucherschutz," *Zeitschrift für Rechtspolitik* 3 (1981): 53–54.

105. Michel Rocard pushed hard to give consumer groups legal recourse against manufacturers whose products injured individual consumers. Consumer organizations, he noted, "are paralyzed both by their weakness and by the fact that they are not permitted to take the role of a consumer as a legal entity [*un consommateur nominal*]. We must undo this lock." Interview with Michel Rocard, *Combat*, 8 November 1972.

on the damages that they could claim. Specifically, French consumer groups were not permitted to act on behalf of specific consumer interests. Instead, they were permitted to recover only for damages to the general interests of consumer organizations. In practice, consumer groups often pursued their own cases alongside individual consumer cases in order to offer legal and technical support. One consequence of this limitation was that French consumer groups could not rely on high legal damages and fees to defray the costs of their legal actions, as U.S. consumer groups could. Of the 1,300 lawsuits brought by consumer associations from 1973 to 1982, 87 percent resulted in rewards of less than 5,000 francs.[106] In 1979, consumer groups filed 450 legal cases that returned combined damages of only 440,000 francs.[107] Moreover, consumer groups wishing to pursue legal suits had to be accredited by the French government. Accreditation required proof that a consumer group had at least 10,000 members and that consumer protection was its primary function. This high threshold gave consumer groups a strong incentive to attract individual members. (Similar accreditation in Germany required that a group have only sixty members.) By 1979, twelve national and sixty-two regional consumer groups had been accredited to pursue civil actions.

Consumer group litigation became a staple of French consumer association activity. In a 1989 survey of French consumers, 76 percent reported that consumer associations were either very or fairly accessible for help with consumer litigation, whereas only 29 percent felt that the government administration was equally capable. While only 2 percent of respondents reported that they personally would rely on the government for support with a consumer grievance, 17 percent reported that they would use consumer associations.[108]

A related legal consideration concerned the treatment of consumer protest. Consumer groups in both countries used boycotts to protest dangerous or highly priced goods. French boycotts were generally greeted with strong popular acclaim, often with support from French trade unions. But the French legal system was generally hostile to these actions. In 1978, for example, the UFC called for a boycott of the Shell Company in response to the wreck of the Amoco-Cadiz oil tanker off the coast of Brittany. When Shell sued the UFC for lost sales, the courts found in Shell's favor (an appeals court eventually suppressed the fines but did not change the ruling).[109] Part of the problem was that French consumer groups were often focused more on confrontation than on technical analysis. On 16 June 1975, for example, the Villejuif Association populaire des familles (APF) distributed brochures to a hospi-

106. Anne Morin, "L'action d'intérêt collectif exercée par les organisations de consommateurs avant et après la loi du 5 janvier 1988," in *Group Actions and Consumer Protection*, ed. Thierry Bourgoignie (Brussels: Story Scientia, 1992), 65.

107. European Consumer Law Group, *Reports and Opinions: September 1977–March 1984* (Louvain-la-Neuve, Belgium: Cabay, 1984), 272–73.

108. "Les Français et les organisations de consommateurs," *Inc Hebdo* 633 (7 April 1989), 9–13.

109. "La cour d'appel confirme l'interdiction du boycottage des produits Shell," *Le Monde*, 15 June 1978.

tal warning that according to the Ministry of Health, Schweppes was adding the chemical E330 to their beverages. Schweppes sued the group and won, on the grounds that E330 was simply the designator for citric acid.[110]

German product boycotts were less common than their French counterparts, but they also typically achieved a greater level of success, especially in cases of dangerous products or excessively high prices. The German legal system was also more permissive with boycotts than its French counterpart, so long as a boycott was not intended specifically to distort economic competition. The first large consumer boycott, which occurred in September 1973 as a protest against the high price of meat, was supported by trade unions and was relatively successful.[111] A 1980 boycott against estrogen in veal, in which French consumers also participated, was the first in which environmental and consumer protection groups worked together. Nestlé and Lacroix responded by taking their veal products off the market.[112] In 1982, the consumer center of Stuttgart launched a boycott of Aral and BP because of their high oil prices, and they managed to get the prices reduced.[113] None of these actions resulted in successful legal challenges.

This difference in the courts' stances toward consumer boycotts to some extent reflected differences in the perceived technical competency of these groups. In Germany, where consumer centers had cultivated a high level of familiarity with product markets, the boycotts launched were typically well informed and targeted at flagrant transgressions. In France, where consumer groups had little technical expertise, courts systematically sided with business in boycott cases, although higher courts typically reduced fines to a token 1 franc on appeal.[114] For French consumer groups, these legal cases became a symbol of their autonomy, advertising that they had not been co-opted by industry and that they were operating at the leading edge of the consumer struggle.

France's Experiment with Negotiated Protection

Early efforts by the French government to harness independent consumer groups to participate in policy creation, combined with a legal treatment that allowed consumer groups to highlight their opposition to industry, made French consumer groups into a political force that had no analogue in Germany. The dynamism and legitimacy of France's consumer movement became the basis upon which Econom-

---

110. "C'est Schweppes!" *Rouge,* 1 December 1976.
111. Wolfgang H. Glöckner, "Verbraucherpolitik im Aufwind," *Die Neue Gesellschaft* 5 (May 1974): 424.
112. "Autofahrer gegen Ölkonzerne: Boykott letzte Waffe der Konsumenten," *Frankfurter Rundschau,* 24 July 1982.
113. Wolf Renschke, "Der Boykott: Sein Möglichkeiten und sein Grenzen," *Verbraucher und Markt '82,* 4 November 1982.
114. Roger-Xavier Lanteri, "Prix: Que peuvent faire les consommateurs?" *L'Express,* 20 September 1976.

ics Minister René Monory opted, in 1978, to pursue a new approach to consumer protection. Consumer groups would negotiate directly with producers to set quality and safety standards for products. This experiment would eventually fail, but the protection strategy that later emerged in France depended on the prior experiment with negotiation.

Already in the early 1970s, France's industry associations were becoming interested in making contact with France's official consumer associations. Some early regional agreements had shown promising signs of success. For example, in Alsace, the consumer association ACOR (Associations des consommateurs organisés), with 130,000 families as members, signed agreements directly with retailers calling, among other things, for them not to charge more than 25 percent profit margins and to provide their accounts to a "Commission des usagers." In exchange, ACOR provided retailers with its label to be included in their advertising and advertised on their behalf in their own journal, "Le Consommateur," which enjoyed a circulation of 80,000.[115]

Such success stories led France's central industry associations to open ongoing discussions with consumer associations. Many of the early efforts failed. Over the period between 1971 and 1973, the association of small and medium-sized firms, Confédération générale du patronat des petites et moyennes entreprises (CGPME), met with the INC, the UFC, and ORGECO to discuss consumer issues. They were unable to reach an agreement.[116] In 1973, the Paris Chamber of Commerce and Industry (CCIP) proposed the creation of a new Centre de concertation industrie commerce consommateur (CCICC) that would bring together consumers and producers within the context of the CCIP. One of its goals would be to show "that the protection of consumers is an essential goal of producers and distributors and that state intervention is not always indispensable for resolving problems of consumer information and defense."[117] This initiative was never achieved.

Real progress began in 1974, when, in the context of the first oil shock, CNPF president François Ceyrac announced that the CNPF wished to work together with consumers.[118] The following year the CNPF appointed Paul Simonet to lead a new Commission on Industry, Trade, and Consumption (CICC) with the goal of presenting a united front to consumer organizations. Simonet appears to have been extremely open to constructive discussions with consumer groups. "Consumerism is a deep and enduring movement that marks the evolution of societal life," he wrote, "with which we should establish an open and constructive discussion."[119] The CNPF was, in the words of Simonet, "very open to all forms of concertation, especially in the domain of information."[120] It was a view also shared by many mem-

---

115. Pons, *Consomme et tais-toi,* 98.

116. Garrigou, *L'assaut des consommateurs,* 53–54.

117. Chambre de commerce et d'industrie de Paris, "Problèmes de la consommation," 24 May 1973, 15.

118. Garrigou, *L'assaut des consommateurs,* 53–54.

119. Gérard Lavergne, "Eux, les clients," *CNPF Patronat* 429 (November 1981): 22.

120. "Opinions sur la fonction consommation et la libre entreprise," *Humanisme et entreprise* 102 (April 1977): 16.

bers of the CNPF. Jean-Georges Marais, for example, the director of customer relations at Air France, affirmed in 1977 that *concertation* with consumer groups was
"indispensable."[121]

By the mid-1970s, the French government began to take an interest in consumer-
business negotiations. In 1974, National Consumer Committee (CNC) President
Francis Pécresse requested the creation of a special working group on "Commerce-
Consommation" to consider approaches to consumer protection. The group proposed to create a trial forum for consumer-producer negotiations in Toulouse. The
new organization, called CRICC (Comité de recours et d'information commerce
consommation), was set up in 1975. Consumers were represented by two family-
focused consumer groups—many other groups still refused to sit down at the table
with businessmen. On 24 March 1976, the first meeting took place, with Christiane
Scrivener, France's new secretary of state for consumption, in attendance. It was the
first truly equal meeting of consumers and producers in France, and it resulted in
agreements covering laundries and the furniture retail trade.[122] In another signal of
growing government interest in consumer-producer negotiations, the Commissariat
du plan in 1975 created a new consumption committee that would address consumer
issues for the first time in the Seventh French Plan. Consisting of consumer and
producer representatives, the committee concluded that France should support the
development of a dialogue between consumers and producers (although business
representatives to the committee also reported a "certain climate of hostility" among
the consumer representatives to the Consumption Committee).[123]

Inaugurated in 1978, the Raymond Barre government placed consumer groups
squarely at the center of its consumer protection policy. Instead of relying on government administration to meet consumer demands, the new economics minister
René Monory called instead for consumer associations to function as a counterweight to industry. Consumer associations in this new confrontational approach
were to be full partners in the production process, not just in providing product information but also in defining product quality and price.[124] In a sense, this approach
simply gave official sanction to what was a reality. Many of France's consumer associations and businesses already had some degree of interaction. In a 1977 survey
conducted by the Ecole supérieure de commerce of Lyons, 24 percent of French
companies reported having engaged in dialogue with consumer associations; 49 percent reportedly still viewed consumer groups with hostility. Looking to the future,
59 percent of companies expected for consumers to take on a consultative role with
industry, and 38 percent felt that dialogue with consumer associations should ex-

121. Jean-Georges Marais, "Le consommateur, cet inconnu?" *Humanisme et entreprise* 102
(April 1977): 69.

122. Garrigou, *L'assaut des consommateurs*, 161–62.

123. Commisariat General du Plan, *Rapport du comité consommation: Préparation du 7ème plan*
(Paris: Documentation française, 1976), 16; and Jacques Dubois, "Les consommateurs dans le
7ème plan," *Information consommation ORGECO* 15 (March–April 1976): 1–2.

124. Jean Marchand, "M. Monory veut des consommateurs puissants," *La croix*, 28 September 1979.

tend to issues "dealing with production, the quality of products, and advertising."[125]

Danièle Achach, appointed head of the newly created Mission consommation within the Economics Ministry's Direction de la concurrence et de la consommation, advocated extensive business-consumer negotiations.[126] From 1979 to 1981, the CNPF's CICC hosted a series of bipartite meetings with consumer associations. A first meeting of fourteen consumer groups with the CNPF took place in December 1979.[127] In these meetings, the parties discussed both general and sectoral standards, including advertising, auto sales, post-sale service, and furniture.[128] Other professional associations also began direct negotiations with consumer groups. Between 1980 and 1983, the Conseil national de la publicité (CNP) negotiated with consumer associations to set standards for the advertising industry. The meetings brought together eleven consumer organizations and as many representatives of the media, plus representatives from INC, BVP, and RFP (Régie française de télévision). The media and advertising professionals favored the discussions, saying that it helped them track the interests of consumer groups on subjects that could change over time.[129] Another voluntary agreement was signed between consumer associations and UDAC, the largest retail store association. According to this agreement, retailers following a set of negotiated guidelines would be allowed to post in their storefront a sticker of a *tricolore* fleur-de-lis that read: "*Engagement du commerce, j'adhère.*"[130] The guidelines required marking rebates as a percentage of the proper price, indicating prices "*tout compris*" including services and other charges, clearly posting information about post-sale services, and guaranteeing to replace goods that did not function properly or were damaged in delivery. Like many such accords, the program was well received but not very widely used. A study in April 1981 of 663 stores in Marseilles found that only twenty-seven stores (4 percent) had placed the *fleur tricolore* in their windows.[131]

Industry was happy with these early experiments with negotiated consumer protection so long as they applied primarily to issues of consumer information. But producers were also concerned that consumer groups increasingly wanted to participate in negotiations bearing on product design decisions. Initiatives like the 1978 quality certificates program, although formally a labeling program, increasingly impinged on product quality and design features in ways that industry found unduly intrusive. By the time François Mitterrand was elected president in 1981, tensions over voluntary consumer-producer negotiations had come to a head.

125. "Que fera le premier pas: l'entreprise . . . ? l'association de consommateurs . . . ?" *Libre service actualités* 624 (6 May 1977), 45–46; and "Le consumerisme," *Libre service actualités* 632 (30 June 1977), 134–36.

126. Formerly the Direction de la concurrence et des prix. Jean Marchand, "Une 'mission consommation' au ministère de l'économie," *La croix*, 17 June 1978.

127. *Les Échos*, 7 February 1980.

128. Gérard Lavergne, "Eux, les clients," *CNPF Patronat* 429 (November 1981): 22.

129. "La guerre est finie," *CNPF Patronat* 447 (July 1983): 71–72.

130. "La charte 92," *50 millions de consommateurs* 122 (February 1981).

131. *Consommateurs actualité* 282 (3 April 1981).

Consumers, for their part, were frustrated with businesses' unwillingness to adopt the voluntary standards negotiated by the industry associations to which they belonged. By the early 1980s, many such standards simply restated existing government regulation. Consumer advocate François Lamy expressed this concern: "It's as if we consumers were asked to sign agreements for all of the laws we already have to follow. For example: I agree to not shoplift, or, I agree to drive on the right, or, I agree to file my taxes."[132] Efforts to make workable agreements between industry and consumer would continue for several years (see chapter 2 and chapter 7), but the potential that both sides had perceived during the 1970s for a nongovernmental approach to consumer protection appeared to have been lost.

The strategies of consumer mobilization in France and Germany could hardly have been more different. French consumer associations organized around the provision of consumer services and competed on consumer mobilization. Many of these groups published their own consumer protection magazines, the combined circulation of which grew to over two million by 1980. Through protests and mobilizations, they cultivated a distinctive identity for the French consumer as politically active and economically threatened. German consumer groups shunned grass-roots membership. Instead, they hired technically trained staff that enabled them to advise consumers on product choice and to consult on committees within industry. What the two movements shared was a common basis of public esteem. A 1996 survey conducted in France found that 74 percent of respondents paid attention to the recommendations of consumer organizations.[133] Similarly, in Germany, a 1995 survey by *Focus* magazine found that 41 percent of respondents trusted consumer protection organizations more than *any* other political or social institution.[134] Thus, while different in organizational strategy, the consumer movements in France and Germany were both perceived to be highly effective.

The student and worker mobilizations of 1968, which acted as a cultural backdrop for the consumer movements to come, also engendered new theoretical accounts of popular mobilization. New analyses in sociology and political science focused on the organizational logic of social movements. Assuming that grievances in effect always lay below the surface, these "resource mobilization" theories emphasized the availability of resources that would allow advocacy organizations to prosper: financial support, technical expertise, political allies, and so forth.[135] In later extensions to this approach, researchers attentive to "political opportunity

132. *Le Figaro*, 10 January 1980.

133. Bénédicte Epinay, "Le lobby consommateurs veut monter au filet: ses moyens le contraignent en fond de court," *Les Échos*, 3 October 1996.

134. Verbraucherzentrale NRW, *Das Jahr '95*, 5.

135. John McCarthy and Mayer Zald, "Resource Mobilization and Social Movements: A Partial Theory," *American Journal of Sociology* 82/6 (May 1977); J. Craig Jenkins, "Resource Mobilization Theory and the Study of Social Movements," *Annual Review of Sociology* 9 (1983): 527–53; and Harold R. Kerbo, "Movements of 'Crisis' and Movements of 'Affluence': A Critique of Deprivation and Resource Mobilization Theories," *Journal of Conflict Resolution* 26/4 (December 1982): 655.

structures" incorporated more nuanced political and institutional variables. These included resources, as in the earlier resource mobilization theories, but also a loose assemblage of new political ingredients: institutional arrangements, historical precedents for social mobilization, access to the political system, and a context of shifting political alignments.[136]

The findings from the French and German cases confirm central insights of the political opportunity structure approach. First, government resources were important in both cases, but the level of funding did not correspond to the political strength of the movements. German consumer groups received greater funding than their French counterparts but enjoyed less policy influence. Second, political allies appeared to matter. French consumer groups forged working relations with labor unions and large retailers, and these groups lent broad legitimacy to their agenda. In Germany, neither of these potential allies took a lasting interest in the consumer movement. Third, political institutions mattered, although in unexpected ways. In Germany, a political culture that encouraged automatic policy access for economic interest groups led its consumer groups to eschew a broader strategy of mobilization. In France, where the political system was more exclusionary, consumer groups pursued more confrontational approaches.[137]

Finally, national traditions of protest appear to have mattered. In Germany, the student protests of 1968 were grounded to a large degree in the neo-Marxist sociology of the Frankfurt School.[138] This approach—propounded by Theodor Adorno, Max Horkheimer, Herbert Marcuse, Walter Benjamin, and others—emphasized the dangers of materialist culture and of social commodification. Indeed, the few consumer protests that did arise in Germany were often explicitly anticonsumerist.[139] In 1970, for example, the Aktion Kritischer Konsum brought together 250 protesters in the Munich shopping district to encourage Christmas shoppers to give money to charities rather than purchase presents. In France, by contrast, the protesters of 1968 shared an orientation toward concerns about social justice, access to opportunity, and control.[140] This set of concerns appears to have been more com-

---

136. Herbert P. Kitschelt, "Political Opportunity Structure and Political Protest: Anti-Nuclear Movements in Four Democracies," *British Journal of Political Science* 16 (1986), 58; Sidney Tarrow, *Power in Movement: Social Movements and Contentious Politics* (Cambridge: Cambridge University Press, 1998); J. Craig Jenkins and Charles Perrow, "Insurgency of the Powerless: Farm Worker Movements (1946–1972)," *American Sociological Review* 42 (April 1977): 249–68; and Charles Tilly, *From Mobilization to Revolution* (Reading, Mass.: Addison-Wesley, 1978).

137. Kitschelt, "Political Opportunity Structure," 67.

138. Wilfried Mausbach, "Historicizing 1968," *Contemporary European History* 11/1 (2002): 177–87; Wolfgang Kraushaar, *Frankfurter Schule und Studentenbewegung: Von der Flaschenpost zum Molotowcocktail, 1945–1995* (Hamburg: Rogner and Bernhard, 1998).

139. Christian Schütze, "Kampagne gegen die Kauflust," *Süddeutsche Zeitung*, 11 December 1970.

140. Roy Pierce and Philip E. Converse, "Attitudinal Sources of Protest Behavior in France: Differences between Before and After Measurement," *Public Opinion Quarterly* 54/3 (Autumn 1990): 298; Melvin Seeman, "The Signals of '68: Alienation in Pre-Crisis France," *American Sociological Review* 37/4 (August 1972): 285–402.

patible with later mobilizations around the quality-of-life issues evoked by value-for-money consumerism.

These findings suggest that consumer-interest mobilization was a highly contingent phenomenon. It depended on the complex interaction of a number of important variables: alliances, resources, and institutional and ideological context. For the purposes of this book, the important point is that the organization of consumers in France and Germany was causally independent either of producer interests or of cultural traditions. It is this independence—or exogeneity—that allows us to treat the preferences of consumer groups as causally independent of producer preferences in the process of policy formation.

CHAPTER FOUR

Consumer Risk

What needs to be explained is how people agree to ignore most of the potential dangers that surround them and interact so as to concentrate only on selected aspects.

—MARY DOUGLAS AND AARON WILDAVSKY, 1982

Inevitably, the decision about how much risk to tolerate with products . . . is a political one that balances the interest group pressures on all sides.

—ALAN O. SYKES, 1995

Europe's consumer movement grew out of the perception in the 1960s and 1970s that products were becoming increasingly dangerous. The sense of heightened risk was partly real and partly subjective. On the one hand, increasingly complicated products made it difficult for consumers to assess their safety or design. One of Europe's most devastating products, the drug Thalidomide (Contergan), was marketed from 1957 to 1961. Prescribed as a remedy for morning sickness in pregnant women, it was later found to produce major birth defects.[1] In Germany, where the drug was developed by Chemie Grünenthal and where the first cases of birth defects emerged, it claimed nearly three thousand victims.[2] Contergan was not licensed in France, so it is difficult to make a direct comparison of the responses in the two nations. But France had its own catastrophic failures. In 1972, for example, a talcum power marketed as "talc Morhange" made 240 children sick and left 36 dead.[3] Such dramatic product failures, especially those affecting young children, be-

1. Contergan was the German brand name for Thalidomide, which was marketed in the United States as Kevadon and in Great Britain variously as Asmaval, Distaval, Tensival, Valgis, and Valgraine.
2. Widukind Lenz, "The History of Thalidomide," from a lecture given at the UNITH Congress, 1992 (http://www.thalidomide.ca/en/information/history_of_thalidomide.html).
3. "L'affaire du talc Morhange," *Le Monde,* 1 August 1978.

came a potent symbol of the risks of new products. Yet the scale of such disasters did not necessarily dictate the degree of consumer or regulatory response. Whereas the talc Morhange case helped to mobilize consumers across France, Contergan never became the focus of concerted consumer activism in Germany.[4]

Indeed, the general correlation between product failure and consumer mobilization appears to be surprisingly weak. Similar cases are commonly perceived differently in different countries. The strut design of the Corvair that Ralph Nader criticized as an instance of dangerous engineering in his book *Unsafe at Any Speed* continued to be used without apparent notice in the German cars from which Chevrolet had originally borrowed the design.[5] Indeed, formative incidents do not even have to be real events. In the United States, Upton Sinclair's fictional account of the Chicago meat-packing industry, *The Jungle,* was directly credited with applying pressure to pass the Meat Inspection Act and the Pure Food and Drug Act in 1906.[6] By contrast, even the most catastrophic product failures have sometimes elicited little or no mobilization. In 1955, the Japanese Morinaga Milk Company distributed milk formula laced with arsenic that left 130 children dead and 12,131 mentally disturbed. When an initial trial absolved the company of responsibility, public opinion turned against the victims, and it took 20 years for them to receive compensation.[7]

On the other hand, consumer perceptions of risk appear to have increased with affluence. The reasons for this parallel evolution have been disputed.[8] Economist Albert Hirschman proposed in his 1976 book *Shifting Involvements* that modern consumption tended to create its own grievances. Hirschman's point rested on a specific psychological analysis in which human pleasure was understood to derive from the temporary abatement of discomfort. Hence, as new consumer durables reduce individuals' general level of discomfort, they also thereby reduce consumers' potential pleasure. For Hirschman, this implied that the proliferation of mass-produced durable goods (refrigerators, for example) would "generate a great deal of vaguely felt disappointment."[9] Sociologist Ulrich Beck suggested a different explanation for the rise of public concern with product risk. Whereas industrialization

---

4. Strikingly, thalidomide-related birth defects solidified the reputation of the U.S. Food and Drug Administration, which had pushed hard to block the drug from commercialization in the United States.

5. Ralph Nader, *Unsafe at Any Speed: The Designed-in Dangers of the American Automobile* (New York: Grossman, 1965).

6. Upton Sinclair, *The Jungle* (New York: Grosset and Dunlap, 1906).

7. Bernd-Dieter Pioch, "Verbraucherschutz in Japan," *Mitteilungen des Instituts für Asienkunde* 112 (1980): 21.

8. Harvey M. Sapolsky, "The Politics of Product Controversies," in *Consuming Fears: The Politics of Product Risk,* ed. Harvey Sapolsky (New York: Basic Books, 1987), 200.

9. He writes: "The modern, mass-produced durable consumer good subverts the way in which consumers extracted pleasure from their purchases in the preduable era. Along with their extraordinarily useful services, these goods are likely to generate a great deal of vaguely felt disappointment, particularly at the time of their first massive diffusion in a society." Albert O. Hirschman, *Shifting Involvements: Private Interest and Public Action* (Princeton: Princeton University Press, 2002), 35–38.

during periods of scarcity had been dominated by the theme of wealth distribution, with the onset of prosperity this emphasis changed, according to Beck, to the theme of risk distribution.[10] He reasoned that postwar consumers, no longer bound to focus their energy on basic sustenance, could turn their attention to the new risks that accompanied their new affluence.

Whatever the cause of increased consumer risk perception, national governments responded by institutionalizing strategies for managing product risk through legal and regulatory reforms. This move represented a dramatic shift from earlier risk management strategies that European governments had adopted. By the early twentieth century, most European countries had recognized the risks inherent to industrialization, including industrial accidents, environmental damage, and product failures. Their responses emphasized broad social insurance schemes. For industry, new programs guaranteeing medical and welfare support distributed the costs of industrialization widely in society. Because these programs *externalized* the risks of production, they often provided a social subsidy to developing industries, especially those that were most risky or volatile.[11] Instead of externalizing these risks through insurance schemes, the new consumer protections of the 1970s moved to *internalize* product risks to the company.[12] With this shift came a new perspective on the nature of industrial production. Product-related losses that had previously appeared inevitable were now perceived to be the responsibility of producers. Risks that had previously been socialized were now to be minimized by placing responsibility on the least-cost avoider—typically understood to be the producer.[13] This transformation was accomplished first through the legal system, by increasing business liability for product-related loss, and subsequently through government regulatory initiatives that helped to set and monitor new product safety standards.

The move to make private economic actors responsible for dangers related to their products had the effect of making product design political. Under previous social welfare insurance solutions, the sources or risks were irrelevant so long as their actuarial impact was accounted for. With the internalization of risk, the details of production became the focus of public scrutiny. Ulrich Beck writes: "Socially recognized risks contain a peculiar political explosive: what was until now considered unpolitical becomes political—the elimination of the causes in the industrialization process itself. Suddenly the public and politics extend their rule into the private sphere of plant management—into product planning and technical equipment."[14] Once product risk became politicized, popular perceptions of risk started to be fil-

10. Ulrich Beck, *Risk Society: Towards a New Modernity* (London: Sage Publications, 1992), 20–24.

11. David Moss, *When All Else Fails: Government as the Ultimate Risk Manager* (Cambridge: Harvard University Press, 2002); and Isabela Mares, *The Politics of Social Risk: Business and Welfare State Development* (Cambridge University Press, 2003).

12. Spiros Simitis, "Products Liability: The West-German Approach," in *Comparative Product Liability*, ed. Christopher J. Miller (London: Comparative Law Series, 1986), 100.

13. Richard A. Posner, *Economic Analysis of Law* (Boston: Little Brown, 1972).

14. Ulrich Beck, *Risk Society*, 24.

tered through national social and regulatory institutions. This meant that consumer risk was open to various interpretations—interpretations that depended on the outcome of a struggle over the very nature of the consumer in society and the economy.

For industry, this shift in responsibility did more than remove a subsidy. The impact of the new institutions on companies' product market strategies depended upon how that risk was allocated. By the mid-1980s, French courts and policymakers had adopted a strategy of insulating consumers as much as possible from risk. In product liability, they granted consumers virtual indemnity against product-related loss. In product safety, extensive efforts were undertaken to ensure that products that reached the market were indeed safe. For French producers, this high level of risk protection required that they work closely with government agencies and take into account a higher level of liability if products failed. For French consumers, this strategy implied that they could presume that any product in the market was safe. Of course, the system was far from perfect. Because it relied on political oversight, the French approach was often slow to respond to new kinds of product crisis. Cases of product failure that did occur, such as the French blood scandal and the sale of BSE infected beef, tended to be highly political in their consequences. Nonetheless, product safety in the French system rested in the hands of business and government agencies, not with the consumer.

Germany adopted a strategy that granted producers far greater autonomy in issues of product safety. In product liability law, it retained a negligence standard of liability that offered a variety of grounds for exculpation even when a faulty product caused loss. In product safety law, it granted a quasi-legal status to safety standards elaborated by industry-led standard-setting bodies. German producers responded to this regulatory environment by conforming closely with industry-wide technical and safety standards, a practice which granted them virtual immunity from product related liability. German consumers, their protection not guaranteed, paid close attention to what they purchased. Branding, labeling, and advertising all played important roles in informing consumers about the likely reliability and safety of products. In Germany, the consumer was an integral part of the product safety system.

These divergent approaches created differences in the product market strategies in the two countries. Some of the most interesting evidence comes from the impact of their product liability regimes. In France, the strict standard of liability placed an absolute responsibility on industry by excluding exculpatory evidence for product-related damage. For consumers, strict liability reduced the duty of care. Because product risk was incorporated into the price of any good, all products at all price levels were assumed to offer the same (economically optimal) level of safety. While high-end goods might offer additional quality, features, or durability, the higher price did not signal a higher level of safety. Hence, under the system of strict liability, the consumer had no safety-related incentive for preferring high- over low-quality goods. Moreover, consumers in this regulatory environment faced no safety-related incentives to avoid potentially risky new classes of products. As one legal observer noted: "With the customer facing a lower probability of being liable [under strict liability], relatively hazardous designs would be less unattractive to him, and the demand curve for such products would rise relative to the demand curve for comparatively safe products."[15]

The most striking evidence of the impact of a strict liability regime comes not from France—where there have been few studies on the subject—but from the United States, where industry faced a similar standard of liability to that applied in France.[16] In the U.S. context, considerations of product liability clearly influenced the kinds of products that reached the market. In a 1985–86 survey, for example, 47 percent of all manufacturers in the United States reported the removal of product lines from the marketplace, 25 percent reported the discontinuation of product research, and 39 percent reported decisions not to introduce new products, all because of the threat of increased product liability exposure.[17] More importantly, the high level of responsibility for product-related loss in the United States encouraged companies to engage in more research and innovation. In their study of U.S. product liability and industry, economists Kip Viscusi and Michael Moore conclude that "for most levels of liability costs, a higher liability burden fosters additional product-related research."[18]

Germany's negligence standard of product liability generated a different set of product market pressures. Under this legal standard, the consumer shared the burden of product risk with the producer, which obliged consumers to play a more active role in product safety. Consumers selected higher-end products in the expectation that their higher level of quality also reflected a greater degree of safety. Conversely, to purchase low-end or potentially dangerous new products was to accept a greater degree of product-related risk, since that risk has not been fully incorporated into the price and design of the product. In Germany, consumers managed concerns about product safety by purchasing more expensive goods of higher quality.

The specific way in which the negligence standard of product liability was applied in Germany helped to reinforce industry-wide standards of quality production. First, producers were generally exempt from liability claims based on product design if they followed industry standards. Typically, this meant standards set by the industry standards board, the German Institute for Standardization (Deutsches Institut für Normung, DIN). Second, industries were exempt from liability for acci-

15. Roland N. McKean, "Product Liability: Implications of Some Changing Property Rights," in *The Economics of Legal Relationships*, ed. Henry G. Manne (St. Paul, Minn.: West Publishing Company, 1975), 267.

16. Procedural differences in the United States, including contingency fees, jury trials, and the use of punitive damages, has led to higher average damages than in France.

17. Jules L. Coleman, *Risks and Wrongs* (Cambridge: Cambridge University Press, 1992), 407–8.

18. Exceptions to this finding are cases in which the level of liability is overly punitive. The most famous of these cases was the U.S. private aircraft industry, which was virtually eliminated by the high cost of product liability suits during the 1970s. W. Kip Viscusi and Michael J. Moore, "An Industrial Profile of the Links between Product Liability and Innovation," in *The Liability Maze: The Impact of Liability Law on Safety and Innovation* (Washington, D.C.: Brookings Institute, 1991), 84.

dents caused by their employees if these employees were hired and managed in appropriate ways. In practice, companies that hired unionized workers with recognized technical training were not liable for accidental damage caused by these employees, so long as they could show that these workers had been managed responsibly. Companies complying with industry-wide design and production norms faced a diminished threat from product liability suits. The shelter provided by conformity with industry standards thereby created a strong incentive to maintain a uniform and high level of design and production quality in industry. "Fault-based liability," observes legal scholar Bernd Hohlbein, "gives an additional quality incentive because it opens the exculpation door to avoid liability, provided the product was blameless."[19] By using product liability law to enforce industry-wide standards of design and production, Germany was in effect equating product safety with product quality.

This quality incentive imposes a cost on more radical kinds of innovation. By encouraging companies to pursue a collective approach to product safety, the negligence standard tends to stifle innovative efforts on the part of smaller companies. Product liability standards enforce compliance with DIN technical standards on all producers. DIN technical committees have invited industry representatives to participate in setting industry technical standards. But participation in DIN technical committees demands company resources and technical expertise, so only large, established companies tend to participate. This means that both small and new producers have limited access to the process of setting technical standards in Germany.[20] Since new designs frequently emerge from new companies, this system of liability grounded in collective quality standards tends to favor traditional products and inhibit innovative products.

Product Liability

Product liability was introduced as a comprehensive legal concept in France and Germany in the 1960s. The German term for product liability, *Produkthaftung*, was coined as late as 1968. Prior to that, consumers in these two countries could sue companies under either tort law or contract law. But these approaches placed a high burden of proof on the aggrieved consumer, who was required to show that the producer was at fault and, in the case of contract law, was a direct contracting party. Before the 1960s, nearly all industrialized countries employed a negligence standard in evaluating company behavior. Under this approach—the legal application of the principle of caveat emptor—producers were held responsible for product-related damage or loss only if the consumer could prove that his or her loss was caused by a defect in the product *and* that the defect resulted from negligent behavior by the

19. Bernd Hohlbein, "Product Safety and Product Liability: The Relevance of Insurance," in *National and European Law on the Threshold to the Single Market*, ed. Günter Weick (Frankfurt: Peter Lang, 1993), 262.

20. Hohlbein, "Product Safety," 246.

producer. Barring cases of obvious fraud, proving producer negligence was typically difficult, since the activities of producers are often hard to observe. Further, courts typically gave considerable latitude to producers. A 1956 German case in which a bike collapsed and injured its rider was typical. While the German Supreme Court agreed that the accident was due to a product defect, it found against the consumer, noting that "common experience . . . suggests that such technical defects cannot be prevented."[21]

By the early 1980s, the legal environment for consumers had changed entirely. France had imposed a strict standard of product liability. Under this standard, companies were liable for damage caused by a product defect even if no amount of care by the company could have prevented the defect. Germany continued to apply a negligence standard of product liability, but had reversed the burden of proof. According to this approach, companies were legally liable for injury only if it resulted from negligent behavior of the producer, but—a key difference—in the absence of exculpatory evidence the producer was presumed to be guilty. Once a consumer had shown that a product defect had caused injury, responsibility fell to the company to prove that they were not at fault.

Rethinking Producer Responsibility

As in the United States, product liability doctrine in France and Germany arose primarily through judicial interpretation of existing contract law and tort law. These two areas of law are conceptually different, and each has created challenges for product liability reform. Tort law governs absolute rights such as life, health, and property and typically focuses on the conduct of people. Contract law governs the terms of agreement between two parties and addresses the qualities of the product itself.[22] Although France and Germany have grounded product liability reform in a legal reinterpretation of both areas of law, France has tended to rely more on contractual product liability while Germany has relied more on tort-based product liability.

French product liability has predominantly been grounded in contract law. The earliest text in contractual liability in France is the 1 August 1905 law against hidden defects (*vices cachés*).[23] The law was originally intended to apply only to producers who knowingly sold goods with defects. The courts gradually reinterpreted the law to embrace a stricter standard of liability. In 1965, professional sellers were presumed to know of defects.[24] So the fact of a defect implied knowledge—and therefore liability—but the notion of defect was applied narrowly. In 1978, the manufacturer was found to have a duty "to deliver an effective product appropriate for

21. Geraint Howells, *Comparative Product Liability* (Aldershot, U.K.: Dartmouth, 1993), 123.

22. Christopher Hodges, *Product Liability: European Laws and Practice* (London: Sweet and Maxwell, 1993), 3–6; Droste Killius Triebel (law firm), *Business Law Guide to Germany,* 3d ed. (Oxfordshire, U.K.: CCH Editions, 1991), 124.

23. Luc Bihl, *Une histoire du mouvement consommateur* (Paris: Editions Aubier Montaigne, 1984), 214.

24. *Cour de Cassation* 14/1/65 D, 389

the user's needs."[25] This interpretation expanded the meaning of defect to include any aspect of design or production that did not meet consumer needs.[26] Together, these two cases marked the transition in France to a strict standard of liability.

Yet even with this new strict standard of contractual product liability, three legal obstacles impeded effective consumer redress, of which two were eventually removed through new legislation and case law. First, contractual privity limited liability to persons directly engaged in a contract. This meant that any individual product defect would create a chain of lawsuits, in which the consumer sued the retailer, the retailer sued the distributor, and the distributor sued the manufacturer. A 1972 case broke this chain of legal suits when French courts ruled that consumers could bring legal suits directly against the manufacturer, a procedure called direct action (*action-directe*) in cases based on the 1905 law on fraud.[27] The 21 July 1983 law on product safety extended this direct action procedure to all product liability cases pursued under general contract law.[28]

A second obstacle to contractual product liability in France was the increasing incorporation of clauses into consumer contracts that explicitly excluded producer liability. As courts increased producer liability, producers began requiring consumers to forego their right to make claims. Legal interpretation restricted this practice. In a 1966 case, such exclusions were found not to apply in cases of gross negligence (*faute lourde*), which was treated under criminal law and was therefore not possible to exclude. Finally, in March 1983, a government decree declared contractual clauses excluding product liability to be null and void.[29] (See chapter 6 below for more detail.) The third obstacle to contractual product liability, its extension to third parties, was never successfully overcome in France. Such claims arise when a product injures someone who is not a contracting party. Because no contract exists, third-party claims in France must be made under tort law.[30]

Tort law is less commonly used in French liability cases, primarily because of the high level of protection afforded by contract law. But tort law also has been extended from a negligence standard to a strict standard of liability.[31] In 1962, a French court found that "the simple act of putting a defective product on the market is considered an act of negligence."[32] A 1975 court ruling found that manufacturers could be found liable without fault based on their status as "guardian of the structure" (*gar-*

25. *Jurisclasseur périodique* 1979, II, 19139

26. Geneviève Viney, "The Civil Liability of Manufacturers in French Law," in *Comparative Product Liability*, ed. Christopher J. Miller (London: Comparative Law Series, 1986), 77.

27. Konrad Zweigert and Hein Kötz, *Introduction to Comparative Law* (Oxford: Clarendon Press, 1987), 171; *Jurisclasseur périodique* 1972, II, 197280.

28. Viney, "Civil Liability," 80.

29. Ibid., 82.

30. Based on § 1382 of the *Code civile.*

31. In the French system, based on the principle of "non-cumul des responsabilités," plaintiffs are not allowed to bring suit under both tort and contract law for the same grievance.

32. *Cour de Cassation* 21 / 3 / 62, I, 155.

dien de la structure) of the product.[33] This obscure formulation meant that producers retained responsibility for the functioning of a product even after it was sold, although the purchaser became responsible for the way in which it was used.

Unlike France, Germany has offered only narrow grounds for product liability under contract law. In 1902, German courts did find the basis for a positive breach of contract analogous to the 1905 French law governing hidden defects. But unlike in France, German law has continued to require that the plaintiff demonstrate a fraudulent concealment of the defect. Moreover, German courts have never eliminated privity, meaning the plaintiff is required to have had a direct contractual relationship with the defendant in order to claim contractual liability.[34] These restrictions placed severe limitations on the applicability of contractual solutions to product-related loss, although they were occasionally applied.

Instead of broadening the contractual obligations of producers, as France did, German courts instead grounded product liability reform in tort law (*Deliktrecht*).[35] The turning point for tort-based liability in Germany was the 1968 asian flu suit (*Hühnerpestfall*), in which a chicken farmer lost several thousand chickens due to contaminated inoculations administered by a hired veterinarian. Because the farmer was not in direct contractual relation with the inoculation manufacturer (no privity) and because the veterinarian was not in a position to have known of the contamination (no negligence), the farmer had no legal recourse under contract law. The farmer therefore sued the inoculation manufacturer directly—but under tort law. In an unusual move, the court recognized that it was nearly impossible for an individual outside of a company to evaluate whether the company had acted negligently or not. It therefore reversed the burden of proof in the case. Once the farmer had shown that a defect in the inoculation had killed his chickens, the court then called on the producer to prove that it had not acted negligently in manufacturing the inoculation. Although reversing the burden of proof did not change the legal standard of negligence, it did signify that this standard could be broadly applied. In 1975, this presumption of negligence was extended to all manufacturers of industrial products.[36]

Germany's presumption of negligence (reversed burden of proof) fell short of strict liability because it admitted several routes of exculpation for the producer. First, German companies were not always responsible for defects caused by their

---

33. Based on § 1384, section 1 of the French Civil Code. Agnès Chambraud, Patricia Foucher, and Anne Morin, "The Importance of Community Law for French Consumer Protection Legislation," in *European Consumer Policy after Maastricht*, ed. Norbert Reich and Geoffrey Woodroffe (Dordrecht, The Netherlands: Kluwer Academic Publishers, 1994), 218; and *Jemaine Juridique* 1976, J., 18479.

34. Howells, *Comparative Product Liability*, 124; and Henricus Duintjer Tebbens, *International Product Liability: A Study of Comparative and International Aspects of Product Liability* (The Hague: Asser Institute, 1979), 67.

35. Based on § 823 I of the Bürgerliches Gesetzbuch (civil code).

36. Warren Freedman, *International Products Liability* (Buffalo, N.Y.: William S. Hein, 1995), 77.

employees. Although Germany's civil code called for vicarious liability by employers for product-related damage caused by their employees,[37] the courts found that companies could avoid this liability through proper organization of the workplace: "The duty to compensate does not arise if the employer has exercised ordinary care in the selection of the employee, and, where he has to supply appliances or implements or to superintend work, has also exercised ordinary care as regards such supply or supervision."[38] This interpretation has tended to favor union-sanctioned worker training programs, in the first instance, and large companies with several levels of management, in the second. One legal scholar summarizes the practical consequence of this approach: "The risk of unexplained runaway products fell upon the injured party when a large and duly organized enterprise had manufactured them."[39]

A second basis for exculpation in the German system was that companies were held responsible only for those design defects that could be foreseen given the current state of science and technology. This "development defense," also elaborated in the 1968 avian flu case, exonerated producers when the present state of knowledge would not have permitted them to foresee the damage caused by their product.[40] This development defense placed pressure on companies to comply with voluntary industry standards, as these were commonly, although not necessarily, accepted by the courts as embodying the present state of knowledge.

Other provisions in Germany limited the liability of producers under tort law even if they were not able to exculpate themselves. For example, their liability could be reduced by showing a contributory negligence by the product user. Contributory negligence was interpreted broadly in Germany, so that even an omission by the consumer to mitigate the damage caused by a product could reduce the liability of the producer. A third form of exculpation, the "outlier" (*Ausreißer*) clause, exempted product defects that occur as a normal result of mass production (although this defense was in practice rarely used). Finally, Germany imposed a financial ceiling both on the damages that could be claimed by a single plaintiff and on the total cumulative claims on a single product. This ceiling, set at 160 million DM per product, ensured that a single product defect would not undermine a large company.

Explaining Product Liability Reform

Why did France and Germany make these reforms? Product liability can in general be understood to serve two economic functions. First, it serves as insurance, spreading the cost of product loss for a single consumer across a large population by push-

37. BGB § 831 states: "A person who employs another to do any work is bound to compensate for any damage which the other unlawfully causes to a third party in the performance of this work."

38. Arthur Taylor Von Mehren and James Russell Gordley, *The Civil Law System: An Introduction to the Comparative Study of Law* (Boston: Little, Brown, 1977), 340.

39. Tebbens, *International Product Liability*, 74–75.

40. Oliver Berg, "La notion de risque de développement en matière de responsabilité du fait des produits défectueux," *La semaine juridique* 27 / 2945 (1996): 273.

ing some or all of that cost into the price of the product. Construed as insurance, product liability operates alongside national health care plans, social welfare provisions, and individual insurance policies of consumers. Second, product liability serves as a form of deterrence. By holding companies responsible for harmful products, product liability claims give manufacturers an incentive to invest in safer products at a level that is proportional to the damage that the products inflict. Construed as deterrence, product liability operates in conjunction with national safety codes, voluntary industry standards, and local and regional product inspection services to ensure a high level of product safety.[41]

In the United States, product liability reform has often been justified through the insurance function that it serves. The greater ability of companies over individuals to acquire inexpensive comprehensive insurance was highlighted as a main reason for reforming product liability in the United States. As Jules Coleman commented on the U.S. system: "Tort law became, in effect, a vehicle by which public authorities and courts created a private insurance scheme. Manufacturers insure product users—period."[42] In the context of the United States, where no universal health care program had been established, the need to ensure an adequate private approach to insurance against product-related damage was felt more acutely.[43] But the insurance logic was not a strong incentive for reform in either France or Germany. Both countries had already created strong national health care and social security systems.[44] In these countries, the justification for product liability reform was grounded in an effort to give companies greater incentives to produce safer products.[45]

In theory, of course, the negligence standard of producer liability that both France and Germany had embraced prior to the 1970s reforms might have provided an adequate level of product safety. Under this standard, producers were viewed to be negligent when they did not take consumer interests adequately into account in their production decisions. Increasingly an "adequate" level of safety was interpreted economically, as a socially efficient level of investment. For individual com-

41. Product liability in the United States has increasingly served a punitive function to chasten companies for past damage. Because this punitive function is virtually unknown in European countries, it will not be considered as a factor in national policymaking.

42. Jules L. Coleman, *Risks and Wrongs* (Cambridge: Cambridge University Press, 1992), 412–13.

43. Of course, individuals could have simply opted to pursue private insurance of their own without relying on producers to, in effect, bundle insurance with their products. But it was commonly argued that consumers were simply not good at estimating product risk. Given apparent biases in consumer risk perception, strict liability in the United States was intended to help consumers make rational decisions about product risk by including the entire cost of that risk in the price of the product. Anthony J. Duggan, "Saying Nothing with Words," *Journal of Consumer Policy* 20/1 (1997): 79–80.

44. Droste Killius Triebel, *Business Law Guide*, 121; and Hans-Wolfgang Micklitz, "Produzentenhaftung: Ein Problem des Verbraucherschutzes? Thesen zur Ergänzung der Reformdiskussion," *Journal of Consumer Policy* 3/3–4 (1979): 330.

45. Richard A. Posner, "A Theory of Negligence," in *The Economics of Legal Relationships*, ed. Henry G. Manne (St. Paul, Minn.: West Publishing Company, 1975), 216.

panies, this meant that they were not considered legally negligent so long as total company investment in product safety exceeded the expected value of consumer loss due to product failures.[46] Conversely, a company was understood to have acted negligently if its marginal investment in prevention fell short of the marginal cost of product-related loss. The problem was that this economic test for negligence placed a high burden both on plaintiffs and on the courts. Plaintiffs had to demonstrate producer negligence, while the courts required a high level of technical expertise to apply the negligence principle properly. These challenges in application meant that companies were in practice commonly permitted to shirk on investment in product safety.

The move to reform product liability law also reflected a critical reevaluation of the cost and benefits of industrialization.[47] Although industrial production was understood to impose social costs, the sense about how those costs should be managed over time changed. A critical turning point came with Ronald Coase's now famous 1960 article entitled "The Problem of Social Cost."[48] Coase argued that private parties could negotiate socially optimal solutions regardless of the initial allocation of costs. While the theory was interpreted as a broad indictment of government regulation, in the legal field it suggested that it was a matter of economic indifference if companies or consumers bore the burden for product externalities. If the burden fell on consumers, they would pay more for less risky products and contract external insurance for the remaining risk. If the burden fell on producers, they could charge more for additional investment in safety and also contract out for insurance. The Coase theorem suggested that these two approaches were economically equivalent.

French and German courts reformed their approaches to product liability in the late 1960s primarily in order to force companies to invest sufficiently in product safety. However, they found different strategies for doing so. The French responded by forcing companies to internalize the full costs of their products. The strict standard of liability created economic incentives for each firm to secure the optimal combination of investment and insurance. Faced with the actual cost of the damage caused by its products, the producer would then invest in an efficient combination of safer design and outside liability insurance in order to minimize the total risk premium. Companies themselves, rather than the courts, would be left to judge whether the marginal expenditure on product safety improvement met the marginal savings in the area of product-related accidents. Germany responded by reversing the legal burden of proof necessary to establish negligence. Under this new procedural standard, a consumer had only to show that a product defect had caused damage. The legal burden then fell to the producer to prove that the product defect had not resulted from fault. By requiring that defendants prove that they had not acted negli-

46. Christian Gollier, "Le risque de développement, est-il assurable?" *Risque* 14 (April–June 1993): 51.

47. Lynn J. Loudenback and John W. Goebel, "Marketing in the Age of Strict Liability," *Journal of Marketing* 38 (January 1974): 63.

48. Ronald H. Coase, "The Problem of Social Cost," *Journal of Law and Economics* 3 (October 1960).

gently, the courts were able to compel all producers to comply with accepted standards of good practice.[49]

Both approaches addressed the concerns of consumers. But they embodied very different approaches to consumer protection. In Germany, the producer faced an obligation of means, requiring that appropriate care be taken in production. In France, the producer faced an obligation of ends that could not be diminished by any level of care in production.[50] Why did the two countries adopt different kinds of regulatory reforms? It is tempting to see the divergence as emerging from distinctive national legal traditions, but closer examination suggests that this interpretation is incorrect. Rather, court decisions bearing on product liability law can best be understood, in both France and Germany, as optimizing consumer safety by taking into account the broader institutional context of protection in interpreting the appropriate national standard of product liability to apply. In Germany, product liability law enforced a collective approach to product safety that gave producers incentives to participate in industry-wide product standards and worker training. In France, by contrast, the courts placed the burden of product safety wholly on individual companies, in the expectation that they would make appropriate investment decisions.

It is worth noting that many countries did not rely at all on product liability law as a form of consumer protection. In Britain, the Royal Commission on Civil Lia-

---

49. Product liability is a complex area of law. The presentation in this chapter is necessarily abbreviated. Countries commonly apply different standards of liability for different product dimensions, including design, manufacturing, product information, and the legal requirement to survey the market after a product is sold. It is interesting to note some exceptions to the predominant standards of liability adopted in France and Germany. France, for example, has retained a negligence standard in liability for providing accurate product information. Germany applies a reversed burden of proof only to liability for product design and manufacturing. See the table below.

Table 4.1　Comparison of product liability regimes in France and Germany

	France	Germany
Design	Strict	Reversed burden
Manufacturing	Strict	Reversed burden
Information	Negligence	Negligence
Surveying the market	Strict	Negligence

Source: Kalman Leloczky, "General and Specific Features of Certain European Product Liability Laws," in *Product Liability: Prevention, Practice, and Process in Europe and the United States,* ed. Rudolph Hulsenbek and Dennis Campbell (Boston: Kluwer, 1989).

Kalman Leloczky, "General and Specific Features of Certain European Product Liability Laws," in *Product Liability: Prevention, Practice, and Process in Europe and the United States,* ed. Rudolph Hlusenbek and Dennis Campbell (Boston: Kluwer, 1989), 67; and Patrick Kelly and Rebecca Attree, *European Product Liability* (London: Butterworths, 1992), 138.

50. Berg, "La notion de risque," 276.

bility and Compensation for Personal Injury convened by Prime Minister Edward Heath in 1972 issued the Pearson Report, which advocated a move to strict liability similar to that pursued in the United States and in France. The proposed reform was never adopted, and the United Kingdom retained a negligence standard.[51] In Sweden, the Product Liability Committee proposed the adoption of a similar strict liability standard for medicines in 1973. Here, too, the proposal was set aside when pharmaceutical producers and importers organized to advocate an alternative system of collective insurance.[52] The British and Swedish cases serve as a reminder that product liability reform was not a necessary outcome in either France or Germany.

Legal Culture and Consumer Rights

Why did Germany and France pursue different solutions to the shirking encouraged by a simple negligence standard of product liability? Such differences of legal approach are typically attributed to differences in the legal systems of the two countries. In the case of product liability, the legal culture argument fails. National legal traditions played only a small role in determining national product liability practice, despite the fact that national product liability standards were elaborated almost entirely through the courts. It is true that France and Germany found different legal foundations for product liability law. Whereas France relied primarily on contract law, Germany relied primarily on tort law. Yet comparison with the U.S. and British cases suggests that such legal differences should not have played a decisive role in the persistent divergence of national product liability standards. It would therefore be inaccurate to attribute the difference of French and German treatments solely to the different legal cultures.

Western legal traditions are commonly divided into those grounded in common law, as in Britain and the United States, and those based on civil codes, as in France and Germany. In general, civil code countries form and modify their legal standards through legislative decisions. Common law countries rely instead on courts to adapt old standards through reinterpretation of legal precedent. The distinction has been perceived as the root of differential national financial systems, even of differential national economic performance.[53] Yet product liability law confounds this distinction. Although France and Germany are commonly grouped into the civil law category of legal traditions, product liability is an unusual policy area in which dramatic

51. Thomas V. Greer, "Product Liability in the European Community: The Legislative History," *Journal of Consumer Affairs* 26/1 (Summer 1992): 168.

52. In Germany, pharmaceutical companies also received an exemption from the general product liability regime. Howells, *Comparative Product Liability*, 151–52.

53. Caroline M. Fohlin, "Economic, Political, and Legal Factors in Financial System Development: International Patterns in Historical Perspective," California Institute of Technology, Social Science Working Paper No. 1089 (2000); Edward L. Glaeser and Andrei Shleifer, "Legal Origins," Harvard Institute of Economic Research Working Paper No. 1920 (April 2001); and Rafael La-Porta, Florencia Lopez de Silanes, Andrei Shleifer, and Robert Vishny, "Legal Determinants of External Finance," *Journal of Finance* 2/53 (1997): 1131–50.

changes in legal standard have been directed almost exclusively through the interpretation of legal case history.[54] Indeed, contrary to what the common law/civil law
distinction might predict, common law United States has adopted a standard most
similar to civil law France. The OECD, in a 1995 survey of national approaches to
product liability, found no practical link between types of national legal system and
the standard of product liability they adopted: "As a matter of practice, it appears
that the distinction between civil law systems and common law systems has little affect on those elements of liability important to consumers."[55]

Even if this broad legal categorization has not been decisive, the very fact that
product liability law was created in France and Germany through judicial interpretation should have helped to isolate those decisions from the logic of political and
economic interests. It should strengthen, not weaken, the case for an explanation
based on distinctive national legal cultures. Indeed, there are important historical
differences between the two legal systems. France's emphasis on contract law in its
approach to product liability, and Germany's emphasis on tort law, appears to have
origins in different historical treatments of associational and contractual rights
within the two national legal systems.

German law is grounded in strict Roman law as interpreted and normalized by the
nineteenth-century pandectist ("all receiving," comprehensive) school of legal history. French law, by contrast, combines elements of Roman law (*droit écrit*) as applied
in the south of the country with a common law tradition (*droit coutumier*) that was
recorded and consolidated by the long tradition of French legal nobility (*noblesse de
robe*) in the north of the country. These different heritages are evident in the extreme
formalism of the German civil code (*Bürgerliches Gesetzbuch*, BGB) as compared to
the briefer and more elegant treatment of the French civil code (*Code civil*).[56]

They have also generated different traditions of association and contract, which
in turn have influenced the later treatment of product liability reform. In German
law, as under Roman law, associations are treated as legal entities with the same rights
as individuals. French law, by contrast, assigns rights only to natural persons. Moreover, contracts in the German legal system are not inviolable, as they are in the
French legal tradition, but must meet a legal standard of appropriateness that pre-
cludes exploitative contracts. In effect, the German legal tradition draws a different
line between legal concepts of individual and contractual agency than the French legal tradition does. The French legal individual is more narrowly defined, but her
contractual agency is greater. The German legal individual is construed more
broadly to include organized groups of people, but she enjoys a diminished set of
contracting rights. It is precisely this limited conception of contractual sovereignty

---

54. Germany's 1968 Drug Law, which imposed a strict standard of liability on pharmaceutical
companies, was one of the few cases in which a national legislature directly shifted the standard of
liability for a product prior to the EU's 1985 Product Liability Directive and national implementing legislation.

55. *Product Liability Rules in OECD Countries* (Paris: OECD, 1995), 28.

56. For a more extensive treatment, see Konrad Zweigert and Hein Kötz, *Introduction to Comparative Law* (Oxford: Clarendon Press, 1987), 80–81, 146.

that raised obstacles to adopting a strict standard of liability under contract law in Germany.

Yet a look at the United States suggests that these different historical legal traditions did not necessarily dictate different standards of product liability in France and Germany. In the United States, strict liability has been grounded equally in tort law and contract law. Contractual liability in the United States evolved, as in France, by extending an implied warranty. Historically, this developed in two stages. In the 1916 *MacPherson v. Buick* case, contractual privity was abrogated by extending a duty of care to third parties. This opened the way for liability claims for innocent bystanders injured by producer negligence. Then, in the 1960 *Henningsen v. Bloomfield Motors, Inc.* case, the court found the producer responsible based on an implied warranty against product-related damage.[57] This finding was standardized in the 1972 U.S. Uniform Commercial Code and has become the basis of strict liability in contract.[58] However, most U.S. states have also found a strict standard of product liability in tort law. The 1965 Second Restatement of Torts imposed strict product liability by extending responsibility to "any product in a defective condition unreasonably dangerous to the user or consumer" (§ 402A).[59] In this new doctrine of "res ipsa loquitur" ("let the thing speak for itself"), the fact of a defective product was taken to be sufficient evidence of producer negligence. This presumption of negligence under tort law was extended to wholesalers and distributors in the 1970 *Price v. Shell Oil* case.

In sum, national legal traditions do appear to have influenced the legal approach that France and Germany have taken to product liability, but they do not appear to have placed insurmountable barriers to the adoption of different standards of liability. The case of the United States suggests that a strict standard of liability was in principle compatible with the legal logic of either tortious or contractual product liability. Germany could have adopted a res ipsa loquitur doctrine under tort law that would have opened the door to a strict standard of product liability.[60]

This suggests that the courts in France and Germany have adopted different standards of product liability not in order to conform to national legal traditions but rather to conform to a particular conception of the consumer's role in the economy. German courts saw the consumer as integrated into the economy and were willing to rely on—indeed, enforce—existing institutions of production to promote safer products. French courts came to see the consumer as economically vulnerable and operating outside of the economy; the courts therefore placed the entire burden of product-related risk onto producers.

57. Roland N. McKean, "Product Liability: Implications of Some Changing Property Rights," in *The Economics of Legal Relationships*, ed. Henry G. Manne (St. Paul, Minn.: West Publishing Company, 1975), 261.

58. Fred W. Morgan, "Marketing and Product Liability: A Review and Update," *Journal of Marketing* 46 (Summer 1982), 69–78.

59. Zweigert and Kötz, *Introduction to Comparative Law*, 713–16.

60. A contract approach does not necessarily imply a strict standard. England, which employs a contractual approach to product liability, has nonetheless retained a negligence standard of liability.

Product Safety Regulation

Product liability law helped to set the terms by which product safety was understood in France and Germany. Nevertheless, governments have rarely been content to rely on the deterrence effect of private law solutions in order to keep producers from selling dangerous goods. Both countries therefore also acted to set general safety standards that products must meet *before* they arrive on the market. These accompanied monitoring and recall systems for products that fell short of the necessary level of safety. Despite these similarities, however, the nature of product safety regulation has differed in a systematic way in the two countries.

The French approach has been characterized by government input into product safety. The German system granted industry a strong voice in ensuring the safety of products. Legal scholar Christian Joerges summarizes the difference succinctly: "French product safety law is hard to fit into a market-oriented approach. The French analytical framework, conceived from a State or administrative viewpoint . . . cuts straight across a German market-oriented category frame of market-related rules, setting of standards and follow-up controls."[61]

French Product Safety through Administrative Intervention

Over the course of the 1970s and 1980s, France experienced a shifting standard of product safety. Early efforts at imposing product safety focused on surveying the marketplace for dangerous products. Starting in the early 1970s, the French government began to regulate individual classes of products that were felt to be especially dangerous. This kind of legislation, targeting products such as toys or drugs, typically appeared in response to a particularly public incident of product failure. Such administrative intervention at the sectoral level constituted the major strategy of product safety in France in the late 1960s and early 1970s. Only in legislation of 1978 and 1983 did the French government move to a general standard of product safety that applied to all products placed on the market.

Beginning in the early 1960s, any product that was not specifically targeted by government safety regulation was covered by general prohibitions against fraudulent business practice. This approach had its roots in a 1963 decree that extended the competency of the Service for the Repression of Fraud, created in 1907 to implement the 1905 law prohibiting "hidden defects," to include the control of product quality.[62] The resources and impact of the Service for the Repression of Fraud were impressive. In 1971 alone, its 1,000 inspection agents evaluated over 400,000 products. Fifty regional laboratories tested product samples removed during such inspections. Twelve thousand products were found to have been fraudulent or unsafe in that year, and half of these cases ended up in court.[63]

61. Christian Joerges, Joseph Falke, and Hans-W. Micklitz, *Die Sicherheit von Konsumgütern und die Entwicklung der Gemeinschaft* (Baden-Baden, Germany: Nomos, 1988), ch. 2, p. 1.

62. Charles Castang, "Consommation: prévenir ou réprimer," *Figaro,* 4 March 1975.

63. Gérard Cas, *La défense du consommateur* (Paris: Presses universitaires de France, 1975), 70.

However, the French government was not content merely to survey the market for dangerous products. In the early 1970s industries with particularly dangerous products faced specific sectoral regulation, often in response to a particularly dramatic instance of product failure. One such case was the talc Morhange affair of 1972, in which thirty-six children died and eight remained crippled for life after having been given a talcum powder containing too much hexachlorophene.[64] The U.S. Food and Drug Administration had already shown this chemical to be dangerous in 1971, and these findings appear to have been known in France.[65] The Morhange affair led directly to the creation on 10 July 1975 of the Law on Cosmetic and Hygiene Products requiring that information about all new products of this kind be compiled and distributed to anti-poison centers across France. The products also had to be approved by the Ministry of Health, after which the labeling of the product was determined by subsequent decrees and regulations of 15 April and 28 December 1977. Noncompliance was punishable with fines and imprisonment.[66]

Similarly, for the drug industry, a technical commission on pharmaco-vigilance (Comité technique de pharmacovigilance) was created on 2 October 1976. Its goal was to "systematically collect in the greatest possible number of hospital locations information on all dangerous accidents, apparently connected to the use of pharmaceutical products, and certainly those incidents and accidents for which there is reason to think that they are related to the use of a pharmaceutical product." Its members were eminent professors. In 1978, under the influence of the Barre government, the Ministry of Family Health created a new Consumer Organization Liaison in which this new commission would be able to consult with consumer groups.[67]

A third example of direct government intervention was children's toys. The toy industry in France, the second-largest exporter of toys in the world at the time, had revenues of 6.6 billion francs and employed 10,500 workers. In a regulation of 22 June 1976, the French government required that formerly voluntary AFNOR standards for toy manufacture be made obligatory.[68] This approach was particularly at-

64. The Morhange case also highlighted problems of consumer access to justice in France. In 1978, the families of the children hurt by the Morhange talcum powder were awarded 25 thousand francs for children who had died, a few thousand francs for children that had been incapacitated for up to a month, and 1.5 million francs for the four children who survived but were considered 100 percent handicapped. Shocked by the small remuneration, the families came together in 1979 to form a *comité des familles victimes du talc Morhange* in order to launch a class action suit against the Morhange company. While such class action was in principle permitted under the 1973 law, the courts ruled that the committee of families did not constitute an acceptable legal party. Two consumer groups, the UFC and the UNAF, also brought legal suits against the company but were allowed to sue only for damages that the case had caused their organizations, not the damage to consumers as a whole. The courts awarded them 40 thousand francs each. Denise Nguyen Thanh-Bourgeais, "La sécurité des consommateurs: Réflexions sur l'affaire du talc Morhange," *Recueil Dalloz Sirey* 12 (1981): 89–94.

65. "L'affaire du talc Morhange," *Le Monde,* 1 August 1978.

66. Rosemonde Pujol, "Cosmétique et santé: nouvelle législation," *Le Figaro,* 25 January 1979.

67. Rosemonde Pujol, "Une antenne pour les consommateurs au ministère de la santé," *Le Figaro,* 8 November 1978.

68. Cas, *La défense du consommateur.*

tractive to the government because it permitted regulation to take into account the latest technical developments without having to be redrafted. French toys had to be certified by a testing laboratory to conform to AFNOR's safety standards. This regulatory approach was similar to that employed to enforce safety standards in Germany, but with the important difference that certification in France was mandatory.

This difference was highlighted with the 1988 European Directive on toy safety, which required that all toys on the European market include a "CE" mark to indicate that they conform with European toy safety standards. The problem was that the CE symbol came about through autodeclaration by the producer rather than from systematic laboratory testing. Many foreign toys included the CE label but did not even possess a manufacturer's label, so that it was impossible to know if they were truly in compliance. Alan Bryden, general director of the French National Testing Laboratory (Laboratoire national d'essais, LNE), warned that "the directive will afford a level of security equivalent to that which we possess only if the administration exercises an extreme vigilance over the use of the CE mark."[69]

Two pieces of legislation adopted in 1978 and 1983 marked a transition away from the selective regulation of dangerous products and toward a general standard of product safety that would apply to all producers. The 1978 Law for the Protection and Information of Consumers, or *loi Scrivener,* required that products be safe under "conditions of proper use" (*"conditions normales d'utilisation"*). The more rigorous 1983 law on product safety extended that standard to include product safety given any "reasonably foreseeable use." Producers were required to ensure safety not only when the product was used properly but also when consumers used the product in an incorrect way that might reasonably have been foreseen by the producer.[70] France remains the only European country to incorporate in an explicit way foreseeable misuse into its general standards of safety.[71]

Beyond setting general standards of product safety, the 1978 and 1983 laws also extended the powers of the government to intervene in the market to enforce the new standards. The 1978 *loi Scrivener* permitted the government to regulate dangerous products and even to have them removed from the market if they were found, by study of an independent testing lab, to be dangerous "in their normal use."[72] If a product presented an immediate or serious threat to the health or safety of consumers, a *"procédure d'urgence"* allowed the government to have the product immediately barred from sale, import, or manufacture. This new right was first used in June 1978, when pajamas treated with the chemical TRIS were removed from the

69. Françoise Vaysse, "Jeux dangereux," *Le Monde,* 8 December 1992.

70. In parliamentary debate over the 1983 law, consumer groups pushed for a wording that would have extended the standard of safety even further to include "improper misuse," which meant consumer misuse that was not foreseeable. While industry was willing to accept a standard of foreseeable misuse, they strongly opposed a further extension of their responsibility to include improper use.

71. Joerges et al., *Die Sicherheit,* ch. 2, p. 5.

72. The first of the two Scrivener laws treated consumer credit, granting consumers a seven-day grace period during which consumers could opt to break off the agreement.

market. The *procédure d'urgence* could exceed one year. (Hence on 20 June 1979 a specific decree was issued prohibiting the treatment of pajamas with TRIS.)[73]

Such a high level of government intervention in production proved unpopular with both the political left and right. The Communist Party, concerned that government recall actions could lead to firings or workforce displacement, abstained from voting on the 1978 law.[74] At the other end of the political spectrum, the conservative Rassemblement pour la République (RPR) warned of an "administrative inquisition," arguing that manufacturers should have greater rights to oppose public intervention if they felt that the criticism of their product was unjustified.[75] But no legislator wanted to be seen voting directly against consumer protection; when Scrivener threatened to call for a public referendum on the issue, the RPR acceded.[76]

If the 1978 legislation introduced the notion of greater government intervention in order to ensure product safety, the April 1983 law on product safety supplied the tool for enforcing safety. It created a Consumer Safety Commission (Commission de la sécurité des consommateurs, CSC), modeled broadly on the U.S. Food and Drug Administration, that was charged with investigating products that posed a threat to public safety. The CSC proved successful. In 1991, its seventh year of operation, the CSC received 207 requests—of which 159 fell within its area of expertise—and handed down twenty-one decisions. Of the requests, 31 percent came from consumer associations and 61 percent from individual customers. The CSC itself was not given regulatory power, as the FDA in the United States enjoyed. But it did have impressive police powers. Agents could enter day or night into industrial or corporate property, could enter the residence of individuals with court approval, and could demand communications and documents of any kind, held by anyone, that they felt necessary.[77] It also appears that the CSC was widely respected. When it published a warning against heating baby food in microwave ovens, for example, thirty manufacturers and importers of baby foods included the warning in their user instructions.[78]

Industry had strongly opposed the creation of new Consumer Safety Commission. They feared that they would be held responsible for damage from consumers using their products in stupid ways. They also felt that it granted government agencies too great an ability to investigate. And they expressed concern that the CSC would become a further forum for employee opposition, with labor unions filing complaints against management.[79] They argued, along with the Federal Consumers'

73. Cas, *La défense du consommateur*, 27. See also *Journal officiel*, 24 June 1979.

74. Michele Thimert, "L'information du consommateur," *L'Humanité*, 28 July 1978.

75. *La croix*, 16 April 1983.

76. Patrick Francès, "La protection et l'information des consommateurs," *Le Monde*, 12 December 1977.

77. Jean-Claude Fourgoux, "Le projet de loi sur la sécurité des consommateurs inquiétant, dangereux," *LSA* 885 (15 April 1983), 29.

78. Françoise Vaysse, "Les anges gardiens de la sécurité," *Le Monde*, 14 April 1992.

79. Chambre de commerce et d'industrie de Paris, *Projet de loi sur la sécurité des consommateurs* (21 April 1983), 8–11.

Union (Union fédérale des consommateurs, UFC), that the composition of the CSC should be limited to independent individuals rather than including representatives of consumers, producers, and distributors.[80] In accordance with this request, the new CSC was staffed by impartial academic experts in an effort to insulate product studies from political or economic pressures.[81] In most other ways, however, it was a case in which ministerial initiative had imposed a significant constraint on business that business was powerless to throw off.

German Product Safety through Industry Self-Regulation

Consumer safety in Germany rested on a combination of food regulation and equipment regulation, supplemented by additional regulations applying to particular sectors of unusual potential harm such as automobiles and pharmaceuticals. The two pillars of consumer protection, enacted in 1975 and 1980, each embodied a focus on market solutions and producer sovereignty. They nonetheless operated quite differently. The Food Act (Lebensmittelgesetz), enacted in 1975, relied primarily on product labeling and industry self-policing to ensure the safety of products. It imposed national safety, quality, and information standards but placed enforcement with the federal states. The 1980 amendment to the Law on Equipment Safety (Gerätesicherheitsgesetz, GSG) made standards created by Germany's standardization board DIN effectively mandatory for producers of equipment used by consumers. Hence, both areas of regulation tended to emphasize industry self-regulation, and neither the law nor the subsequent amendment provided for a legal recall responsibility for the producer.

On 18 June 1974, the Bundestag unanimously passed the Law on Food and Commodities (Lebensmittel- und Bedarfsgegenständegesetz, LMBG), which went into effect on 1 January 1975.[82] Seen at the time as the "basic law of consumer protection," the new law replaced a variety of nation- and state-level quality regulations. Extraordinarily broad in scope, it imposed standards on labeling, safety, and sanitation for food; regulated additives and advertising; and applied not only to food but also to tobacco and cosmetic products. Dozens of private testing labs throughout Germany were to perform chemical tests for the safety and conformity of food products. The law also provided for foods not meeting required safety standards to be kept from distribution.[83] The 1981 Food Labeling Law (*Lebensmittelkennzeichnungs-*

---

80. "Levée de boucliers," *Les Échos*, 28 January 1983.

81. When the new members of the CSC were appointed by the administration on 17 November 1987, one member was not readmitted. Professor Fournier, head of the antipoison center in Frenand-Vidal, had argued forcefully during his tenure to have Bergasol tanning cream removed from the market. INC lobbied hard to have him retained, but without success. "La nouvelle commission de la sécurité des consommateurs," *Consommateurs actualités* 570 (20 November 1987), 11.

82. Formally the law was entitled "Gesetz zur Neuordnung und Bereinigung des Rechts im Verkehr mit Lebensmitteln, Tabakerzeugnissen, Kosmetischen Mitteln und sonstigen Bedarfsgegenständen" or simply "Gesetz zur Gesamtreform des Lebensmittelrechts."

83. Susanne Langguth and Matthias Horst, "Zum Schutz der Konsumenten," *Verbraucher und Markt '83* 34 (18 August 1983), 10.

recht) further required that the full contents of food products be included on the packaging and that all perishable products include an expiration date.[84]

Unlike the French product safety laws, however, Germany never created a central authority with a mandate and regulatory capacity to apply the new food law. Indeed, all enforcement was delegated to the federal states, which were given no additional funding for enforcement. One reason for this weak enforcement was the opposition by both the FDP and the CDU to the legislation. The FDP argued that the new law only multiplied the number of legal texts that would have to be enforced, maintaining that the same goals could be achieved by enforcing existing laws.[85] For its part, the CDU argued that the regulation was overly intrusive. For example, the CDU opposed any advertising restrictions on tobacco products on the grounds that this would not limit smoking, as the SPD claimed. In the end, as in France, no member of parliament could be seen to oppose such broadly popular legislation.[86]

The lack of centralized enforcement of the new food law was due in part to CDU opposition, but it also suggested the ways that the SPD itself justified the legislation. They focused primarily on the economic advantages the law would bring by normalizing safety standards across Germany's states. Until 1975, each state regulated foods in its own traditional way. The SPD argued that the new law made economic sense because it promoted market transparency. Even the AgV, the leading consumer association, argued that one of the big advantages of the new food law was that it would reduce the burden on retailers, who until then had to track and apply over two hundred different laws and regulations.[87] Hence, the 1975 Food and Commodities Law, conceived as the "basic law of consumer protection," was pushed by the SPD on the grounds not specifically of consumer safety but rather for its unifying effect on the marketplace.

Regulation of consumer safety for equipment required a different strategy, one drawing on a more extensive application of existing technical standards within industry. The government initiatives of 1977 and 1980 were crucial. After seven years of attempting to establish a product safety standard, the Federal Minister of Labor in 1977 created the "GS" (*Geprüfte Sicherheit,* "tested safety") label for products to indicate conformity with all relevant (primarily DIN) technical standards. Permission to use the GS symbol would be granted by private test centers throughout Germany. By the mid-1980s, 16,000–17,000 testing certificates were issued annually. In December 1985, 85,000 kinds of equipment and machines carried the GS symbol.[88]

84. Ibid.

85. Gerhard Wilhelm Bruck, *Perspektiven der Sozialpolitik: Synopse sozialpolitischer Vorstellung der Bundesregierung, SPD, FDP, CDU, CSU, DAG, des DGB und der Bundesvereinigung der Deutschen Arbeitgeberverbande* (Göttingen, Germany: Verlag Otto Schwartz, 1974), 134–36.

86. Ingeborg Jahn, "Neues Lebensmittelrecht soll die Verbraucher besser schützen," *Frankfurter Rundschau,* 19 June 1974.

87. Katharina Olbertz, "Beim Verbraucherschutz hängt alles an der Kontrolle," *Handelsblatt,* 8 September 1975.

88. Josef Falke, "Post Market Control of Technical Consumer Goods in the Federal Republic of Germany," in *Post Market Control of Consumer Goods,* ed. Hans-Wolfgang Michlitz (Baden-Baden, Germany: Nomos, 1990), 364–65.

Companies that applied for GS certification and failed were referred to the trade supervisory offices (Gewerbeaufsichtsämter) for mandatory testing.

Although the GS program was considered a success, the administration remained unsatisfied with the voluntary nature of the GS symbol; in 1980 it moved to make industry standards of safety mandatory for all technical products on the market. The core of this legislation, named the Equipment Safety Act (Gerätesicherheitsgesetz, GSG), was a general safety requirement (*allgemeine Sicherheitspflicht*) that read: "The producer or importer of technical equipment may only display or circulate goods such that, in accordance with the generally recognized rules of technology as well as the labor protection and accident avoidance regulations, the user or third party to its specified application is protected against all kinds of risk to life and health, as specified by the manner of its particular application."[89] Unlike France's 1983 law, Germany's GSG employed a standard of safety based on the "specified application" of a product—and hence was not intended to cover the "foreseeable misuse" included in the French standard.

The "generally recognized rules of technology" described in the law had the effect of making industry standards quasi-mandatory. While the GSG did provide the possibility for manufacturers to avoid existing standards in favor of new technical approaches that offered equivalent or greater levels of safety, for most producers the effect of the GSG was to enforce compliance with DIN standards. By 1981, 637 DIN standards and 101 other kinds of technical standards fell under the GSG.[90] These standards, in turn, were set in technical committees that included representatives from the major manufacturers in the relevant field. Thus, the effect of the GSG was to force all competitors in a particular market to compete on technical standards that had been set by the industry leaders.

The GSG was to be applied by the trade supervisory offices (Gewerbeaufsichtsämter), of which Germany had 71 in 1986, with a total staff of nearly 3,000. With an estimated 180,000 new products coming on the market each year, the trade supervisory offices were only able to evaluate a fraction of all products. Over half of these were tested at trade fairs and exhibitions, with most of the remaining tests coming from referrals from Germany's comparative product testing organization, Stiftung Warentest, from industry works councils (Betriebsräte), or from other private testing laboratories.[91] The Stiftung Warentest and product testing organizations such as those granting the GS accreditation were required by law to refer nonconforming products to the Gewerbeaufsichtsämter for further testing.

If the danger of a product was deemed particularly acute, the GSG did permit the use of a prohibition decree (*Untersagungsverfügung*). These notifications, however, were only published in the GSG's own technical journal, which had a circulation of 500 copies. Starting in 1981, they were allowed to distribute the notifications

89. *GSG*, section 3, paragraph 1.

90. Annemarie Bopp-Schmehl, Uwe Heibült, and Ulrich Kypke, *Technische Normung und Verbraucherinteressen im gesellschaftlichen Wandel* (Frankfurt: Haag and Herchen Verlag, 1984), 101.

91. Falke, "Post Market Control," 359–69.

more widely, but they did so in only about ten cases each year.[92] Moreover, the GSG had no authority to force companies to recall products. Indeed, when a directive on product recall was proposed at the European level, the idea was quickly quashed by Germany. This kind of recall action was forcefully opposed by both industry and labor on the grounds that the process of safety evaluation inherent in product recall, currently managed by technical experts in standardization boards and the Gewerbeaufsichtsämter, would become politicized and transferred to experts in other fields.[93]

The Idea of Risk

State intervention into product risk and consumer safety transformed the environment into which producers sold their goods. Externalities of faulty or dangerous products were suddenly internalized to the company. Aspects of product design and manufacturing became the focus of government scrutiny. This new extension of state power suggests the limits of producer interests in guiding consumer regulation. Indeed, most of the legal and regulatory changes to the management of risk were strongly opposed by industry. Moreover, since producers in France and Germany shared similar preferences with respect to these new policies, a focus on producer interests alone fails to explain the differences in approach that emerged between the two countries.

In response to the pure interest group accounts of economics, sociologists argued that the ways in which societal risks were defined in a given polity were often socially constructed.[94] What one country perceives as a risk another may simply ignore.[95] In an early examination of this phenomenon, sociologists Mary Douglas and Aaron Wildavsky suggested that countries emphasize those risks that reflect the cultural organization of their societies. "Once the idea is accepted that people select their awareness of certain dangers to conform with a specific way of life, it follows that people who adhere to different forms of social organization are disposed to take (and avoid) different kinds of risk."[96] Specifically, they trace national differences in risk perception to cultural attitudes about equality and hierarchy. As Wildavsky later

92. Joerges et al., *Die Sicherheit von Konsumgütern*, 161–67.

93. Hans-Wolfgang Micklitz, "Comparative Analysis of the National Country Reports on Post Market Control and Perspectives for a European Setting of Post Market Control," in *Post Market Control*, ed. Micklitz, 415–18.

94. Niklas Luhmann, *Risk: A Sociological Theory* (Berlin: de Gruyter, 1993); and Lee Clarke and James F. Short, "Social Organization and Risk: Some Current Controversies," *Annual Review of Sociology* 19 (1993): 375–99.

95. Although smoking kills an estimated half-million people in Europe each year, it is the (so far) innocuous genetically modified organisms that have become the focus of more intensive political scrutiny. Alice H. Cooper and Paulette Kurzer, "Rauch ohne Feuer: Why Germany Lags in Tobacco Control," *German Politics and Society* 21/3 (Fall 2003).

96. Mary Douglas and Aaron Wildavsky, *Risk and Culture: An Essay on the Selection of Technical and Environmental Dangers* (Berkeley: University of California Press, 1982), 9.

summarized, "across-the-board concern with technological danger stems from commitment to an egalitarian way of life . . . whereas support for technology as largely benign bespeaks commitment to hierarchy and individualism."[97] Yet the case of consumer protection policies in France and Germany make clear that such sweeping cultural accounts may be misleading. France and Germany recognized similar risks—and then managed them in different ways that had little to do with national legal cultures.

National approaches to product liability and product safety instead reflected emergent ideas about how consumers should be protected from product-related risk. The issue in each case hinged on whether public policy should focus on establishing acceptable procedures or on ensuring acceptable outcomes. Germany opted for a procedural interpretation. The goal of legal and regulatory treatment in Germany was to enforce a set of industry practices and standards that would draw on the knowledge of industry to ensure safe products. In product liability, companies were able to exculpate themselves by demonstrating that they had organized production properly: by following industry standards in design, by hiring appropriately trained workers, and by managing their company well. In product safety regulation, the state opted to make mandatory the safety standards established by industry. Under this approach, all producers in a sector would be held to standards established by representatives of leading firms in the context of Germany's standardization board, the DIN. In both cases, the German approach relied on procedural rules to achieve legitimate outcomes.

In France, the approach to product risk might be described as consequentialist. The goal of both legal and regulatory treatment of products has been to ensure an end state of appropriate safety, the characteristics of which are defined in advance. In product liability law, the intentions and actions of producers were seen as irrelevant in assigning responsibility. In the French standard, a company was liable for product-related damage even if no level of producer care could have avoided the damage caused by their product. A similar interpretation came to be adopted in product safety regulation. This set of policies evolved over time, from a focus exclusively on products that were particularly dangerous to a general set of product safety standards that applied to all products. The goal of the general standard that was eventually adopted was to ensure that any product that reached the market would be safe. The French approach focused on ends rather than means. Fault would be judged not by the actions or intent of individuals but by the mere fact of product failure.

How effective were the two approaches in protecting consumers from product-related injury? It is a difficult question to answer. One impact of the narrower German interpretation of industry responsibility for product safety has been a distortion of the estimations of total product-related accidents in the country. One of the few studies of home and leisure accidents in Germany, conducted by the Association of

97. Aaron Wildavsky and David Laitin, "Political Culture and Political Preferences," *Annual Political Science Review* 82/2 (June 1998): 593.

Liability Insurers, Accident Insurers, Automobile Insurers, and Legal Cost Insurers (HUK-Verband), found that 99 percent of all such accidents resulted from mistaken actions by consumers and not from flaws of design or construction in the product itself. Legal scholar Christian Joerges points out how improbable this finding is, given that the Trade Inspection Offices in North Rhine–Westphalia found in a 1984 study indicating that nearly a quarter of all home appliances on the market were in some way defective.[98] Indeed, efforts to assess systematically the number of product-related accidents in Germany have been discouraged, to the point that accidents have become almost unmentioned in discussions of product safety.

98. Joerges et al., *Die Sicherheit von Konsumgütern*, 134.

CHAPTER FIVE

Consumer Information

> In the bazaar information is poor, scarce, maldistributed, inefficiently
> communicated, and intensely valued.
>
> —CLIFFORD GEERTZ, "The Bazaar Economy"

Information has always been the first line of defense for consumers.
Through word of mouth, sales advice from retailers, brand reputation, advertising,
or past experience, consumers use available information about products to make
their purchasing decisions. Until the 1960s, the supply of such product information
was largely a private matter. There were some exceptions. These included the regulation and policing of weights and measures and early moves to restrict outright
fraud, especially in the drug trade. But for most of the nineteenth and twentieth centuries, information about products was seen as a private contractual issue to be
worked out between producers and consumers.

This perception began to change in the 1960s for three reasons. First, a proliferation of new products and brands had made the private acquisition of useful product information more challenging. Entirely new kinds of goods with innovative
features and little track record were quite difficult to evaluate through traditional
information channels. Second, corporate advertising budgets had been increasing
since the 1950s. As advertising techniques became more sophisticated, critics on both
the left and the right argued that advertising could lead to purchases that consumers
did not really *need*.[1] Such academic criticisms were reinforced by popular concern
over new motivational—even allegedly subliminal—advertising techniques that
seemed to treat consumer preferences as highly manipulable.[2] Finally, increasing

---

1. Jürgen Habermas, *The Structural Transformation of the Public Sphere: An Inquiry into a Category of Bourgeois Society,* translated by Thomas Burger (Cambridge, Mass.: MIT Press, 1991),
189; and John Kenneth Galbraith, *The Affluent Society* (London: H. Hamilton, 1958).

2. Vance Packard, *The Hidden Persuaders* (New York: D. McKay, 1957). In the same year, market researcher James Vicary claimed to have induced movie viewers to buy more Coke and popcorn

automobile use and the proliferation of self-service retailing was breaking down customer ties with traditional retailers. As shopping moved from the corner store to the suburbs, consumers enjoyed more options but less professional sales advice. It is probably not a coincidence that early consumer protection legislation in France and Germany followed a period of significant growth in modern large-scale retailing.[3] When these three long-term trends intersected with the economic slowdown of the late 1960s, political pressure for better consumer information came to a boil.

Within the scope of government intervention to improve consumer information, France and Germany confronted similar issues but adopted different approaches. German policymakers focused on providing consumers technically precise product information through a strict set of regulatory policies. French policymakers imposed relatively weak information requirements. Two areas of policy emerged in France and Germany during the 1960s and 1970s to provide consumers with more accurate information. The first approach was to regulate the content of commercial speech so that it would provide consumers with useful information. The second approach was to promote the distribution of objective product information derived from comparative product tests.

In the case of advertising, both countries adopted strong initial legislation. In both instances advertisers responded by creating self-regulatory bodies in the hope of forestalling direct government intervention. The standards for misleading advertising adopted in Germany, however, were interpreted in an extremely strict manner. In France, by contrast—where the government had not hesitated to curtail freedom of advertising for reasons of public morality or public health—the treatment of misleading advertising has been relatively lenient. These differences in approach engendered different advertising cultures in the two countries. In a 1989 study of European attitudes, Françoise Bonnal surveyed the qualities that consumers in six European countries associated with good advertising. France and Germany in particular showed a marked divergence. France placed a strong emphasis on the value of creative advertising. "The French . . . insist on defending the idea of an inventive and aesthetic advertising that creates new languages, sometimes at the risk of forgetting the needs of the product."[4] In Germany, good advertising was seen as honest advertising: "The particularity of German advertising is its severity. Ideal advertising must be honest, informative, and in good taste."[5]

---

by flashing suggestive messages on the screen that were too fleeting to be perceived consciously. Although his results were never reproduced, and Vicary disappeared six months after announcing his findings, the U.S. Federal Communications Commission nonetheless banned subliminal advertising in 1974.

3. France's 1973 *loi Royer* restricting new retail building also provided for collective legal action by consumers. Germany's Building Use Code, which effectively halted green-site retail construction over 800 square meters, was enacted in 1977.

4. Italy, like France, emphasized creativity. "Les Français . . . s'obstinent à défendre une idée de la publicité inventive, esthétique et créatrice de nouveaux langages, au risque parfois d'oublier les exigences du produit." Françoise Bonnal, "Les goûts publicitaires des Européens," in *Six manières d'être européen*, ed. Dominique Schnapper and Henri Mendras (Paris: Gallimard, 1990), 267.

5. Denmark, Spain, and the United Kingdom also placed a strong emphasis on informative

In the case of comparative product testing, producers in France and Germany both fought against independent product tests. They worried about the accuracy of such tests and about their impact on the sales of newly developed products. Courts in both countries tended to support producers' concerns, and in case after case they ruled against private testing organizations. Yet despite these similar concerns, the outcomes in the two countries were strikingly different. In France, two different testing organizations came to thrive under the controversy they generated. Journal circulations grew; with more subscriptions came funding for further tests. In Germany, by contrast, legal challenges forced the state to oversee the arena of comparative product testing. The result has been a pattern of strong state and business intervention in testing in Germany, at odds with the independent and activist testing culture in France.

The available evidence suggests that German consumers came to rely heavily on the results of comparative product tests in making purchases. A survey in 1978 found that 26 percent of Germans reported changing their purchasing choices based on the results of comparative product tests, compared to only 13 percent of French citizens.[6] In both France and Germany, the circulation of magazines featuring comparative product tests had reached half a million in 1975. Twenty years later, in 1995, German circulation had doubled to one million, whereas French circulation had halved, to roughly 260 thousand (see figure 5.1).

Because German consumers have paid close attention to comparative product test results, so too have German producers. In survey of German producers conducted in 1984, over two-thirds of manufacturers of products that had been tested by Stiftung Warentest reported incorporating testing criteria developed by Warentest into the design of new products.[7] Over half of all companies reported using test results to improve existing products; one-third used the test criteria of Warentest for their own internal quality controls.[8] A different survey in 1994 found that 80 percent of manufacturers relied in some way on Warentest information.[9] Seen in this light, industry participation in comparative product testing appears to have encouraged a sort of post hoc standardization. Aware that many consumers pay attention to comparative test results, producers are able to develop high-quality or highly engineered products with confidence that a significant group of consumers will take these qualities into account when they buy. This situation is in striking contrast to

---

advertising: "La particularité du public allemand est la sévérité. La publicité rêvée doit être honnête, informative et de bon goût." Bonnal, "Les goûts publicitaires," 274.

6. Although the circulation of product test magazines was approximately the same, industry representatives report that such magazines are widely shared, estimating that each subscription would eventually be read by five people on average. George H. Gallup, *The International Gallup Polls: Public Opinion 1978* (Wilmington, Del.: Scholarly Resources, 1980), 336.

7. Wolfgang Fritz, Harald Hilger, Hans Raffée, Günter Silberer, and Friedrich Förster, "Testnutzung und Testwirkungen im Bereich der Konsumgüterindustrie," in *Warentest und Unternehmen: Nutzung, Wirkungen und Beurteilung des vergleichenden Warentests in Industrie und Handel,* ed. Hans Raffée and Günter Silberer (Frankfurt: Campus Verlag, 1984), 46.

8. Hans Raffée and Wolfgang Fritz, "The Effects of Comparative Product Testing on Industry and Trade: Findings of a Research Project," *Journal of Consumer Policy* 7 (1984): 427.

9. *Die Welt,* 2 December 1994.

France, where companies do not have access to testing criteria and where consumers have far less interest in test results.

But if Germany's widespread reliance on test results brought an advantage in terms of quality and engineering, this appears to have come at the cost of radical product innovation. First, intensive interaction with producers has extended the duration of the average product evaluation cycle in Germany to two years. While a longer testing cycle helps companies manage the impact of possible negative reviews, it also means that older products with good reviews may overshadow newer products that have not yet been reviewed. Indeed, because many companies report incorporating Warentest evaluation criteria into their product design process, radically new products may be less likely to be developed. Retailers tend to reinforce this restraint on product innovation. In a 1984 survey of 13 department stores and 146 specialty retailers in Germany, 32 percent reported ordering outdated products that had received a "good" rating in Stiftung Warentest's magazine *Test,* even though new versions were available. Twenty-five percent reported keeping high-scoring products in their inventory longer than they would have otherwise.[10]

Second, the central role of German producers in setting the criteria by which products are tested and compared has limited the scope of testing in Germany. Warentest does not, for example, evaluate products such as perfume and champagne, whose qualities are not as amenable to technical measure. By contrast, French testing groups like the Federal Consumers' Union (Union fédérale des consommateurs, UFC) and the National Consumption Institute (Institut national de la consommation, INC), regularly assess such products via surveys of their readers. Producer participation also creates a conservative bias in that comparative tests emphasize conventional product dimensions. In these ways, industry participation in the evaluation process appears to create a bias against entirely new kinds of products as well as against radical innovations in existing products.[11]

In general, it appears that regulations governing the provision of product information have an impact on consumer and producer product strategies. Accurate product information helps ensure that consumers can identify hidden qualities of products. It also encourages companies to offer high-quality products, secure in the knowledge that consumers will recognize the additional quality and take it into account when purchasing. As one set of researchers in the U.S. Federal Trade Com-

10. Harald Hilger, Wolfgang Fritz, Günter Silberer, Hans Raffée, and Friedrich Förster, "Testnutzung und Testwirkungen im Bereich des Konsumgüterhandel," in *Warentest und Unternehmen,* ed. Raffée and Silberer, 191.

11. Interestingly, comparative product tests appear to create a systematic bias in favor of domestic producers. A comparison of six years of Warentest results with survey responses from product manufacturers reveals that equally positive test results tend to increase demand for domestic products more than they do for foreign products (81 percent versus 59 percent). Conversely, negative test scores tend to decrease demand for domestic products only half as much as they decrease the demand for foreign products (19 percent versus 41 percent). While positive evaluations tend to confer greater advantage to domestic producers, negative evaluations tend to confer greater disadvantage to foreign producers. Fritz et al., "Testnutzung und Testwirkungen im Bereich der Konsumgüterindustrie," 94.

mission note, "If price is more easily observed than quality, competition may be skewed toward less expensive, lower-quality products."[12]

Highly accurate product information reporting may also run counter to radical product innovation. Manufacturers that know the criteria by which consumers will be judging their products tend to invest in improvements of their products along these dimensions. Similarly, consumers are more likely to purchase products that fit existing criteria because they can be confident about the quality of the goods purchased. Customers might well avoid new kinds of products that cannot be evaluated according to existing standards. When product information about existing kinds of products is good, the relative risk of new products is high. Thus, as consumers and producers become more reliant on institutional sources of technical product information, new products that do not coincide with existing information sources are unlikely to flourish.

Comparative Product Testing

France and Germany were relative newcomers to comparative product testing. The U.S.-based Consumers Union, which publishes *Consumer Reports*, began the world's first systematic product testing program in 1936. Sweden, the Netherlands, and the United Kingdom all saw the creation of similar testing organizations in the 1950s. Germany's Stiftung Warentest was established only in 1966, and France's two product testing publications *Que choisir?* and *50 millions de consommateurs* first circulated in 1961 and 1970, respectively. As circulation figures suggest, consumer interest in these journals rose rapidly in both countries in the first half of the 1970s (see figure 5.1). By the 1980s, these publications had become extremely popular, even by international standards, although French readership did drop off in the late 1980s and 1990s.

Consumer groups in both countries saw comparative product tests as a source of valuable information for consumers. But such tests also posed challenges. First, producers in both countries expressed concerns that independent product tests would be biased, inaccurate, or unfair to the interests of industry. Early publishers of test results therefore faced a barrage of lawsuits from industry charging them with inaccuracy and defamation. Second, useful product tests were expensive to conduct. Different countries had found different approaches to finance them. The U.S. *Consumer Reports* funded its tests solely through private subscriptions; Sweden's *Råd och Rön* received government subsidies; Austria's *Konsument* was managed by the country's trade union movement.[13] Both France and Germany found solutions to these problems—solutions that embodied distinctive domestic approaches to consumer protection. Germany opted for significant producer participation at all stages

12. Howard Beales, Richard Craswell, and Stephen C. Salop, "The Efficient Regulation of Consumer Information," *Journal of Law and Economics* 24/3 (December 1981): 510.

13. Klaus Wieken, *Die Organisation der Verbraucherinteressen im internationalen Vergleich* (Göttingen, Germany: Verlag Otto Schwartz, 1976), 22.

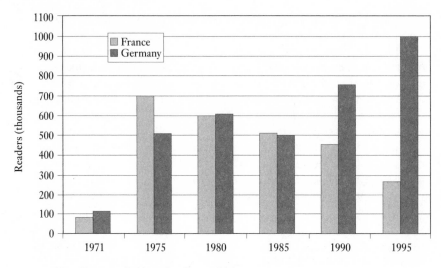

Note: Data compiled by author from multiple sources.

Figure 5.1   Circulation of comparative product test results in France and Germany

of the product evaluation process. France instead granted a great deal of independence to product testers, who established a reputation for their autonomous and often critical stance toward producers. In both countries, governments helped to subsidize product tests.

Industry Collaboration in German Product Testing

Comparative product testing in Germany began with two false starts. In September 1961, former *Der Spiegel* editor Waldemar Schweitzer began publishing the results of product tests in his monthly magazine *DM: Deutsche Mark*. Its circulation grew to 350,000 by 1963, when it changed to a weekly format, reaching a peak of 800,000 in 1964. Between January 1963 and December 1964, *DM* published results on an impressive 215 product categories, including 3,000 product brands.[14] Success proved transitory, however. Circulation fell to 450,000 in 1965, and by 1966 *DM* was shut down altogether.[15] The problem that led to its downfall was not financial, it was legal. *DM* was continually sued, beginning with a chocolate manufacturer that received a negative evaluation in the first issue and ending with a lawsuit filed by Volkswagen. In a driving test that pitted the Volkswagen 1500S model against similar models from BMW, Ford, Audi, and Alfa Romeo, the Volkswagen's engine failed repeatedly, earning *DM*'s "not recommended" evaluation.[16] VW sued *DM* for 10

14. Ibid., 24.
15. Dieter Meiners, *Ordnungspolitische Probleme des Warentests* (Berlin: Duncker and Humblot, 1968), 181–83.
16. Dirk Schindelbeck, "Ist Bonn für gutes Gulasch?" *Damals* 12 (2000): 7.

million DM in what the *Neue Zürcher Zeitung* at the time touted as the "greatest industrial trial in Germany."[17]

The core problem for *DM* was that it financed its product tests not only through magazine subscriptions, which were relatively inexpensive, but also by selling advertising space among its product reviews. This combination created a palpable conflict of interest that undermined both public confidence in their reporting and the legal status of *DM* as a neutral testing organization. *DM*'s experience revealed both the potential size of public demand for comparative product testing and the potential strength of industry opposition to product testing by a for-profit organization.

The second false start came from Germany's umbrella consumer organization, the Association of Consumer Groups (Arbeitsgemeinschaft der Verbraucherverbènde, AgV). The AgV began already in 1959 to make critical product comparisons. In 1962, it created its own product test center that tested eight product categories and 115 product brands over the course of the next two years.[18] This effort was also thwarted, in August 1962, by the German Brands Association (Markenverband), which took AgV to court on charges of brand name defamation. Rather than fight extended legal battles, in 1963 the AgV stopped its testing program. It announced that it had decided "to conduct future tests not in opposition to industry, rather . . . to carry them out in technical collaboration with branded products industries and retailers."[19] While the AgV continued to compile and publish comparisons of product specifications and prices, it never again entered the field of comparative product testing.[20]

These early signs of industry opposition to comparative product testing contrasted sharply with the political enthusiasm for this activity in Germany. As early as 1957, Minister of Economics Ludwig Erhard had made a proposal for institutionalized consumer protection via product tests. In 1962, Chancellor Konrad Adenauer called, in his government's platform, for the creation of a neutral testing body as soon as possible. Minister of Justice Wolfgang Stammberger affirmed that there was a sound legal basis for objective, technical, and neutral comparative tests.[21] The CDU under Adenauer called for the creation of a state-run testing facility for products; the opposition party, SPD, favored an independent public association instead.[22] Under pressure from its coalition partner, FDP, the CDU accepted the SPD proposal, and on 4 December 1964, the Bundestag voted unanimously for the creation and financing of the Stiftung Warentest.[23] By the organization's own account, its founding responded to four emerging consumer concerns: the growing abun-

---

17. Stiftung Warentest, *Zeichen setzen für Verbraucher* (Berlin: Stiftung Warentest, 1996), 7; and Peter Ditgen, *Der vergleichende Warentest als Instrument der Verbraucherinformation*, doctoral thesis, University of Cologne, 1966, 66.

18. Wieken, *Die Organisation der Verbraucherinteressen*, 22.

19. Ditgen, *Der vergleichende Warentest*, 67.

20. "Marktübersicht Waschkombinationen," *Verbraucherpolitische Korrespondenz* 1 (January 1964): 7.

21. Stiftung Warentest, *Zeichen setzen für Verbraucher*, 7–8.

22. Meiners, *Ordnungspolitische Probleme*, 60–63.

23. Stiftung Warentest, *Das Wichtigste in Kürze* (Berlin: Stiftung Warentest, 1996).

dance of products, the growth in advertising, the time-consuming task of comparative pricing, and the increasingly technical nature of products (often precluding expert advice at the point of sale).[24]

The first comparative test results appeared in the new magazine *Test* in 1966. Government funding for the program, originally intended as a five-year startup grant, had to be extended when sales remained disappointingly low. Originally available only by subscription, in 1970, *Test* became available at newsstands. Circulation reached 100,000 in 1972. In 1973, sales receipts began to exceed government financial support.[25] What followed was a boom in circulation that appears to have been spurred in large part by a growing demand from consumers under economic stress from the first oil embargo. *Test* has since become extremely successful. Circulation reached one million in 1995, with government support providing only 13 percent of its operating expenses.

Unlike its failed predecessors, Warentest never lost a legal suit to the companies that it evaluated. This record of success rested in large part on a groundbreaking 1975 ruling by the German Federal Supreme Court (Bundesgerichtshof, BGH). Ruling on a case filed against Warentest's 1967 evaluation of ski bindings, the BGH supported Warentest, finding that the organization served a valuable function of market transparency so long as the tests were carried out in a fair way. The economic logic was stated explicitly in the ruling: "Consumer enlightenment through an increase in market transparency is essential, not only in the interest of the consumer, but plainly also from an economic perspective."[26] In other words, the goal of testing was to combine consumer interests with the interests of a more efficient industrial sector. As product testing was also therefore in the interest of industry, the condition set by the court for fair testing was that industry itself be allowed to participate in the evaluation process.[27]

The charter of the Stiftung Warentest provided industry actors with the ability to participate in product evaluation at all stages of the process.[28] First, the board of trustees (Kuratorium) of Warentest included five representatives from industry, five representatives from consumer associations, and five neutral specialists. A three-quarters vote of this board could veto any test proposal. About 5 percent of all proposals were blocked in this way. This happened most often when the board of trustees felt that the evaluation would depend heavily on matters of taste. Champagnes and perfumes, for example, typically fell outside of Warentest's purview. Once a product category was chosen, Warentest again consulted with industry and consumer associations in selecting specific brands to evaluate. Individual tests nor-

---

24. Stiftung Warentest, *Zeichen setzen für Verbraucher,* 6.
25. Wieken, *Die Organisation der Verbraucherinteressen,* 25.
26. Stiftung Warentest, *Zeichen setzen für Verbraucher,* 14.
27. The test would be illegal when "das Vorgehen des Testveranstalters 'als nicht mehr vertretbar (diskutabel) erscheint.'" Werner Brinkmann, "Rechtsprobleme des vergleichenden Warentests in der Bundesrepublik Deutschland," *Zeitschrift für Verbraucherpolitik* 1 (1977): 257.
28. Roland Hüttenrauch, "Zur Methodik des vergleichenden Warentests," *Journal of Consumer Policy* 1/2 (1977): 143–50.

mally included about twenty similar products. In order to select them, Warentest polled roughly a hundred retailers to find out what brands they stocked. Popular brands were usually included, with the idea that their strong market share was an indication that readers were interested in them. While some manufacturers did not want their products evaluated, it was more common for companies to complain that they had not been included in an evaluation.

Once the test products were selected, manufacturers were then notified of the specific model that had been chosen. This gave them the opportunity either to suggest a different product in their product line that would fit the evaluation better or to announce that a newer and better product would be released in the next few months and should become the target of testing. Warentest also consulted with industry and consumer groups to decide what product properties to evaluate. Criteria proposed by engineers on the staff of Warentest were discussed and amended by a special advisory council (Fachbeirat) with five to ten representatives from industry, consumer associations, and retailers. The criteria were then distributed to all manufacturers whose products were being tested. Manufacturers were encouraged to indicate whether any important criterion—especially one that might show their product in a good light—had been omitted. This reduced the potential of an unfair advantage favoring firms who happened to have a representative on the advisory council.

The final stage of the process was, of course, testing. Warentest had no test facilities of its own. Instead, it relied on ninety independent testing laboratories to carry out the evaluations, based on the criteria identified by the advisory council. The actual evaluation might last from one to six months, depending on the characteristics of the product. Raw results from the tests were then distributed to participating manufacturers for scrutiny. This early notice of findings allowed manufacturers to raise objections before publication in *Test*. Once any objections were dealt with, the Warentest staff then weighed the importance of the different test results and combined them to create an overall evaluation. Individual products were placed according to their evaluation on a standardized five-point scale, running from "very good" to "very unsatisfactory."

This process may have appeared to give industry unwarranted input into what was meant to be objective comparative product tests. It was also a slow process, requiring an average of two years from conception to publication. But German consumers were highly supportive of the results. A 1994 survey found that Stiftung Warentest was the second most popular organization in Germany, behind only the Red Cross.[29] Indeed, Germany's consumer group, AgV, had been a strong advocate of this sort of consumer-business collaboration in product testing, seeing it as a means to avoid bias and to ensure the independence and legitimacy of the testing organization.[30]

---

29. "Interview mit dem Chef der Stiftung Warentest, Roland Hüttenrauch," *Tagesspiegel*, 27 November 1994.

30. "Errichtung eines 'Deutschen Allgemeinen Warentestinstituts,'" *Verbraucherpolitische Korrespondenz* 3 (25 January 1964), 2.

Industry at Arm's Length in France

Comparative product testing in France has long been divided between two organizations that publish competing consumer magazines. The first group, the Federal Consumers' Union (Union fédérale des consommateurs, UFC), began disseminating the results of comparative product tests in its journal *Que choisir?* in December 1961. A second group, the National Consumption Institute (Institut national de la consommation, INC) began publishing the results of product tests in its own journal, *50 millions de consommateurs,* in 1970.[31] While performing roughly the same function, the two organizations took markedly different approaches.

The UFC, the nonprofit consumer association responsible for the *Que choisir?* evaluations, was founded in 1951. For the first eight years of its distribution, circulation did not exceed 5,000 copies. In 1969, the UFC decided that the best way to grow would be to associate with the Belgian Consumer Association (Association belge des consommateurs, ABC), whose journal *Test-Achats* already enjoyed a circulation of 100,000 in the much smaller country. So in 1969, *Que choisir?* began to publish the results of tests conducted for *Test-Achats.*[32] The UFC later revealed that not only the tests themselves, but also most of the production work for *Que choisir?*— including editing, layout, and printing—had been undertaken by the Belgian group.[33] By the end of 1973, French sales began to pick up and the UFC split from ABC. Running its own comparative product tests, though, took a financial toll. Despite the new subscribers, *Que choisir?* nonetheless fell three million francs into debt over the course of their first year on their own.[34]

Ironically, salvation for the UFC came in the form of a lawsuit. In December 1973 the Arthur Martin Company sued *Que choisir?* for a false comparative test report concerning an Arthur Martin refrigerator. In what appears to have been a typographical error, the volume of the refrigerator was reported in *Que choisir?* to be 226 liters instead of its actual 266 liters. On 18 February 1974, the French Commercial Court, a body that oversees industry and retail matters, ordered *Que choisir?* to reimburse Arthur Martin 310,000 francs for damages. Furthermore, they were required to pay for the publication of the court finding in five major newspapers. The decision was upheld on appeal in 1975.[35] This ruling, based on the advertising clause

31. A third organization, the Laboratoire coopératif d'analyses et de recherches, also published the results of product tests, but they did not compare specific product brands. They instead offered general purchasing suggestions based on the findings from products they identified as "brand A" and "brand B."

32. Hans B. Thorelli and Sarah V. Thorelli, *Consumer Information Handbook: Europe and North America* (New York: Praeger, 1974).

33. "Défense timorée du consommateur aisé," *Libération,* 29 May 1975.

34. When the Belgian Consumer Association ran out of money for *Test-Achats* in the summer of 1965, U.S. and British consumer groups offered them financial support. Until 1968, the editors of *Test-Achats* were unpaid volunteers. Jean-Marc de Preneuf, "La crise de *Que choisir?:* Un triste gout d'échec," *La croix,* 15 December 1974; and Jacques Neirynck and Walter Hilgers, *Le consommateur piégé: Le dossier noir de la consommation* (Paris: Editions ouvrières, 1973), 260–61.

35. Mary Blume, "The Rocky Road of Consumerism in France," *International Herald Tribune,* 30 April 1977; "31 millions pour Arthur Martin," *Libération,* 3 March 1977.

of the newly written *loi Royer* of 1973, established a particularly high level of responsibility for the publication of comparative product tests. So long as product evaluations were held to the strict standard that the *loi Royer* set for advertising, plaintiffs had only to prove that an error had been made, regardless of whether or not the error had arisen out of negligence or even intent.[36]

Unlike the lawsuits against Germany's *DM*, however, the Arthur Martin lawsuit proved beneficial for *Que choisir?* Specifically, the well-publicized case helped to establish the UFC's credentials as independent of industry influence and to emphasize antagonistic relations with industry as the organization's central theme.[37]

By the late 1970s, *Que choisir?* had become the scourge of French industry. In April 1977, when *Que choisir?* discovered that many aerosol cans on the market exploded if heated to over 90 degrees Celsius, they called for a consumer boycott of these products.[38] In February 1978, *Que choisir?* evaluated doctors by sending them patients with simulated ailments. One of the doctors, Albert Cohen, brought a defamation suit against UFC.[39] In December of the same year, eleven medical testing labs sued *Que choisir?* for a critical report in their May 1978 edition entitled "Thirty-two laboratory tests, thirty-one errors." In each of these cases, the appeals court in Paris found against *Que choisir?* on the grounds that their methods were not "scientifically incontestable." The fines were kept relatively low, though, and the publicity they generated spurred sales of *Que choisir?*[40]

In one of its most highly public cases in 1979, *Que choisir?* reported on 750 different cases in which automobile tires manufactured by the French Kléber-Colombes company had exploded when cars approached 130 kilometers per hour (81 mph). At the time, Kléber-Colombes enjoyed sales of 2 billion francs, of which 36 percent came from foreign sales, and it controlled 40 percent of the French tire market. Michelin, the leading producer, held 48 percent of Kléber-Colombes stock.[41] In response to the *Que choisir?* criticism, on 28 November 1979 Kléber-Colombes organized an "information meeting" at their testing center in Mirmas. They invited some of France's best race drivers in order to put the suspect tires, the models V10 and V12, through a rigorous workout. One engineer offered an appeal to patriotism: "Journalists, your attack is tragic. What you are attacking is the entire French automobile industry. It is the backbone of France."[42] François Lamy, who had pursued the case during the *Que choisir?* tests, presented himself at the center but was not admitted. When asked why Lamy was not allowed to participate, the CEO of Kléber

36. Jean-Philippe Vidal, "Les organisations de consommateurs peuvent-elles revendiquer le droit à l'erreur?" *Les Échos*, 25 March 1977.

37. Ibid.

38. "L'Union fédérale des consommateurs appelle au boycott des aerosols," *Libération*, 5 April 1977.

39. Elisabeth Rochard, "Peut-on tester un médecin?" *Le Matin*, 15 November 1978.

40. *Le Monde*, 26 December 1978.

41. François Bourbon Destrem, "Kléber-Colombes met toute la gomme," *Quotidien de Paris*, 30 November 1979.

42. "Journalistes, l'attaque est malheureuse. Ce que vous attaquez, c'est toute l'industrie automobile française. Qui fait vivre en épine dorsale la France."

responded: "We do not allow a criminal to speak."[43] The episode was in a sense typical for the UFC, which used controversial test results in order to publicize—and when possible politicize—broader consumer safety issues.

This approach could not have been more different from the strategy adopted by France's other comparative product testing organization, the state-run Institut National de la Consommation (INC). Minister of Economy and Finance Michel Debré had proposed the creation of the INC, and it was approved by a vote of the National Assembly on 15 December 1966. Its organizational tasks, set by government decree in 1967, called for it to provide technical support on consumer issues to the government as well as to consumer associations.[44] The INC was also charged in article 2 of its charter to conduct product tests at the request of these groups. The first test results appeared in 1970 in the organization's monthly magazine, *50 millions de consommateurs* (later renamed *60 millions de consommateurs*). After receiving popular approval, in 1971 the advisory group to the Sixth French Plan recommended that government funding for comparative product tests conducted by INC be increased.[45] Between 1971 and 1975, INC conducted 140 different tests.[46]

INC's approach to product testing was similar to—and partly modeled on—that employed by the UFC. Products to be tested were purchased anonymously, with the test sample generally amounting to three quarters of the total selection of products available on the market. When the price of products and tests permitted, several products of each brand were included in the testing sample. Labels were removed from the products, which were then either tested in-house or, for more complicated tests, sent to external testing labs. The raw test results were then generally sent to the companies whose products had been tested, although *50 millions de consommateurs* writers were not required to take into account company responses. Tests lasted between six months and a year from the date of product purchase to the date of publication—from a quarter to a half of the duration of testing conducted by their German counterpart.[47]

In general, *50 millions de consommateurs* was more popularly oriented than *Que choisir?*[48] The first published product test reported by *50 millions de consommateurs* evaluated cleaning powders, whereas the first test by *Que choisir?* looked at tennis balls. INC also increasingly worked to distribute its test results through the popular media. Each year, INC broadcast ten hours of consumer programming in 126 television spots of the program *D'accord pas d'accord* ("Okay not Okay"). In a 1986 survey, 88 percent of consumers knew of the *D'accord pas d'accord;* 70 percent

43. Patrick Berthreu, "Kléber-Colombes en rechappe," *Libération,* 7 December 1979; Josée Doyère, "Information sélective," *Le Monde,* 1 December 1979.

44. Josée Doyère, "Le dixième anniversaire de l'INC: Un outil au service d'une politique libérale," *Le Monde,* 24 January 1978.

45. Jacques Dubois, "Les consommateurs et le VIe plan," *Information consommateur* 70/5 (1970): 5.

46. Claude Duchamp, "Les essais comparatifs," *Revue des études coopératives* 186 (1977): 81.

47. Ibid., 78.

48. Michel Wieviorka, *L'état, le patronat, et les consommateurs: Étude des mouvements de consommateurs* (Paris: Presses universitaires de France, 1977), 146–47.

avowed interest in such television spots, although 71 percent of viewers said they watched it simply because it happened to be on while they were watching.[49] INC test results also appeared in external magazine and newspaper articles (1,400 times in 1989) as well as on television and radio. Beginning in July 1989, all of INC publications became available over France's digital network Minitel from a service called BINC. This service received 348,900 calls in 1989 alone.[50]

Government financial support for INC raised questions about its objectivity. A consumer survey commissioned by the employers association, CNPF, reported that consumers appreciated the impartiality of *Que choisir?* but regretted its lack of finances. Conversely, consumers recognized the value of *50 millions de consommateurs* but were suspicious that it might be biased in favor of France's state-owned industries.[51] In fact, the first two product tests conducted by INC were never published. The first, on apple juices, found them to be of dubious quality, but it coincided with protests by French farmers in which they dropped bushels of fruit on the highways. A second on washing machines revealed that Italian machines were better than their French competitors. In order to suppress these uncomfortable findings, the first version of *50 millions de consommateurs* was released without any test results.[52] The problem of bias continued to plague INC. In a famous 1979 case, Pierre Fauchon, director of the INC, stepped in to alter the title and text of an article on hormone-treated beef that had originally been edited to read, "Ne suivez plus le boeuf" (literally: "Don't follow the beef").[53] The episode followed immediately in the wake of broad calls by consumer groups to boycott hormone-treated veal. Writers at INC felt that Fauchon had changed the text at the behest of the Ministry of Agriculture, which feared that it would look like a further call to boycott.[54]

In part because of these early experiences, government sponsorship of comparative product testing drew mixed reactions from consumer and producer associations. ORGECO, the consumer association representing the big French labor unions, supported product tests as a counterweight to industry prerogative: "Only comparative tests are capable of truly impeding producers and distributors and thus of permitting an effective defense of the consumer."[55] While most family-oriented consumer associations also favored the INC tests, the UFC voiced concern about the conflict of interest posed by the dual role of the INC as both advisor to the gov-

49. "Les émissions télévisées de l'INC 'D'accord pas d'accord,'" *Consommateurs actualités* 513 (13 June 1986), 3–6.

50. Marie-Hélène dos Reis, "L'Institut national de la consommation," *Revue française d'administration publique* 56 (October–December 1990): 659–60.

51. Alain Poirée, *Les discours consuméristes et leur perception par les Français* (Paris: I.C.C.-C.N.P.F., 1984), 16.

52. Jacques Neirynck and Walter Hilgers, *Le consommateur piégé: Le dossier noir de la consommation* (Paris: Editions ouvrières, 1973), 266.

53. *50 millions de consommateurs* 118 (1979).

54. INC, "Exposé de Pierre Fauchon, Directeur de l'INC," memo of the Conseil d'Administration, 26 January 1981, 16.

55. Jacques Dubois, "L'étiquetage d'information et les essais comparatifs," *Information consommateur* 4 (1970): 2.

ernment and evaluator of products. In part for this reason and in part due to the growing competition *Que choisir?* faced from *50 millions de consommateurs,* in 1972 the UFC withdrew from the governing board of the INC.[56]

Producers had generally opposed INC's move into product testing. CNPF president Paul Huvelin saw all government support to comparative product testing as an unfair intervention in business.[57] The Paris Chamber of Commerce and Industry (Chambre de commerce et d'industrie de Paris, CCIP) did not object to product testing per se but complained that industry had no input into the evaluations. Taking their cue from Germany's Stiftung Warentest, they proposed that INC consult professional associations in drawing up the list of brands to be tested, in studying the "physionomie" of the market, and in establishing criteria for evaluating specific products. They argued that product test results should be distributed to producers with enough advance notice to allow for their responses to be incorporated into the final evaluations.[58] These objections from business were initially rejected. In an October 1973 letter to the President of the CCIP, Minister of Economy and Finance Valéry Giscard d'Estaing rejected the German-inspired approach. Greater company participation in the preparation of comparative tests would, he claimed, "risk to accentuate the disequilibrium in favor of producers who would rapidly become masters of what products were submitted to tests, of the choice of laboratories, and of the results that were diffused." He proposed instead that product testers be held to high standards of quality in product testing that could be contested after a product test was published. The CCIP in turn rejected this *a posteriori* solution as overly burdensome for companies, testing organizations (which would face large fines), and consumers.[59]

What followed was a series of efforts to make INC product tests more responsive to the concerns of business. In March 1975, France's standardization board AFNOR published an experimental standard, known as "NF X 50–005," which was intended to provide "a charter of good relations between organizations conducting comparative tests, producers, and consumers."[60] The voluntary standard called for testing organizations to maintain financial independence from producers and distributors, precluding any form of advertising in the magazine where comparative test results were presented. It also stipulated that tests should cover products from the entire price range, that reviews of subjective qualities should be based on consumer surveys, and that companies implicated by comparative tests should be consulted about the testing procedure and its results.[61] Three years later, the newly created office of the secretary of consumption called in 1978 for access to all *50 millions de con-*

56. Dos Reis, "L'Institut national de la consommation," 656.

57. Jacques Dubois, "L'étiquetage d'information," 2.

58. Chambre de commerce et d'industrie de Paris, "Problèmes de la consommation," rapport présenté au nom de la Commission du Commerce Intérieur par H. Ehrsam [Report of the Commission on Domestic Commerce, H. Ehrsam] (24 May 1973), 7.

59. Chambre de commerce et d'industrie de Paris, "Réglementation des essais comparatifs de produits," rapport présenté au nom de la Commission du Commerce Intérieur par H. Ehrsam [Report of the Commission on Domestic Commerce, H. Ehrsam] (6 December 1973), 8.

60. Duchamp, "Les essais comparatifs," 77.

61. Chambre de commerce et d'industrie de Paris, "Réglementation des essais comparatifs," 6.

sommateurs articles before they were published in order to avoid damage to certain companies.[62]

The issue resurfaced again a decade later, in 1987, when the new right-wing government endorsed business participation in comparative product testing. In a sweeping indictment of both INC and the UFC, the new secretary of consumption and competition, Jean Arthuis, stated in July 1987: "France is cruelly lacking a system of comparative product tests worthy of the name. . . . One need only observe the use made by our German neighbors of their Stiftung Warentest to be persuaded that such an organization is an essential element for economic performance, joining the aspirations of consumers and professionals alike."[63] One of Arthuis's goals was to make INC results available for producers to incorporate into their advertising. Producers, in turn, wanted more input into the process by which their products would be evaluated.[64]

In October 1987, the National Council on Consumption called for the creation of an autonomous Authority on Comparative Tests (Autorité des essais comparatifs, ADEC) to oversee the testing operations at INC. This new oversight body included six members of consumer associations, six members of professional associations, and four neutral professionals.[65] ADEC was assigned three functions in product testing. They would help in the selection of the product categories to be tested, and product categories would be selected two to three years in advance of publication so that interested industries could register their opinions. They would participate in developing the testing methodology, including setting the composition of the expert groups that would oversee particular tests. They would also participate in the effort to draw conclusions from the test results.[66]

Producers applauded the ADEC initiative. Roger Cabal, CNPF vice president for consumer affairs, especially praised the likely effect of lengthening the development period for the tests. This, he felt, would allow companies to change their product designs so that they would better conform to the testing criteria.[67] Consumer groups had a mixed response. Whereas most consumer groups in the CNC assented to the change, the UFC stood in strong opposition to the creation of ADEC. Apparently at the UFC's behest, the new French testing authority was also condemned by the European Office of Consumer Unions (Bureau européen des unions de consommateurs, BEUC) on the grounds that it permitted excessive state intervention in

62. Pierre Pujol, "Un souch' non désintéressé pour les 'consommateurs,'" *Quotidien du peuple*, 25 January 1978.

63. "Intervention de M. Jean Arthuis, Secrétaire d'État chargé de la Consommation et de la Concurrence, devant le Conseil d'Administration de l'INC (26 juin 1987)," *Consommateurs actualités* 558 (10 July 1987), 2–3.

64. Professional representatives had been removed by the Socialist government in 1982 from the Advisory Council of the INC and placed instead in the National Council on Consumption, formerly the National Committee on Consumption, in order to create a high-level forum for concertation between consumers and producers.

65. Drawn from AFNOR, LNE, INC, and the independent testing group Qualitel.

66. "La réforme des essais comparatifs," *CNPF Patronat* 499 (March–April 1988): 78–79.

67. "Mise en place d'une autorité des essais comparatifs au sein de l'INC," *INC Hebdo* 563 (2 October 1987), 5.

product evaluation. BEUC found that the level of industry participation in ADEC far exceeded that in Germany's Stiftung Warentest and warned that "any direct or indirect interference by the state or producers, in the rare cases where that has occurred, throws discredit on product tests for many reasons: because of an arbitrary choice of products to be tested, by the exclusion of foreign competitors, by juggling the relationship between quality and price, by reference exclusively to national standards, or by the uneven use of results by companies or the state."[68]

Despite these dire warnings, ADEC never attained the level of industry collaboration that lay at the heart of Germany's Stiftung Warentest. While industry representatives were represented in ADEC, companies were largely unwilling to contribute at different stages in the evaluation process. ADEC today continues to set broad policies for product testing in *60 millions de consommateurs*, but it has not led to a significant integration of industry into the process of product testing.

Truth in Advertising

The most prominent channel for consumer information about new products was advertising. Levels of advertising spending grew over the 1970s in both France and Germany, with Germany consistently spending more than France, both in absolute terms and as a percentage of economic output. The rise in advertising spending brought with it a growing concern over the negative impact that advertising might be having on consumers. John Kenneth Galbraith's critique of the role of advertising in promoting "unreal" needs first appeared in the United States in his 1958 book *The Affluent Society*. This work, translated into German in 1959 (*Gesellschaft im Überfluß*) and into French in 1961 (*L'ère de l'opulence*), brought attention to the increasing role of advertising in structuring demand for products. Shortly afterwards, in the early 1960s, France and Germany both put in place advertising regulations that prohibited flagrantly false advertisements. These early regulations, aimed at cases of obvious fraud, were only a first step. By the 1970s, manufacturers and consumers in both countries began to push for a higher standard of truth in advertising. Asked if advertising misleads consumers as to the quality of products, for example, a 1974 survey found that consumers in both France and Germany overwhelmingly agreed: 74 percent of French citizens and 77 percent of German citizens said yes.[69] Consumers groups supported more accurate advertising as a source of consumer protection, since better-informed consumers would be better able to defend their interests. Recognizing a growing political pressure for a consumerist agenda, producers saw restrictions on advertising, in particular industry self-regulation, as a relatively painless strategy for managing growing consumer grievances.

New legislative efforts focused on the ambiguous category of "misleading" ad-

68. "UFC-BEUC: Pleins feux sur l'ADEC," *INC Hebdo* 578 (22 January 1988), 3.

69. Jacques-René Rabier, *Euro-Barometer 4: Consumer Attitudes in Europe* (Luxembourg: Commission of the European Communities, October/November 1975) [IPCSR Edition, 1978], 51–52.

vertising. In both countries, new standards were written into law; new regulatory bodies were created to oversee the new standards. Yet the standards came to be applied in different ways. In France, courts interpreted advertising standards loosely, granting advertisers a broad margin for creativity. Advertising enforcement was largely in the hands of the advertisers themselves, who also played a central role in setting standards for appropriate content. Furthermore, advertising in France was addressed under criminal law, which limited the ability of consumer groups to bring direct suits against transgressors, while also encouraging judges to be lenient in marginal cases. In Germany, by contrast, courts held advertisers to a remarkably strict standard that ensured that consumers would not be misled. The law implementing strict advertising standards also granted consumer groups a privileged position to bring legal suits against companies that transgressed. The result was a lenient, creative environment for advertising in France and a rigorous standard of truth in advertising in Germany.

German Advertising Regulation as Competition Policy

The basic law of advertising in Germany was established in the 1965 amendment to the Law against Unfair Competition (Gesetz gegen den unlauteren Wettbewerb, UWG), which required that advertising not be misleading. The wording of the amendment states that "any person who in the course of business and for the purpose of competition makes misleading statements about business-related facts, in particular about the characteristics, origin, mode of production or pricing of any goods or services . . . the mode and source of supply, the possession of warrants . . . may be subject to an injunction."[70] Because Germany's advertising law resides within competition law rather than criminal law, it does not provide for imprisonment, as in France, except in cases of gross negligence. A 1969 amendment to the UWG clarified that the purpose of the legislation was "protection against consumer disappointment, to improve business transactions and to confront the risks that emerge from new forms of advertising."[71] But the ambiguity over what kinds of advertising might be "misleading" left significant room for interpretation by the courts.

Clarification came with the groundbreaking 1971 court ruling against the Philips Company. In this case, the German Supreme Court (Bundesgerichthof) found the advertised claim that the Philips electric razor was "the world's most purchased" ("*der meistgekaufte der Welt*") to be misleading. The court finding was striking because the razor did in fact have the highest total sales in the world. The factual accuracy of the advertising was therefore not in question. Instead, the court argued that the manner in which the information was presented might be interpreted by consumers to mean that the Philips razor was also the most popular in Germany— which was not true.[72] From this case emerged a rule of thumb that any advertise-

70. Gesetz gegen den unlauteren Wettbewerb (UWG), Section 3.
71. *Bundestag-Drucksache* 5/4035 (1969).
72. Gerhard Schricker, "Soll der einzelne Verbraucher ein Recht zur Klage wegen unlauteren Wettbewerbs erhalten?" *Zeitschrift für Rechtspolitik* 8 (1975): 195.

ment in Germany that is thought to deceive more than 10 percent of the population is considered misleading.[73] German courts were unusual in that they admitted surveys as legal evidence of the percentage of the public that an advertisement would mislead. In a 1979 case, for example, the Kontinent Moebel company was sued on the grounds that their name gave the mistaken impression that their products were imported. In a consumer survey asking how respondents interpreted the name, 8 percent felt it implied imported products, 7 percent felt it implied that they also sold products abroad, and 2 percent found it generally indicated "internationalism." Finding against Kontinent Moebel, the court argued that 10 percent of respondents had been misled.[74] While such cases seem extreme, the reasons for setting the bar for public credulity so low appears to have been a concern that advertisements would disproportionately mislead the members of society that were the least educated.[75]

In response to the emerging new court standard for misleading advertising, Germany's Central Committee on the Advertising Economy (Zentralausschuß für Werbewirtschaft, ZAW) created the German Advertising Council (Deutscher Werberat, DW) in 1972. The DW was intended to be a self-regulatory body that could replace direct state regulation.[76] Both consumers and competitors were encouraged to bring complaints to the DW. The DW was not legally bound to respond to these complaints, but it could at its own discretion send notices of possible violation to companies that did not in its appraisal appear to be meeting the strict standards involved with misleading advertising. Producers were not legally bound to respect these notices, but the probability of legal recourse by competitors led most German companies to respect the findings of the DW. While the ZAW did provide a useful filter for court cases, it never met the goal of replacing state regulation with self-regulation, and the number of court cases continued to rise.[77]

Two-thirds of all advertising court cases were brought by companies in direct competition with the defendant. The remainder of the cases were brought by consumer associations, which in 1965 had been granted the right to file associational lawsuits (*Verbandsklage*) in cases of misleading advertising.[78] The main consumer

73. UWG Section 3. Stefan Strassner, *Verbraucherinformationsrecht* (Saarbrücken, Germany: ÖR Verlag, 1992), 35.

74. Strassner, *Verbraucherinformationsrecht*, 43–44.

75. Interview, Hauptverband Deutscher Einzelhandel, August 1995.

76. Klaus Tonner, "The Legal Control of Unfair Advertising in the Federal Republic of Germany," in *Unfair Advertising and Comparative Advertising*, ed. Eric Balate (Brussels: Story Scientia, 1988), 104.

77. Ibid.

78. The 1965 amendment to the UWG permitted established consumer groups to sue producers, but not collections of consumers themselves. An amendment to the UWG submitted by the government on 29 September 1978 placed strong limitations on suits even by individual consumers, requiring that any consumer seeking damages show that misleading advertising was the specific reason they purchased a product, that they would otherwise not have made the purchase. This significantly raised the barrier to claiming compensation based on false advertising, as this burden of proof proved nearly impossible to meet. Alex Stein, "Die Verbraucheransprüche und ihre Geltendmachung durch Verbraucherverbände nach der UWG-Novelle," *Journal of Consumer Policy* 3 (1979): 29–40.

organization charged with bringing suits for UWG infraction was the Consumer Protection Union (Verbraucherschutzverein, VSV), which was established in Hamburg in 1966 and then moved to Berlin in 1974. By 1981, the VSV alone had brought 577 suits against companies for misleading advertising.[79] The majority of such cases started as complaints from consumers. In 1977, for example, 80,000 consumer complaints were lodged with consumer organizations, of which 20,000 concerned advertising. Of these, 400 were pursued by consumer groups, and 150 reached the courts. Once in court, consumer groups enjoyed a success rate of 80 percent.[80] German consumer groups saw accurate consumer advertising as an important pillar of consumer protection and repeatedly argued that Germany's strict standard of advertising was not being adequately enforced.[81] A 1974 study commissioned by the AgV, for example, found that only 35 percent of all advertising in popular magazines was *not* misleading to the consumer. Worst were the advertisements for cleaning chemicals, cosmetics, over-the-counter drugs, and erotica—indeed, advertising for this last group was found to be misleading in 90 percent of cases.[82]

In a typical case raised by consumer groups, a German biscuit company was brought to court on the grounds that the slogan they employed to advertise their low-sugar biscuits, "Nibbling allowed" (*"Naschen erlaubt"*), was misleading. Since the phrase implied that nibbling was in general a bad thing, the plaintiff argued, it therefore implied that something particular about these biscuits made them a unique exception in the broader market for biscuits. Given that the competition also produced similar low-sugar biscuits, the courts deemed the advertisement misleading. By the early 1990s, thousands of such cases were being tried every year. In an evaluation of business opportunities in Germany, the business newsletter *Lloyd's List*

79. Jürgen Bornecke, *Handbuch der Verbraucherinstitutionen* (Bonn: Verlag Information für die Wirtschaft, 1982), 107.

80. Roland von Falckenstein, "Praktische Erfahrungen mit der Verbraucherverbandsklage in Deutschland," *Journal of Consumer Policy* 1/2 (1977): 173–75.

81. In order to evaluate the effectiveness of Germany's self-regulating Deutscher Werberat (DW), one researcher submitted 321 complaints based on advertisements of well-known companies from thirty popular German magazines published from 1976 to 1978. This amounted to nearly half of the DW's yearly total of 670 complaints. Of the complaints listed, 74 percent were simply rejected. The average time for processing the remaining complaints was 32 days. Udo Beier, "Schwachstellen der Werbeselbstkontrolle: Aufgezeigt am Beispiel des Deutschen Werberats," *Journal of Consumer Policy* 3 (1979): 300–313.

82. The study evaluated 2265 advertisements from eighteen magazines: 46 percent made exaggerated claims, 6 percent included double meanings, 6 percent left out basic information, and 7 percent included deceptive information. The ZAW in turn criticized the AgV study for exaggerating its results. Among the advertisements the AgV coded as misleading included one for powdered potatoes that mentioned "grandmothers recipe book," an ad for detergent claiming that it was "unbelievably inexpensive," and cigarette advertisements that did not include a health warning. The ZAW claimed that the AgV had exaggerated the number of infractions in order to raise its own profile. Arbeitsgemeinschaft der Verbraucher, "Verbraucherschutz überwiegend irreführend," *Verbraucherpolitische Korrespondenz* 4 (April 1974); "Verbraucherverband: Zuviel Irreführung," *Handelsblatt*, 14 February 1975; and "Eine 'Studie' voller Vorurteile," *Die Welt*, 2 April 1975.

described the German advertising regulation as "based upon the idea of a totally immature, pathologically stupid, and absent-minded consumer."[83]

Expressive Freedom in French Advertising Regulation

France's first law governing advertising, passed in 1963, prohibited advertising that was "created in bad conscience" (*"faite de mauvaise foi"*). Under this standard, false advertising was punishable only if it was shown to be intentionally false. In 1973, however, Article 44 of the *loi Royer* replaced the lenient bad-conscience standard with a broad proscription against any advertising "of a misleading nature" (*"du caractère trompeur"*). The new standard depended not on the intention of the advertiser but on the actual impact on consumers. Its wording, as transcribed in Law 121–1 of the Consumption Code, appears to make illegal an extraordinarily broad range of advertising content:

> All advertising in any form is illegal that provides false or misleading assertions, information, or provisions when it applies to one or more of the following elements: availability, nature, composition, substantial quality, active content, kind, origin, quantity, means and date of production, ownership, price and conditions of sale of goods or services that are the subject of advertising, conditions of use, results that can be expected as a result of their use, grounds for or means of sale or provision of services, extent of responsibility assumed by the maker, identity, size or ability of the producer, sellers, marketers or providers.[84]

By the letter of the law, France appeared to have enacted legislation to rival that of Germany. The new legislation also provided strong punishments. Responsible parties would be subject to as much as two years in jail, a 250,000-franc fine, and a responsibility to finance additional advertising to rectify misleading claims.[85]

But soon after the 1973 law calling for such stringent restrictions on misleading advertising was passed, French courts softened the law's provisions. In an early case, an advertisement for Samsonite luggage showed bulldozers playing soccer with a suitcase in order to demonstrate its strength. A rival company argued that since in fact Samsonite had had to replace the suitcase several times in making the commercial, the advertisement was misleading. Commenting on the case, the court

---

83. *Lloyd's List,* 17 January 1992.

84. "Est interdite toute publicité comportant, sous quelque forme que ce soit, des allégations, indications ou présentations fausses ou de nature à induire en erreur, lorsque celles-ci portent sur un ou plusieurs éléments ci-après: existence, nature, composition, qualités substantielles, teneur en principes utiles, espèce, origine, quantité, mode et date de fabrication, propriétés, prix et conditions de vente de biens our services qui font l'objet de la publicité, conditions de leur utilisation, résultats qui peuvent être attendus de leur utilisation, motifs ou procédés de la vente ou de la prestation de services, portée des engagements pris par l'annonceur, indentité, qualités ou aptitudes du fabricant, des revendeurs, des promoteurs ou des prestataires."

85. Jean Beauchard, *Droit de la distribution et de la consommation* (Paris: Presses universitaires de France, 1996), 314–16.

noted: "We must take into account the degree of discernment and the critical sense of the average consumer. The law is not intended to protect the mentally feeble."[86] Moreover, they argued that "attractive advertising commonly demands a certain use of fantasy."[87] A 1978 case against General Foods France made this clear. A lawsuit against their advertising claim that the drink Tang had "the taste of freshly pressed oranges" alleged that the statement, and the picture of an orange rind on the product packaging, was misleading. General Foods France too was exonerated, on the grounds that there was no fraudulent intent and that even the statement itself was not purely false.[88]

The courts later spelled out the logic behind these cases in a decision involving the Wonder battery company. Wonder had been sued for claiming that a Wonder battery "loses its charge only when used." Competitors brought suit against Wonder, arguing that this claim was not physically possible, since all batteries naturally lose charge during storage. The Tribunal of Paris found that the slogan was not "of the nature to lead into error" ("*de nature à induire en erreur*"), the standard set by the 1973 law, because the battery also contained an expiration date. Consumers could therefore reasonably be expected to understand that the claim was merely an exaggeration.[89] Advertisements were not bound even to a standard of factual truth, so long as "an average consumer with normal intelligence" might reasonably understand the nature of the exaggeration.[90]

France's permissive standard for truth in advertising was reinforced through a strategy of self-regulation by the advertising industry that helped encourage a liberal interpretation of what might be construed as misleading. France's Office of Advertising Verification (Bureau de vérification de la publicité, BVP), created in 1954, began as a purely self-regulatory body of the advertising industries. (Founded much later, Germany's DW had a similar structure.) Its activities were expanded in 1971 to address truth in advertising, and it was reorganized to introduce the National Consumption Institute (INC) onto its administrative council.[91] But BVP control over individual companies was limited to a published admonishment and the possibility of taking transgressors to court.[92] Its close ties with industry and its weak re-

---

86. Claude Vaillant, "La publicité mensongère et la protection du consommateur en France: bilan d'application jurisprudentielle," *INC Hebdo: Actes des VI journées du droit de la consommation* (12–13 December 1988), 19.

87. Jean-Jacques Biolay, *Le droit de la publicité* (Paris: Presses universitaires de France, 1986), 79.

88. "De nature à induire en erreur le consommateur." "'L'affaire Tang' pourrait remettre en cause la lutte contre la publicité abusive," *Les Échos*, 22 March 1978.

89. "Ne s'use que si l'on s'en sert!" Claude Vaillant, "La publicité mensongère," 18.

90. "Publicité comparative: Mensongère ou non?" *Consommateurs actualités* 505 (18 April 1986), 7.

91. In principle the 1971 reform introduced consumer interests into advertising regulation in the form of three seats on the board of directors allocated to the INC; in reality, the INC was wary of becoming too closely associated with any industry association and opted to occupy only one of these seats. Jean-Jacques Boddewyn, "Outside Participation in Advertising Self-Regulation: The Case of the French Bureau de Vérification de la Publicité (BVP)," *Journal of Consumer Policy* 7 (1984): 51.

92. Biolay, *Le droit de la publicité*.

course in cases of misleading advertising meant that the BVP was not ever able to enforce a very strict standard of truth in advertising.

A later attempt was made in France to introduce a more powerful oversight body that could set and enforce stronger advertising standards. In 1976, the Consumption Commission, organized by the new Secretary for Consumption Christiane Scrivener to make suggestions on consumer-friendly policies, recommended that advertising standards be set through equitable negotiations between consumer groups and advertisers. This proposal led to the creation in 1977 of the twenty-eight–member National Advertising Council (Conseil national de la publicité, CNP).[93] The new CNP included representatives from eleven national consumer organizations and eleven representatives of the media, plus expert witnesses from the government, the INC, and the BVP. The CNP was organized into three permanent committees focusing on ethical "deontology" questions, dialogue, and training, plus special working groups created on an ad hoc basis. The council was funded through a levy on advertising earnings. All meetings of the group were secret.[94] Many of the industry participants in the CNP favored these discussions, saying that it helped them keep track of the interests of consumer groups on subjects that changed over time. They also saw it as a way of reinforcing the mechanism of industry self-regulation.[95] Between 1980 and 1983 consumer and professional representatives negotiated within the CNP to set new standards for advertising. These discussions were spurred on by the 1981 election of François Mitterrand, who had proposed to make any decision arrived at by consumer and professional members of the CNP binding on industry.

With the economic crisis of 1983, however, this corporatist solution to advertising regulation was abandoned, and dialogue under the CNP halted. In the shadow of this failure, French advertising returned to the lenient standards set by, and enforced through, the courts. Behind this failure to enact more stringent standards of advertising lay the opposition of French producers. The leading employer's association, CNPF, opposed state enforcement of advertising standards negotiated with consumers, on the grounds that it would undermine the originality that they felt was fundamental to effective advertisement. They argued instead for self-regulation (*autodiscipline*) by the advertising industry.[96] French unions, by contrast, perceived that more accurate information about products would encourage consumers to purchase higher-quality goods and that this quality emphasis would favor skilled union jobs. The consumer group that represented the major French trade unions at the time, ORGECO, thus called for the government to provide greater funding to consumer associations to help fight false advertising. In the words of Jacques Dubois, president of ORGECO, "If one man warned is worth two, one consumer informed is worth at least ten."[97] In the end a lack of corporatist capacity in French industry

93. Boddewyn, "Outside Participation," 55–56.

94. Biolay, *Le droit de la publicité.*

95. "La guerre est finie," *CNPF Patronat* 447 (July 1983): 71–72.

96. "Le rôle de la publicité," *CNPF Patronat* 359 (May 1975): 47–48.

97. "Si un homme averti en vaut deux, un consommateur informé en vaut au moins dix." Jacques Dubois, "La publicité contre le consommateur?" *Information consommateur* 2 (1971): 4.

combined with a strong opposition from France's top employer association, the CNPF, to undermine the effort to create a system of advertising regulation that would be more responsive to consumer interests and needs.

Lenience in the regulation of misleading advertising was particularly striking given France's lack of reticence to restrict advertising for other reasons. Indeed, this sort of intervention was a staple of French competition and cultural politics. France prohibited the advertisement of product prices that, given the nature of the demand, could not be expected to remain in stock. Legislators were particularly concerned that less expensive French goods might be advertised, only to have more expensive foreign goods sold in their place.[98] France also long condoned government restriction on advertising for cultural reasons. The law requiring that the French language be used exclusively in advertising has its origins in the 1510 ordnance of Louis XII, the 1539 ordnance of Viller-Cotterets, and the law of 2 Thermidor in year 2 of the French Revolution. Practices that have been found illegal under this law include the use of the words "new filter" in the advertisement for French-made cigarettes and the distribution of an English-language handbill by the Paris Opera. Restrictions have also limited advertising in order to manage demand for dangerous or scarce products. Cigarette advertisements can contain images only of the cigarette package itself. Lawyers, doctors, and pharmacies cannot advertise at all. Other restrictions have specifically economic goals. In an effort to keep down the price of government health care, for example, pharmaceutical products reimbursed by social security may not be advertised. In 1974, in response to the first oil crisis, the government banned all advertising for energy.

In cases where advertising might be expected to have a negative effect on consumption patterns, the French government has been quick to regulate. Yet in areas in which only the accuracy of consumer information was at stake, French regulation has been characterized by leniency. This pattern was due in part to early court decisions that embraced a lenient interpretation of misleading advertising and in part to the failure of the subsequent consumer dialogue. A complex interaction of consumer and producer interests left advertising, in the end, as a pocket of regulatory laxity.

The regulation of advertising and comparative product testing offers a critical testing ground for the productionist view of consumer regulation—the view that na-

---

98. Indeed, producers whose goods were so advertised were granted a special dispensation to refuse distribution to the abusing retailers, a practice that is otherwise illegal in France. Advertising restrictions have also in some cases discriminated directly against foreign products. One example is the regulation of advertising of alcoholic beverages, which are classified for this purpose on a scale of increasing strength from 1 to 5. Higher values on the scale entail greater restrictions on advertising. Yet the constitution of the scale is flagrantly discriminatory against foreign spirits. Grade 5 alcohols, which include mainly aperitifs, cannot be advertised at all. Aperitifs, such as whiskeys, gins, and vodkas, are mostly foreign alcohols. Grade 4 alcohols, by contrast, which include digestifs, *can* be legally advertised. Digestifs, including rum and distilled alcohols such as brandy, contain no less alcohol than aperitifs but are primarily French products. This sort of discrimination is in principle not permitted under the Treaty of Rome, but it has not so far been corrected. Biolay, *Le droit de la publicité*, 68, 73.

tional regulations reflect the priorities of producers. First, product information has traditionally been seen as the domain of producers. While product safety involves economic externalities that reasonably invoke the state's interest in public safety, product information is arguably a private matter to be provided at the discretion of producers under the watchful eye of the consuming public. Second, the regulatory contexts in France and Germany were strikingly similar. Business interests shared the same concerns about public intervention in the realm of product information, and governments and court systems responded in similar ways to their objections. Third, German economic policy has commonly been seen to be particularly responsive to the organized interests of business. In the case of product safety and liability, for example, the interests of German industry appear to have been largely accommodated by the government and the German courts. This suggests that, particularly in the area of product information, German industry should have been able to obtain its own preferred policies.

Yet it did not. The French and German cases show that producer influence was uneven at best. In advertising, German producers faced a far tougher standard of misleading advertising than they would have wanted, and their attempt to limit government intervention through industry self-regulation had little effect.[99] French regulators, by contrast, attempted to impose a strict regulatory treatment of misleading advertising—and failed. As in the case of product liability, the role of the courts was critical in dictating the standard of protection that consumers would receive.[100] Through a series of court decisions, they developed a body of advertising law that corresponded to the broader conception of the consumer interest that was emerging in French society at the time.

In comparative product testing, the pattern of business influence was reversed. In Germany, business pushed for and achieved significant business input into the testing process. This allowed them to lower the risk to production lines by controlling the market uncertainty that independent product testing could create. One reason for their success was the support that they received from labor unions. So long as producers had sufficient advance notice about poor test results, undue shocks to the labor force could also be avoided. Through the help of the Justice Ministry, German policy choices were held in close alignment with the economic interests of trade unions and of industry. In France, by contrast, business consistently fought independent product testing and consistently failed. Here too, the role of trade unions proved to be crucial. Unlike in Germany, France's trade unions felt that an independent testing authority would provide a critical counterweight to the power of employers. Organized labor supported the independence shown by *Que choisir?* and opposed industry's effort to gain greater input into the tests conducted by *50 mil-*

99. Tonner, "Legal Control of Unfair Advertising," 104.

100. How exactly the courts arrived at their decisions is difficult to trace. In both France and Germany, judges communicated regularly with other political and economic actors. For this period, however, records of their communications remain closed. What is clear, however, is that the role of judge-made law has played a central role in shaping how some elements of consumer protection have emerged.

lions de consommateurs. The result was a system of product testing in France in which often controversial results helped to support strong consumer and union opposition to producers.

These apparently contradictory outcomes must be understood not in terms of simple producer interest but in light of the broader debate between consumers and producers over the identity of the consumer. In Germany, economic actors came to see support for accurate product information as part of a broader package of reforms that would provide consumer protection while also minimizing government intervention in the economy. In France, where industry also saw an informational approach as the least damaging response to consumer grievance, the provision of accurate product information was perceived to be less important. Even French consumer groups, obviously in favor of better product information, were skeptical that information alone would redress consumer grievances.

CHAPTER SIX

Standards versus Contracts

Among government efforts to regulate the consumer sphere, a number of policies bridged the categories of information and risk. Two such policies—quality labels for products and standard consumer contracts—are the focus of this chapter. In the case of quality labels, French and German efforts to provide consumers with objective information through uniform labeling standards rapidly turned into a debate over what product qualities to include on the label. Producers worried especially that proposals to make quality labels contingent on achieving minimum levels of performance would be tantamount to setting product standards. In the case of standard consumer contracts, the very name suggested the ambiguity. Were these contracts that should be regulated in the interest of fairness and transparency, or were they standards to be set through appropriate public policy? How one answered this question hinged critically on one's view of the economic and social status of consumers in society.

These hybrid consumer policies are analytically valuable because they dramatized the tradeoff that French and German policymakers faced between providing consumers with more information and insulating them from product-related risk. In each case, policymakers had to decide whether their goal was to ensure contractual integrity between producers and consumers or to go further, to set general standards with which all producers would have to comply. The outcome of such disputes depended on the political influence and organizational capacities of consumers and producers.

It should not be surprising that French and German policymakers adopted systematically different solutions. In the case of consumer contract terms, Germany's approach saw them as a set of standards. Germany's legislature explicitly proscribed an extensive set of contractual clauses so as to restrict the discretion of sellers. In France, initial efforts to treat consumer contracts as standards failed. After brief experimentation with negotiated contract terms, France instead moved to a purely contractual view of consumer contracts. While French retailers and producers would be held to a general standard of contractual fairness—for example, banning the exclusion of legal recourse for consumers—they were not to be subject to specific standards concerning product delivery, pricing, post-sale services, or availability. In Germany, treating contracts as standards ensured that consumers knew the terms on which they were acquiring new products. In France, consumers faced uncertainty about the exact contractual terms that would be applied to any new product they purchased.

Part of the justification for regulating consumer contracts was the impact that uncertainty about the content of such contracts could have, not just on shopping consumers, but also on product quality. In 1976, Germany's Justice Minister Philipp Held of Bavaria, an early advocate of regulating consumer contracts, stressed the economic benefit of greater clarity: "Under somewhat more honest, more comparable, and more transparent sales conditions market transparency will be improved; better application of legitimate consumer interests can lead to greater quality competition."[1] German producers appeared to have shared this view. They expressed concern that contractual uncertainty would make shopping less of a science, thereby lowering the overall quality of goods on the market over time.[2] In his analysis of the German AGB law, Michael Adams identifies the problem as one of adverse selection. He argues that producers with lower-quality contract terms have an incentive to charge the same rate as producers with higher-quality ones. Just as uncertainty about the qualities of a product may lead a consumer to favor lower quality, as Akerlof argued, so too may uncertainty about warranties and other after-sale services drive consumers to place a low value even on high-quality products.[3]

A similar pattern of policy formation—and economic outcomes—characterized the area of product labeling. During the 1970s, France experimented with a number of approaches to consumer labeling that would effectively set minimum quality standards for products. By the early 1980s, policymakers, facing resistance from business, concluded that labels should not be employed as a means for stipulating product standards. In Germany, policymakers also saw product quality standards as a logical extension of labeling activities. Industry accepted this approach but feared that including consumers in the process would politicize technical standards. Germany's Economics Ministry therefore adopted a plan for using product labels to convey quality information but gave control of this project to German Institute for Standardization (Deutsches Institut für Normung, DIN), the industry board tasked with setting technical standards.

Research on product labels suggests that they enhance competition in the arena

1. Johann Georg Helm, "Privatautonomie und zivilrechtlicher Verbraucherschutz," in *Verbraucherschutz in der Marktwirtschaft*, ed. Erwin Dichtl (Berlin: Duncker and Humblot, 1976), 79.

2. Joachim Beimowski, *Zur ökonomischen Analyse Allgemeiner Geschäftsbedingungen* (Munich: Verlag V. Florenz, 1989), 15.

3. Michael Adams, "Ökonomische Analyse des Gesetzes zur Regelung des Rechts der Allgemeinen Geschäftsbedingungen (AGB-Gesetz)," in *Anspruche, Eigentums- und Verfügungsrechte*, ed. Manfred Neumann (Berlin: Duncker and Humblot, 1984), 664.

of product quality.[4] Empirical research on regional appellations confirms that such labeling schemes do promote quality.[5] Quality labels in particular appear to perform the function of product standards, lowering consumer search costs for higher-quality goods. These findings have product market implications for the policy outcomes in France and Germany. Germany's emphasis on information as a strategy of consumer protection helped to promote a system of quality labels that provided consumers with better information. The result was a greater competition over quality. In France, which failed to develop a similarly widespread system of quality labeling, the difficulties of attaining information on product quality reduced quality competition.

Product Labeling

The German and French experiences with product labeling reform in the 1970s reveal the divergence of interests in relation to consumer information and risk. In Germany, consumer product labeling grew out of the Reichsausschuß für Lieferbedingungen (RAL), an organization originally created to provide a service to producers by ensuring the quality of raw materials. In France, consumer product labeling began as an equal collaboration of producers and consumers in a new organization, the French Association for Product Labeling (Association française pour l'étiquetage d'information, AFEI). RAL's attempt to negotiate minimum quality thresholds was rebuffed primarily by industry, which was able to have the program eliminated and a more business-friendly system installed in its place. In France, qualitative product labeling failed through a lack of sustained industry support.

French Product Labeling

France's product labeling campaign began relatively innocuously. Since 1967, French conserved and frozen food producers had been employing a complex labeling sys-

4. Phillip Nelson, "Information and Consumer Behavior," *Journal of Political Economy* 78 (1970): 311–29; Howard Beales, Richard Craswell, and Stephen C. Salop, "The Efficient Regulation of Consumer Information," *Journal of Law and Economics* 24/3 (December 1981): 491–539; Randall E. Westgren, "Delivering Food Safety, Food Quality, and Sustainable Production Practices: The Label Rouge Poultry System in France," *American Journal of Agricultural Economics* 81/5 (1999): 1107–11; Hendrik Spruyt, "The Supply and Demand of Governance in Standard-Setting: Insights from the Past," *Journal of European Public Policy* 8/3 (2001): 367; Thomas Reardon and Elizabeth Farina, "The Rise of Private Food Quality and Safety Standards: Illustrations from Brazil," *International Food and Agribusiness Management Review*, forthcoming.

5. Tyler Coleman, "Quality and Competition: The Political Economy of the Wine Sector," paper presented at the annual meeting of the Society for the Advancement of Socio-Economics, Amsterdam, the Netherlands, 28–30 June 2001; Richard Locke, *Building Trust*, manuscript (http://web.mit.edu/polisci/research/locke/building_trust.pdf); and Maria Luz Loureiro and Jill J. McCluskey, "Assessing Consumer Response to Protected Geographical Identification Labeling," *Agribusiness* 16/3 (2000): 309–20.

tem to discreetly indicate the age of their products. For these products, the date of preparation was printed using a system of coded letters so that distributors and retailers would be able to decipher them—but not consumers. Years received an arbitrary letter (the years 1967–72 were indicated by the sequence PCAEDL). Months of the year were coded by another arbitrary sequence of letters (NFUOCPDBSHTL from 1969 to 1972; a different sequence was used prior to 1969). Days of the month were indicated by the corresponding letters of the alphabet, excluding the letters *Q*, *V*, and *W*, with the numbers 2 through 9 standing for the days 24 through 31. Thus a frozen food labeled with "LF7" was produced on 29 February 1972.[6] This patently obscure system galvanized early consumer groups to push for regulatory reform. On 12 October 1972, the "Décret Pons" applied the law of 2 August 1905 on labeling to prepackaged foods, requiring that labeling include information about what the product is, the name of the producer, weight, date of expiration, and the contents and additives.[7] French consumer groups supported the initiative. On 20 November 1973, eight national consumer groups led a "label" campaign, encouraging consumers to buy only products that were correctly labeled according to the new law.[8]

This early focus on product labeling struck a political chord, evoking further discussions of what information might be provided to consumers on product labels. France's leading employers' organization, the National Council of French Employers (Conseil national du patronat français, CNPF) undertook a joint program with the National Consumption Institute (Institut national de la consommation, INC) to develop useful and informative product labels. In September 1970 they founded AFEI, a nonprofit organization for the public interest with the goal of designing and distributing product labels. The content of the labels was to be strictly factual and negotiated among consumer and industry representatives. Different kinds of labels would be negotiated for different product lines, and their use was strictly voluntary. At first, industry was less than enthusiastic. Henri Estingoy, the head of the INC, explained the program's slow start in 1971: "We don't sense delirious enthusiasm among the industrial sectors, and proposals [for new labels] are insufficient in number."[9] Nonetheless, the first model product label appeared in 1972. By 1974, AFEI had issued 300 labels, a figure that grew to 1000 by 1978, 1300 by 1980.[10]

The success of AFEI and the growing concern over product quality in the mid-1970s led consumer groups and the French government to push to extend the range of informative labeling beyond objective product dimensions to include measures of

6. Alain Gaussel, *Un panier de mensonges* (Paris: Editions du Seuil, 1973), 11.

7. Michel Bernard and Jacqueline Quentin, *L'avant-garde des consommateurs: luttes et organisations en France et à l'étranger* (Paris: Editions ouvrières, 1975), 100.

8. *Combat*, 22 November 1973.

9. "Promouvoir la function consommation," *Vos clients* 9 (1971), 11.

10. AFEI was eliminated in 1984. Pierre Frybourg (president of AFEI), "L'étiquetage d'information," *Revue de la concurrence et de la consommation* 12 (1980): 14–16; "L'étiquetage informatif vous aide dans vos achats," *Information consommation OR-GE-CO* 27 (March–April 1978): 3–4; and Jacques Dubois, "L'affichage des prix . . . ne doit être qu'un premier pas," *Information Consommateur* 1 (1972): 3–4.

more subjective product qualities. These would include composite indicators that would approximate qualitative characteristics of interest to the consumers, such as durability and usefulness. The model for this initiative was the Swedish VDN-Skala (Varudeklarationsnämnd-Skala, named for Sweden's Value Declaration Office). Established in 1951, the VDN-Skala provided relative product quality information on five-point scales. By 1971, the VDN-Skala had been successfully applied to 110 different kinds of products.[11] Following this lead, the French Ministry of Industry and Research under Michel d'Ornano in November 1975 created a Quality Service (*Service de la qualité*) designation under the Direction des Mines.[12] This *Service de la qualité* would work with AFEI to design the new qualitative product labels. The French president, the Ministry of Commerce, and the National Consumption Institute (INC) all endorsed the proposal. The association of companies that produce electrical goods (CEDEF-GIFAM), likely to be heavily influenced by the new label format, also gave its restrained approval: "We accept this project rather favorably but we remain concerned by the modality of the dialogue with the consumers."[13]

In 1976, the newly appointed state secretary of consumption, Christiane Scrivener, took over the qualitative labeling project. She saw it as a flagship for her campaign to promote consumer interests. After protracted closed-door discussions with industry, she helped to write and pass a law on consumer information on 10 January 1978 that provided the legal basis for product quality certificates (*certificats de qualification*). The content of such quality certificates would be negotiated among industry, consumers, and the administration. Shoes were among the first products to be labeled under the new scheme. Each kind of shoe would be described on three separate scales, measuring comfort, durability, and a third composite category they labeled "*finition*" for overall quality. In addition to offering measures of quality, the project also proposed to enforce a minimum level of guaranteed quality, to be set by the Ministry of Industry.[14] Product testing to establish product quality levels was to be carried out by the National Testing Laboratory (Laboratoire national d'essais, LNE), a state-run product safety organization that, with 350 employees and a budget of 44 million francs, was probably not prepared for the magnitude of the task it had been handed.[15]

French industry was also less than enthusiastic about a broad labeling project that would include qualitative indicators and a minimum cutoff level of quality. Of greatest concern, French producers appeared not to be producing products that were likely to perform well in any qualitative labeling scheme. Many products were expected to fall short of the requisite level of quality specified by the Ministry of In-

11. Adrian Weser, *Warenkennzeichnung: Ein Mittel der Verbraucherinformation* (Göttingen, Germany: Verlag Otto Schwartz, 1976), 126–33.

12. *Le Monde,* 22 November 1975.

13. "Nous accueilons plutôt favorablement ce projet mais nous demeurons préoccupés par les modalités du dialogue avec les consommateurs." Rosemonde Pujol, "Protection du consommateur: d'Ornano intervient," *Le Figaro,* 20 November 1975.

14. Jean Calais-Auloy, *Le droit de la consommation* (Paris: Editions Dalloz-Sirey, 1992).

15. Gisèle Prevost, "Qualification de produits industriels," *Les Échos,* 27 September 1979.

dustry. One study projected that if the quality certificates program were fully implemented, 280 product brands would disappear entirely from the market.[16] Moreover, industry resisted participating in many of the committees for setting labeling standards. Without greater industry support, the ambitious goal to have all products relabeled in this way by the end of 1981 seemed increasingly implausible.

When François Mitterrand's Socialist government took office in 1981, the qualitative labeling project was quickly eliminated. The new Mitterrand government did not put an end to the principle of a producer-consumer dialogue to negotiate product qualities. But it had a different approach. Rather than pursue qualitative labeling, it attempted to engage consumer groups to negotiate quality standards directly with industry. Their idea was to integrate consumers explicitly into the process of product standardization. Thus, France's qualitative labeling effort was set aside in order to make way for a program designed to address product quality directly. However, in following a gradual progression from the logic of informative labeling to direct consumer input into product design, France had taken on a project that, in the end, would prove much too ambitious. The outcome is discussed in chapter 8. The overall effect, however, was to put an end to the French project of providing consumers with more informative product labels.

German Product Labeling

Product labeling followed a more constructive trajectory in Germany. The German Institute for Product Safety and Labeling (Deutsches Institut für Gütesicherung und Kennzeichnung, RAL) initiated informative product labels in 1964.[17] Founded in 1925 with the goal of certifying raw materials for production, RAL was discontinued in 1942, when wartime production conditions caused quality levels to sink below the acceptable threshold set by RAL. The organization was resurrected in 1952 under the influence of Ludwig Erhard's Economics Ministry within the organizational umbrella of the German Standards Committee (Deutscher Normenausschuss, DNA), the precursor to the German Institute for Standardization (Deutsches Institut für Normung, DIN). The main goal of the new RAL was to create product quality symbols for both industrial and consumer products that assured conformity with a minimal level of safety and quality. RAL recognized 68 such symbols in 1960, 103 in 1978, and 145 in 1995.[18] Over half of these quality symbols applied to building materials, with the rest applied to consumer products and, to a lesser extent, agricultural products.[19] Although RAL focused its efforts primarily on quality symbols, it also issued standard specifications for product colors (RAL-

16. Elisabeth Rochard, "Pour informer les consommateurs: un 'certificat de qualification,'" *Le Matin*, 27 June 1979.

17. The RAL retains the acronym of its earlier incarnation, the Reichsausschuß für Lieferbedingungen (Imperial Committee for Delivery Conditions).

18. RAL Deutsches Institut für Gütesicherung und Kennzeichnung, *70 Jahre RAL-Gütezeichen: Eine moderne Idee feiert Geburtstag* (Sankt Augustin, Germany: RAL, 1995), 22.

19. Weser, *Warenkennzeichnung*.

Farben) and certificates of provenance (*Herkunftsgewährzeichen*), such as for Lübecker Marzipan and Münchner Bier.[20]

RAL began issuing a series of informative product labels called *RAL-Testate* in 1964. Like the proposed French quality certificates, these informative labels included scales for those properties of the product that consumer and producer representatives agreed would be most helpful to the consumer. The characteristics of the product being sold were marked on a scale that indicated its position relative to the full range of products on the market. Companies interested in including an *RAL-Testate* on their product packaging were required to submit the product to a testing center for evaluation. Any products that did not meet minimum DNA standards were not allowed to incorporate the *RAL-Testate* on their packaging. By 30 April 1974, RAL had created quality scales for 122 product types, including household electronics (vacuum cleaner manufacturers were prominent users of the scales), cooking wares, metal goods, plastic and leather goods, textiles, and cleansers. Interestingly, one in four *RAL-Testate* labels was requested by Germany's mail order companies, who apparently sought a means to convey more information to their consumers, who did not have direct access to their products. One category of products, heat storage units, were in effect required to be sold with *RAL-Testate*, as Germany's electric companies allowed only products with this mark to be installed. The *RAL-Testate* were also gradually growing in public recognition. A 1976 survey by the University of Giessen reported that one in six housewives was familiar with the *RAL-Testate* label.[21]

In a sense, the *RAL-Testate* initiative proved too successful. On 26 August 1973, RAL was kicked out of the DNA. The impetus came neither from RAL nor from the staff or administration of the DNA. The organizations had worked well together and continued to collaborate even after the separation. Pressure for separation came instead from Germany's top association for the household equipment industry (Hauptgemeinschaft der deutschen Hausgeräteindustrie, HDHI). As an industry member of DNA, the HDHI was concerned that the rising prominence of consumer politics would soon draw political scrutiny to RAL activities. If RAL remained within DNA, they argued, the entire process of standardization in consumer goods threatened to become politicized. This could lead to consumer groups and the government to request greater input into the standardization process (something that would soon happen in any case). While most members of DNA made industrial products that would be unaffected by consumer politics, they nonetheless acceded to the wishes of the HDHI and banished RAL.[22]

This move appears to have stimulated precisely what the HDHI most feared. Under its new charter as an independent organization, in 1973 the RAL invited participation from diverse economic interests in order both to maintain its neutrality

20. Jürgen Bornecke, *Handbuch der Verbraucherinstitutionen* (Bonn: Verlag Information für die Wirtschaft, 1982).

21. Weser, *Warenkennzeichnung*, 124–25.

22. Annemarie Bopp-Schmehl, Uwe Heibült, and Ulrich Kypke, *Technische Normung und Verbraucherinteressen im gesellschaftlichen Wandel* (Frankfurt: Haag and Herchen Verlag, 1984).

and to establish its legitimacy as an entity separate from DNA. Consumer organizations, trade unions, production associations, and chambers of commerce now all participated in *RAL-Testate* design. Consumer and producer groups met in a new RAL committee on *RAL-Testate* (Ausschuss RAL-Testate im RAL) to set priorities for the products to be considered and the product values to be included on the labels. This new negotiating forum became a focus for new minimum quality and safety levels.[23] The effect was to create a negotiating arena outside of DNA for product standardization—one that was more open to political pressures. The AgV in particular applauded the move and began an initiative to spread knowledge of the program, which it saw as an important component of consumer protection.[24] The business response to this move was hostile. Even the consumer council (Verbraucherrat, VR) of DIN opposed the new *RAL-Testate* format. When RAL applied in 1974 for a contract from the Economics Ministry to help finance the cost of the new independent *RAL-Testate* system, the proposal was turned down. Under sustained pressure from industry as well as from the Economics Ministry, RAL abandoned the *RAL-Testate* program altogether in 1975, returning to its earlier narrow focus on content symbols.

As in France, Germany's initial effort to negotiate quality labels had failed. Unlike France, Germany did not abandon its effort to create an informational labeling system that could address the needs of consumers. When the Economics Ministry turned down RAL's request, it also approached Germany's leading industry association (Bundesverband der Deutschen Industrie, BDI) and other economic groups for proposals for an alternative product information system. After two years of discussion, a group representing the top consumer association AgV, the Economics Ministry, and Stiftung Warentest came together with RAL to support a 1977 law setting guidelines for the provision of product information in Germany (*Richtlinien für Produkt-Information in der Bundesrepublik Deutschland*).[25]

In order to implement this new set of guidelines, in 1977 a working group of prominent social and economic associations created an alternative set of informational labels that would provide end consumers with standard, objective measures of the most important qualities of a product.[26] This new product information system (*Produktinformationssystem*, PI) was distinct from the *RAL-Testate* in that it focused on measurable qualities of products rather than attempting to create a composite scale. To ensure that the information provided was both accurate and useful to consumers, the PI had two standing committees, each with representation from industry, consumer groups, and the retail sector. The community board for

---

23. "Grundsätze für Gütezeichen," *Bundesanzeiger*, 23 March 1974.

24. "Mehr RAL-Testate!" *Verbraucherpolitische Korrespondenz* 7 (12 February 1974).

25. Willi Laschet, "Verbraucher sind auch Kunden," in *Verbraucherpolitik Kontrovers*, ed. Hartwig Piepenbrock and Conrad Schroeder (Cologne: Deutscher Instituts-Verlag, 1987).

26. The group included the Economics Ministry (BMWi), RAL, the leading consumer association (AgV), the Stiftung Warentest, the leading industry association (BDI), trade associations, DIN, and the Federal Association for Materials Testing (Bundesanstalt für Materialprüfung, BAM).

product information (Gemeinschaftsausschuss für Produktinformation, GA-PI) was responsible for setting the operating guidelines of the PI system. A second group, the technical committee for product information (Fachausschuss für Produktinformation, FA-PI) was responsible for the content and form of the PI as well as the enforcement of guidelines set down by the GA-PI. Both committees were kept small so that they could work effectively. Critically, representatives of industry outnumbered consumer representatives two-to-one.[27]

In January 1979, RAL and DIN collaborated to create a private company, the German Society for Product Information (Deutsche Gesellschaft für Produktinformation, DGPI), which took over management and promotion of the PI system. This new private management arrangement helped to ensure that neither the government nor consumers would interfere in PI labeling.[28] In 1980, DGPI signed a contract with the Economics Ministry to provide product information and to transpose Europe-level environmental quality requirements into German product information labels.[29] By 1984, twenty PI labels had been produced, and an additional sixteen were in production. DGPI was later amalgamated into DIN. The PI system continues to be used in Germany, particularly for white goods, electronics, gas, oil and coal equipment, heating pumps, and solar panels.[30]

Perhaps the most striking feature of both French and German efforts to promote a system of product quality labels was the lack of successful regulatory guidance. In France, ministry officials had looked to the successful VDN-Skala in Sweden as a policy model but failed to translate it to the French context. In Germany, the economics ministry dismantled a successful labeling system under pressure from industry. Far from embodying the considered opinions of technical experts within relevant government ministries, the French and German labeling policies emerged from periods of experimentation and failure with policy solutions that reflected the broader priorities of producers and consumers on the treatment of consumer protection.

Consumer Contracts

Consumer contracts specify the conditions to which shoppers assent when they purchase products or services. Like product quality labeling, consumer contracts are particularly interesting from a policy perspective because they combine issues of

---

27. Members included five producer representatives, three from BDI, two from retailing industries, five from AgV, one from DIN, and one from BAM. Bornecke, *Handbuch der Verbraucherinstitutionen*, 326.

28. Bopp-Schmehl et al., *Technische Normung*, 86.

29. Reinhard Hector, "Verbraucherpolitische Aspekte aus Sicht der Gebrauchsgüterindustrie," in *Verbraucherpolitik in der Sozialen Marktwirtschaft*, ed. Jürgen Bornecke (Cologne, Germany: Verein für wirtschaftliche und soziale Fragen, 1984), 28.

30. Hans-Wolfgang Micklitz, "Three Instances of Negotiation Procedures in the Federal Republic of Germany," *Journal of Consumer Policy* 7 (1984): 213.

product information and product risk. On the one hand, consumer contracts generally cover terms of warranty as well as legal conditions that affect the liability of the producer and consumer. On the other hand, these contracts may also define details concerning product pricing, conditions of delivery, the cost and availability of repairs, and many other post-purchase eventualities.[31] Standard contracts have become the norm for most product sales.[32] Printed unobtrusively on sales slips or accompanying documents, they constitute the fine print of any purchase. While many countries have subjected such contracts to a standard of clear writing, in practice consumers often do not learn the implications of the terms they have agreed to until long after they purchase a product, if ever.[33]

Although few reliable data exist, use of standard term and adhesion contracts appears to have grown rapidly beginning in the 1960s. Just as rational manufacturing depended on standardized parts and worker functions, rational financial management of large firms also required standardized contractual relationships with both suppliers and consumers. Standard contracts offered three specific advantages over ad hoc contracts negotiated at the point of sale. First, they reduced the costs of individual contract negotiations and subsequent legal fees. Second, companies using standard term contracts could accurately evaluate and control their risk exposure. Third, standard contracts could work to the advantage of consumers, who could purchase branded products with the certainty of finding the same contract conditions everywhere. This meant that manufacturers and distributors that could provide this kind of contractual uniformity were likely to be favored by customers. For all of these reasons, manufacturers in the postwar period increasingly employed standard form contracts in their relations with consumers and also with suppliers.[34]

As competition intensified through the 1960s and was further aggravated by the economic downturn of the 1970s, companies began looking to the specific terms of their contracts to improve their price competitiveness. By rewriting standard contracts so as to limit risk exposure, for example, a company could reduce the unit sales price of products without making any changes to production. In principle, this development should not have posed a problem for consumers. After all, they could shop for the combination of product quality and contractual terms that best fit their needs. So long as an industry did not drift into monopoly, market forces should create competition for an appropriate level of contractual security.

31. Erika Schork, "Geschäft mit den Geschäftsbedingungen," *Süddeutsche Zeitung,* 13 July 1972.

32. When the conditions of such contracts are prepared in advance by a producer or retailer—often with the help of a lawyer—they are called standard form contracts or, when consumers are given no room for negotiation, adhesion contracts.

33. One German consumer group estimated that reading an average consumer contract would take seventeen minutes.

34. Standard form contracts have also played an important role in distributing contractual responsibilities between producers and their suppliers. Steve Casper, *Reconfiguring Institutions: The Political Economy of Legal Development in Germany and the U.S.,* Ph.D. dissertation, Cornell University, 1997.

However, two parallel developments stifled this sort of market competition for contract terms. First, an extraordinary growth in the number and complexity of products in the 1970s meant that consumers often did not know enough about them to be able to judge the value of the contracts that accompanied them. What was the likely lifetime and repair schedule for a microwave oven, for example? In many cases, even the producers did not really know what to expect from new kinds of products. Second, the parallel growth in self-service shopping made it difficult for consumers to seek professional sales advice.[35] Just as adhesion contracts were becoming more complex, sales personnel who might have been able to share customer experiences with different kinds of contracts were giving less advice. Taken together, these two trends meant that companies could dilute their contractual responsibilities without consumers being able to detect the difference. This prospect was especially worrisome from a social justice perspective, since those consumers who were least capable of discerning often complicated differences among competing contract terms were most likely to be hurt by the practice.

By the mid-1970s, political pressure to regulate the terms of consumer contracts had risen all over Europe. Sweden had already made provisions for its consumer ombudsman to regulate consumer contracts in 1971. Germany's Justice Ministry suggested the need for analogous regulation in Germany in 1972.[36] France advocated similar regulation in its Seventh Plan beginning in 1974.[37] The British disallowed personal injury exemptions in consumer contracts in 1973. By 1975, the topic had become so pervasive that the European Economic Community proposed a directive for a Europe-wide approach to regulating consumer contracts. Policymakers believed that regulating the content of consumer contracts would not only protect consumers but also improve the knowledge with which consumers shopped, thereby fostering greater economic efficiency. So long as consumers did not fully understand what they were buying, they were likely to make nonoptimal purchases.[38]

The move to regulate consumer contracts posed a profound challenge to western private law doctrine. Most European countries held the sanctity of contract as the core principle of their legal system. Public interference in privately signed contracts thus marked a significant shift in the boundary between public and private law. Such a move was not entirely novel. France and Germany had already begun regulating private labor contracts through labor legislation enacted in the nineteenth century. Indeed, some policymakers in France drew an explicit analogy between consumer contract reform and these earlier labor policies. Jacques Ghestin, a French consumer activist, argued that consumer groups might mimic labor unions in negotiating col-

35. Michel Trochu, Yannick Tremorin, and Pierre Berchon, "La protection des consommateurs contre les clauses abusives: Étude de la législation française du 10–1–1978," *D.P.C.I.* 7/1 (March 1981): 37–38.

36. "Die Parteien entedecken die Verbraucher," *Süddeutsche Zeitung,* 31 October 1972.

37. Jacques Dubois, "Les consommateurs dans le 7ème plan," *Information consommation OR-GE-CO* 15 (March–April 1976): 1–2.

38. Joachim Beimowski, *Zur ökonomischen Analyse Allgemeiner Geschäftsbedingungen* (Munich: V. Florenz, 1989), 18–19.

lective consumer contract agreements directly with industry associations.[39] Sweden and the Netherlands had both adopted this negotiation approach to regulating consumer contracts.[40]

Germany's solution was to regulate only standard consumer contracts—those that were prepared by producers in advance. Its 1976 Law on General Business Conditions (Gesetz zur Regelung des Rechts der Allgemeinen Geschäftsbedingungen, or AGB-Gesetz) detailed a "blacklist" of clauses that could not be used in such contracts. This approach still left ample room for variation. By 1984, German consumers faced an estimated 250,000 different standard contracts.[41] France, by contrast, applied a standard of contractual fairness to all consumer contracts, whether standardized or not. In this approach, French courts evaluated the fairness in legal cases brought by individual consumers on a case-by-case basis. The result was a solution that gave all consumers access to justice but that provided few guidelines about the specific clauses they were likely to encounter while shopping.

The French Experience

As with other areas of consumer policy, France's efforts to regulate consumer contracts shifted over time from the information model to the negotiation model and finally to the protection model. France's early legislation to regulate consumer contracts followed the information strategy. Consumer contracts were first regulated by the 1977 *loi Scrivener,* named after France's newly appointed secretary of consumption (secrétaire d'état à la consommation), Christiane Scrivener. It was the product of two years of consultations between the Economics Ministry and France's professional associations. By the end of 1977, Scrivener had formulated and submitted for parliamentary discussion a proposal for the creation of an administrative body to evaluate and control the use of abusive contract clauses in consumer sales. A new commission on abusive clauses, created in January 1978 and installed in February, had fifteen members, each named for three years, including three magistrates, three legal consultants, three representatives of the administration, plus three representatives each from professional and consumer associations.[42] Neither consumer groups nor producers had significant input in the commission's decisions.

The group went to work quickly, and in March 1978 it recommended that four

39. "Négociation collective: Le point de vue des juristes," *Que savoir* 43–44 (June–July 1982): 50–60.

40. Elisabeth Maillot Bouvier, "L'ombudsman dans la politique de concurrence et de consommation en Suède," *Revue de la concurrence et de la consommation* 17 (1982): 40–42; and Thierry Bourgoignie and Jean Gillardin, *Droit des Consommateurs: Clauses abusives, pratiques du commerce et réglementation des prix* (Brussels: Facultés Universitaires Saint-Louis, 1982), 129.

41. Belgium, Spain, and Italy all came to adopt this information approach. "Les clauses abusives dans les contrats conclus avec des consommateurs," *Bulletin des communautés européennes,* Supplement 1/84 (Luxembourg: Office des publications officielles des communautés européennes, 1984), 14.

42. Jean Marchand, "Le consommateur mieux protégé contre les pièges des contrats," *La croix,* 1 February 1978.

kinds of contract clauses be prohibited immediately: limitations on guarantees (defined by articles 1641 and 1645 of the Civil Code protecting against *vices cachés*), changes in price between sale and delivery, allowance of open delivery dates, and restricted access to justice. Over the next decade, the commission made twenty-eight additional recommendations concerning particular kinds of clauses that they felt were abusive and should therefore be banned from consumer contracts.[43]

However, the legislation that created the Abusive Clauses Commission gave it little power. Clauses that the commission found to be unfair could be found null and void (*réputée non écrite*) in court, but such a finding provided no basis to have them removed from other standard contracts. Only the government had the right, based on a recommendation of the Council of State (Conseil d'État), to prohibit the use of certain kinds of clauses by companies. Using this power, the Council of State on 23 March 1978 issued a decree proscribing three of the first four terms that the Commission had identified as abusive.[44] Yet, after this initial move, the government was, in the words of Calais-Auloy, "extremely hesitant to use this regulatory power."[45] The only other decree to be issued based on the commission's recommendations, concerning warranties accompanying white goods, came eight years later, on 22 December 1987.[46] Frustrated that their recommendations were not being heeded, the commission attempted to use the courts to apply their findings. They lobbied for penal sanctions against professionals who continued to use contract terms that the commission had declared abusive.[47] This effort also failed. Consequently, nearly all of the clauses that the commission had identified as being abusive could still legally be included in consumer contracts.

Consumer groups became frustrated with this first attempt at regulating consumer contracts. In principle, article 46 of the "*loi Royer*" of 27 December 1973 introduced group legal actions (*actions d'intérêt collectif*) for consumers. Specifically, it granted registered consumer associations the right to take civil action in all jurisdictions against activities that prejudiced, directly or indirectly, the collective interests of consumers. The problem was that the collective interest provisions of the *loi Royer* limited their right to recover claims only to the interests of consumer organizations, not to the collective interests of individual consumers.[48] While consumer associations could bring suit in support of individual claims of abusive contract terms, they were not permitted to bring a suit on behalf of all consumers injured by a particular standard contract. In practice, this meant that abusive con-

---

43. "Rapport du 22 mars 1991 à Madame le secretaire d'état chargé de la consommation," *Bulletin officiel de la concurrence, de la consommation et de la repression des fraudes: Bulletin officiel des services des prix* 8 (8 May 1991), 119; *Bulletin officiel de la concurrence, la consommation, et de la repression des fraudes,* various years.

44. Jean Marchand, "Contrats commerciaux: La commission demande des sanctions pénales contre les clauses abusives," *La croix,* 15 June 1979.

45. Jean Calais-Auloy, "Towards New Laws for Consumer Protection: Proposals of the French Reform Commission," *Journal of Consumer Policy* 8 (1985): 63.

46. "La commission de clauses abusives a dix ans," *INC Hebdo* 597 (10 June 1988), 4.

47. Josée Doyère, "Les clauses abusives dans les contrats," *Le Monde,* 21 June 1979.

48. Calais-Auloy, "Towards New Laws," 65.

tract terms could not be eliminated in all of their occurrences, only nullified one at a time.

Amid growing consumer group frustration, the government of François Mitterrand decided to make consumer contract terms the object of industry-consumer dialogue, an idea that had long been supported by business. Indeed, a study commissioned on the topic by the CNPF's working group on enterprise and consumerism proposed on 6 May 1976 that the CNPF work together with France's largest consumer organization, the National Consumption Institute (INC), to study contracts between professionals and consumers. The CNPF argued that this would help restore consumer confidence in the wake of the first oil shock. François Ceyrac, president of the CNPF, wrote: "Even if, with rediscovered growth, the French have returned for a time to their old habits, producers and distributors should not be deceived. The consumer in crisis is the consumer of tomorrow."[49] Thus, in 1977, five professionals and five representatives of consumer groups met under the auspices of the CNPF to put together a list of abusive clauses that the CNPF then distributed to its members. Paul Simonet, president of the CNPF's Commission on Industry, Trade, and Consumption, wrote that "for the present, concertation offers the best hope of solution."[50]

Most French interest groups supported the negotiation strategy proposed by the CNPF and agreed that the protection of consumer rights in contract clauses could be achieved through negotiations between industry and consumer associations. Even the Communist consumer association Indecosa-CGT argued that consumer contracts should be negotiated in this way.[51] The Paris Chamber of Commerce and Industry (Chambre de commerce et d'industrie de Paris, CCIP) also supported negotiated contracts, seeing them as a better alternative to government intervention, which was likely to be incomplete, as well as to court enforcement, which would result in arbitrary treatment. The CCIP suggested that model contracts should be optional for businesses, with their adoption signaled to the consumer by a special label.[52]

This negotiated approach became government policy under the Calais-Auloy committee appointed by President Mitterrand in 1982. Under this new scheme, business and consumer groups met frequently to negotiate sectoral standard contracts. Yet, just as these negotiations were beginning, industry backed down. Paul Simonet, who had headed the CNPF's push to negotiate directly with consumer groups, was removed from the CNPF's Commission on Consumption. His replacement, Jean Levy, strongly opposed collective conventions on the grounds that they would unfairly restrict business: "To transfer into the domain of consumption

49. "Accord patrons-consommateurs," *Information consommation OR-GE-CO* 16 (May–June 1976): 6.
50. Paul Simonet, "La commission des clauses abusives," position paper, 1976, 11.
51. "39 clauses abusives à éliminer," *Informations Indecosa-CGT* 12 (January 1986): 2.
52. Chambre de commerce et d'industrie de Paris, "Les clauses abusives dans les contrats de consommation," rapport présenté au nom de la Commission du Commerce Intérieur par M. Gibergues (adopted 8 April 1976), 7–11.

a system inspired by labor law is unacceptable."[53] No further concrete progress was made on negotiated contracts.

With the failure of the negotiation approach, France came to rely increasingly on legal decisions to protect consumers against abusive consumer clauses.[54] On 5 January 1988 the legislature passed a law extending the rights of consumer associations to take civil action against abusive retail clauses—even if consumers had not themselves brought a complaint.[55] The law also specified that contract terms not brought to the attention of the consumer at the time of signing were considered invalid, meaning in practice that the terms could not be hidden on the back of the contract, on a sign, in a brochure, or in unsigned annex documents.[56] In 1991, the French Supreme Court affirmed the right of a judge to declare autonomously a consumer contract clause abusive.[57]

This new reliance on the courts to restrict abusive consumer contracts helped reduce the regulatory burden on the state. It also reflected a failure of the strategies that had been advocated by government ministries. While the Abusive Clauses Commission still met to identify classes of clauses that they deemed abusive, their findings had little formal status. Only in 1993 did a government decree grant judges the right to seek advice from the Abusive Clauses Commission, including expert testimony in court.[58] Thus while French consumers came to enjoy strong legal recourse against abusive contract clauses, they could still not be certain exactly what kinds of clauses they were likely to find when they went shopping.

German Intervention

Political support for regulation of standard contract terms in Germany was bipartisan, crystallizing in 1972. Bavarian Justice Minister Philipp Held (CDU) proposed in early 1972 to the Federal Ministry of Justice a legal protection of consumers in standard contracts.[59] Held was concerned was that court treatment of standard contracts had become so diverse as to create enough uncertainty to damage the econ-

---

53. Elisabeth Rochard, "Le CNPF ne veut pas de conventions collectives de la consommation," *Le Matin,* 19 February 1982.

54. A commission established in 1987 to systematize and rewrite the French consumption law (Commission de refonte du droit de la consommation) proposed to create red and pink lists similar to the black and grey lists that Germany had adopted in 1976. The red list would specify clauses that were absolutely forbidden, whereas the pink list would include clauses that must be explicitly justified as not abusive before the judge. The government disbanded the commission in 1988 without implementing their proposals, and the red and pink list proposals were dropped. Jean-Michel Rothmann, "Clauses abusives: a revoir. . . ." *Consommateurs actualités* 543 (20 March 1987), 14.

55. Articles L. 421–1 to 421–9 of the *Code de la consommation.*

56. The law did not, however, specify whether the courts were extended the right to apply recommendations of the Commission on Abusive Clauses. Jean Beauchard, *Droit de la distribution et de la consommation* (Paris: Presses universitaires de France, 1996), 325.

57. Ruling in the Lorthoir Case, 14 May 1991. "Les clauses abusives et la présentation des contrats dans la loi no. 95–96 du 1er février 1995," *Receuil dalloz sirey* 14 (1995): 99–108.

58. OECD, *Consumer Policy in OECD Countries: 1991–1992* (Paris: OECD, 1995): 101–2.

59. "Die Parteien entedecken die Verbraucher."

omy. In May 1972, he wrote: "We can say without exaggeration that standard form contracts have threatened both legal security and legal equality. I have no doubt that, in view of this situation, lawmakers must take action."[60] In 1974, German Economics Minister Hans Friedrichs concurred: "Freedom is the choice among alternatives. When I do not or cannot know the alternatives, then the room for freedom becomes limited. Freedom is even further restricted, when anticompetitive sales practices attempt to push the choice of consumers in a particular direction."[61] Employer and worker unions also recognized the need to reduce the legal uncertainty associated with the recent growth in contract terms.[62]

Different policy actors had very different ideas about how such regulation should be managed. The SPD proposed at a legal-political congress of their party in 1972 to form an administrative body that would certify standard contracts before they were promulgated.[63] Germany's trade unions affirmed the need to certify contracts but called instead for an independent institute, the Federal Institute for Consumer Protection and Food Safety (Bundesanstalt für Verbraucherschutz und Lebensmittelsicherheit, BVL) to perform the certification. When the FDP-controlled Economics Ministry opposed pre-certification, the SDP suggested instead that the competition office (Kartellamt) regulate this area.[64] The opposition CDU feared that government regulation would lead to a form of price control, as companies would be monitored to ensure that they were indeed offering reduced prices for the reduction in liability in the AGB.[65] Producer groups in Germany also opposed the SPD approach. The industry group BDI advocated a system of industry self-control, to this end creating an AGB Oversight Committee in December 1973 that would help to resolve consumer disputes. Concerned that regulations focused solely on consumer contracts would hurt retailers, the Association of German Retailers (Hauptverband des Deutschen Einzelhandels, HDE) proposed that existing consumer advice centers should be staffed with lawyers who would help settle consumer claims.[66] The central consumer association, the AgV, proposed extending greater legal rights to consumer associations to pursue companies using unfair adhesion contracts, including the right to sue companies that did not comply.[67]

In the end, the SPD/FDP coalition agreed to draft legislation that would clearly define what kinds of clauses might be included in standard contracts. To do so, they

60. Cited in "Die Parteien entdecken das 'Kleingedruckte,'" *Süddeutsche Zeitung*, 24 May 1972.

61. Hans Friedrichs, "Aufgaben der Verbraucherpolitik," *Bulletin des Presse- und Informationsamtes der Bundesregierung* 146 (5 December 1974), 1465.

62. Marianne Schatz-Bergfeld, *Verbraucherinteressen im politischen Prozess: das AGB-Gesetz* (Frankfurt: Haag and Herchen, 1984), 49.

63. Gerd Rinck, "Die Empfehlung Allgemeiner Geschäftsbedingungen, deren Kontrolle und Registrierung," *Wirtschaft und Wettbewerb* 5 (1974): 293.

64. Schatz-Bergfeld, *Verbraucherinteressen*, 65–71.

65. Gerd Rinck, "Die Empfehlung Allgemeiner Geschäftsbedingungen," 293.

66. Heribert Schatz, *Verbraucherinteressen im politischen Entscheidungsprozess* (Frankfurt: Campus Verlag, 1984), 66.

67. Erika Schork, "Geschäft mit den Geschäftsbedingungen," *Süddeutsche Zeitung*, 13 July 1972.

pushed for the contents of this legislation to be negotiated between consumers and producers. The Ministry of Justice convened a meeting of interest groups in 1975 to hear their views on the contents of the new legislation. The meeting was attended by 150 economic associations, including labor unions, producers, and consumers.[68] Although the meeting included representatives from many of Germany's consumer groups, the outcome was widely perceived to reflect the interests of producers.

The Law on General Business Conditions (Gesetz zur Regelung des Rechts der Allgemeinen Geschäftsbedingungen, or AGB-Gesetz) was passed in December 1976. Its general goal was to ensure that information and power asymmetries between contracting parties did not cause them to reach agreements excessively in favor of one party.[69] The AGB-Gesetz went further, however, enumerating a "blacklist" of seventeen specific kinds of contract clause that were expressly forbidden (AGB-Gesetz § 11). A second list contained 23 kinds of contract that were provisionally forbidden unless the consumer explicitly agreed to them (AGB-Gesetz § 10). The most common of these exclusions concerned product warranties, liability, delivery, and jurisdiction (*Gerichtsstand*).[70]

The scope of application of these restrictions was also different than in France. First, the AGB-Gesetz applied only to "adhesion" or standard form contracts, meaning contracts that had been formulated in advance of the sale and were not negotiable as a part of the sale. Individual agreements struck between buyer and seller were therefore not subject to AGB-Gesetz control. Second, the AGB-Gesetz applied equally to consumer as well as to professional contracts. Indeed, 30 percent of AGB-Gesetz litigation was between professionals.[71] There were also some sectoral exclusions from the AGB-Gesetz. It applied only in limited cases to contracts with state-owned industries, such as transportation.[72] Another interesting exception was the German automobile industry, which had been granted an exemption in order to be able to negotiate contract terms with consumer associations.[73]

The primary form of enforcement was by legal suits filed by consumer associations, although Germany's federal cartel office (Bundeskartellamt) also retained the

---

68. Schatz, *Verbraucherinteressen im politischen Entscheidungsprozess,* 68.

69. This goal was implemented in two ways. On the one hand, the AGB-Gesetz imposed a requirement of clarity in standard contracts that ruled out surprising conditions that were not immediately obvious from the text of the contract (AGB-Gesetz § 3). On the other hand, the AGB imposed a standard of appropriate content matter to which standard contracts must conform. As expressed in the General Clause (AGB-Gesetz § 9), standard contract terms were inappropriate if they unreasonably prejudiced the contracting party against the command of good faith.

70. Schork, "Geschäft mit den Geschäftsbedingungen."

71. Anne Fily and Philippe Guillermin, "Les politiques de la consommation dans les états membres de la CEE," *Revue de la concurrence et de la consommation* 70 (November–December 1992): 43–50.

72. "Jetzt wird 'Kleingedrucktes' der Verwaltung überprüft," *Der Tagesspiegel,* 13 September 1977.

73. "Les clauses abusives dans les contrats conclus avec des consommateurs," *Bulletin des Communautés européennes, Supplément* 1 / 84 (Luxembourg: Office des publications officielles des communautés européennes, 1984): 8.

right to file suits. Section 13 of the AGB-Gesetz granted consumer associations with more than seventy-five members the right to file such lawsuits. Cases were brought not on behalf of a single consumer but in their collective interest. Companies found guilty were therefore required to modify or withdraw the offending adhesion contract. They also faced fines of 5,000 DM per offending clause, 10,000 DM for super-regional firms, and 20,000 DM for particularly important infractions.[74] Most contraventions of the AGB-Gesetz did not result in court cases, however, because consumer associations were usually able to negotiate with the offending company to make appropriate modifications. A 1979 study of ninety-eight cases in Baden-Württemberg and Stuttgart revealed that only twenty-seven went to court, the rest having been resolved when consumer associations called attention to the problem.[75]

The regulation of product labeling and of consumer contracts combined concerns about product information *and* product risk. Because of this, each case offers a microcosm for understanding how the tradeoff between risk and information was negotiated in the two countries. They show that national responses emerged from the interplay of producer and consumer interests but with a contributing role for innovation, experimentation, and failure. They also suggest how difficult it is to map simple determinative theories—based on institutional legacies or producer interests—onto the frequently contingent process of consumer policy formation.

In Germany, industry and consumer groups agreed that consumer contracts and labels should serve a function as product standards. They differed, however, on how this should be achieved. In each case, Germany's consumer groups pushed for a seat at the table where the new standards would be crafted. In each case, the weakness of Germany's consumer associations left them with little influence. Both in standard contracts and in product labeling, consumer efforts to participate in the standardization process were rebuked. The result was a set of policies that embraced a high standard of consumer information, but one that was also dominated by the interests of organized industry.

In France, consumers in both policy areas began by embracing a strong information standard. As consumer groups mobilized, however, the pure information approach was replaced by an effort to negotiate specific standards that would be mutually beneficial to consumers and producers. It quickly became clear that individual firms opposed such negotiated solutions. As the negotiation strategy failed, the government stepped in to implement administrative solutions—ones that embraced a contractual view of the consumer marketplace. Hence quality labels were typically left to founder; consumer contracts were left to a case-by-case evaluation in the French courts. These were not necessarily the outcomes that French industry had initially desired. Had French producers been endowed with stronger central associations, ones that could represent their economic interests more forcefully and

74. Walter Stillner, "Praktische Erfahrungene mit dem AGB-Gesetz," *Zeitschrift für Verbraucherpolitik* 4/2 (1980): 148.
75. Ibid., 143.

discipline their members more actively, they might well have embraced a standards-based approach to consumer contracts and labeling. In the absence of such organizational capacity, however, France ended up with a solution that seemed to cater to the least common denominator, which, in turn, would hinder consumer demand for high-quality products.

CHAPTER SEVEN

Price and Quality

Should any person brew, or otherwise have, other beer than March
beer, it is not to be sold any higher than one Pfennig per Mass.

Furthermore, we wish to emphasize that in future in all cities, markets
and in the country, the only ingredients used for the brewing of beer
must be Barley, Hops and Water.

—Reinheitsgebot für Bier, Bavaria, 1516.

Our analysis of consumer protection has focused so far on new areas
of public policy, ones that emerged virtually ex nihilo during the period beginning
in the 1970s when the consumer was reinvented as a category of national citizenship
with its attendant rights. Yet at least two areas of consumer protection are among the
oldest classes of regulation in the world: product quality standards and the regulation of product prices. European quality regulations find their origins in the Middle Ages. Among the most famous and enduring was Germany's Beer Purity Law
(*Reinheitsgebot für Bier*), which was enacted by Bavaria's Wilhelm IV in 1516 to restrict the ingredients in beer to barley, hops, and water. Similar quality standards
pervaded medieval European craft production, increasing in number during the six-
teenth century as governments increasingly stepped in to regulate the formerly self-
monitoring trade guilds. Price regulations have even deeper roots. One of the longest
enduring of these concerned bread. France's Charles V ("Charles the Wise") fixed
the price of bread in the Edict of 1372. This price cap endured for several centuries,
even though, somewhat confusingly, the weight of the loaf was allowed to fluctuate
considerably.[1]

What distinguishes these early instances of product regulation from the consumer
protection policies that emerged in the 1970s is their primary preoccupation with
issues of production and distribution rather than of consumption. Many early qual-

1. Luc Bihl, *Une histoire du mouvement consommateur* (Paris: Editions Aubier Montaigne,
1984).

143

ity regulations used private or government-mandated standards to limit entry to a sector and to set the terms of producer competition. Others had distributive goals. Sumptuary laws restricted the use of scarce or imported materials in clothing and other personal goods.[2] Even Germany's Reinheitsgebot had as its primary goal to limit the use in beer of scarce wheat and rye grains, which were needed for bread.[3]

With the rise of industrial manufacturing in the nineteenth century, centralized national standardization bodies emerged to help industrial producers coordinate product specifications with their suppliers and competitors.[4] While such standards undoubtedly benefited end consumers, their primary goal was to address new challenges of technical mass production. In the case of price regulation, the goal had more to do with issues of distribution. Before the rise of the modern welfare state, price fixing provided a rudimentary safety net. In early modern Europe, food prices and availability were among the single greatest sources of social upheaval and public violence. Governments responded by deploying price restrictions to limit hording and to ensure wide distribution of basic necessities.[5] Even with the advent of modern welfare provisions, scarcity during times of war often created pressures for governments to implement extensive price controls. Each great power engaged in World War II employed a system of price restraints to ration scarce goods.

In the postwar period, ideas about the purpose of price and quality regulation began to evolve in ways that placed affluent consumption, rather than production or distribution, at the focus of policymaking. Several overlapping reasons explain this change. A growing saturation of markets for consumer durables led to concerns that producers might be intentionally designing obsolescence into their products. The inflation of the late 1960s followed by new price pressure from the first oil shock in 1973 focused attention on the role that informed consumers might play in keeping prices in check. Mounting inflation also drove concerns that manufacturers were taking advantage of their dominant position to impose unfair prices on consumers. At the same time, policymakers worried that efforts to restrain prices—especially France's strategy of fixing prices—could lead manufacturers to lower the quality of their products. These fears seemed to be reinforced by economic studies, based on the results of new comparative product tests, that found little or no correlation between price and quality within classes of products.[6]

2. French physiocrats worried that luxury goods would detract from agriculture, which they saw as the source of national wealth. Cissie Fairchilds, "Fashion and Freedom in the French Revolution," *Continuity and Change* 15/3 (2000): 421.

3. Beer posed a particular public policy challenge in that it was difficult to tax the inputs to beer without also taxing bread production. Since barley had few uses apart from beer, the Reinheitsgebot facilitated taxation. Use of wheat was eventually permitted, in the seventeenth century, but licenses were granted only to certain noblemen, not to mass producers. Communication with Ron Pattinson, March 2005.

4. Johannes Backherms, *Das DIN Deutsches Institut für Normung e. V. als Beliehener: Zugleich ein Beitrag zur Theorie der Beleihung* (Cologne, Germany: Carl Heymanns Verlag, 1979), 48.

5. E. P. Thomson, *The Moral Economy of the English Crowd in the Eighteenth Century* (1971); and Manfred Gailus, "Food Riots in Germany in the late 1840s," *Past and Present* 145 (1994): 162.

6. Monroe P. Friedman, "Quality and Price Considerations in Rational Consumer Decision

Yet similar pressures generated divergent outcomes. How price and quality regulation came to be reinterpreted in France and Germany depended on the emerging politics of consumer citizenship. French responses emphasized price restraint while abandoning product quality to producer discretion; German responses emphasized high quality standards for products while leaving pricing largely to the discretion of producers. These national approaches both reflected and reinforced the emerging conception of the economic role of the consumer in each country. In France, where the consumer came to be perceived as a new class of political citizenship, pricing was regulated through a standard of fairness. Efforts to achieve consumer participation in product standardization failed. In Germany, where the consumer was conceived as an economic citizen, the regulation of price focused on restrictions to ensure that product prices conveyed useful information about the costs of production. Further, over the objections of industry, the German Economics Ministry helped consumers provide technical input into setting technical product standards.

Fixing Prices

In both France and Germany, the 1973 Middle East oil embargo made prices a political issue. In France, pricing became a political obsession. The Socialist and Communist trade unions each began publishing their own consumer price surveys based on the basket of goods they felt a working family would consume and using these surveys as the basis for wage increase demands. France's state-financed comparative product testing organization INC tracked overall price increases in "*Le panier de '50,*'" a survey that measured the prices of a basket of roughly thirty consumer products, and published the results in each issue.[7] In Germany, where inflation was regularly half of the level experienced in France, pricing was less political. Like its French counterpart, Germany's leading consumer association, AgV, tracked product prices in stores and published the results in its monthly journal. These price indices were not systematic, however, and were primarily used to criticize specific product sectors—in particular the farm sector—rather than as part of a broader politics of price restraint.

For both countries, the heightened attention on consumer prices led to two kinds of response. The first was an effort to promote pricing transparency. In the past, retailers had set prices differently for different patrons, depending on their perceived need and ability to pay. While this practice helped retailers to maximize profits, it

Making," *Journal of Consumer Affairs* 1 / 1 (1967): 13–23; Ruby Turner Morris and Claire Sekulski Bronson, "The Chaos of Competition Indicated by Consumer Reports," *Journal of Marketing* 33 / 3 (1969): 26–34; George B. Sproles, "New Evidence on Price and Product Quality," *Journal of Consumer Affairs* 11 / 1 (1977): 63–77; and Peter C. Riesz, "Price versus Quality in the Marketplace," *Journal of Retailing* 54 / 4 (1978): 15–28.

7. Institut national de la consommation, *Rapport annuel du directeur au conseil d'administration du 24 octobre 1974* (Paris: INC, 1974), 50.

discouraged consumers from undertaking comparative shopping, thereby blocking the downward pressure that comparative shopping could impose on price. Efforts to promote price awareness included legislation to require product price labeling as well as active campaigns encouraging consumers to compare prices.

A second set of policies directly restricted how retailers and producers could set product prices. Governments in France and Germany banned resale price maintenance (RPM), the practice whereby producers dictated the price at which retailers would sell their goods. Resale price maintenance drove a wedge between consumers and retailers, since retailers favored manufacturers that offered higher retail margins, while consumers favored lower overall prices. RPM also helped to restrict retail competition, since different retailers sold the same products for the same prices. France and Germany also intervened in other ways that were intended to control pricing.

Despite these common initiatives, however, French and German approaches to consumer prices were different in ways that were informed by the emerging consumerist discourse. In Germany, prices were seen to provide consumers with important information. During a brief period in the mid-1970s, consumers mobilized to help restrain inflation. These efforts largely failed, and Germany retained distinctive laws and institutions designed to ensure that consumer prices genuinely reflected underlying qualities of products. In France, the idea of the *prix juste* (fair price) came to dominate policymaking. Concern about persistent inflation drove successive governments to emphasize price restraints as a policy response. At the height of price regulation in the late 1970s, the government was setting prices for hundreds of thousands of individual products. In part, this kind of intervention was seen as a necessary response to the industrial consolidation that the French government had also encouraged. It also offered a politically appealing response to price inflation, since history showed that price increases in France were likely to be attributed to a lack of government action rather than to shifting conditions of supply and demand.[8]

Price Information

France and Germany both imposed regulations in the 1970s to ensure that all consumer products were displayed with their prices in order to facilitate comparative shopping. In Germany, the 1973 Price Information Act (Preisangabenverordnung) accompanied the prohibition on resale price maintenance, since retailers were then, in principle, allowed to offer the same goods for different prices. In France, product labeling was required by decree in 1971 and reinforced by supporting regulation in 1976. In both countries, clear price information was seen to be a key to holding down retail prices. Whereas in France this new emphasis on comparative price shopping enjoyed enthusiastic endorsement from both government and consumer organiza-

---

8. Price increases in 1911, for example, led to consumer boycotts that resulted in three deaths, 136 injuries, and 396 arrests. Bihl, *Une histoire du mouvement consommateur,* 214–16.

tions, similar efforts by consumer organizations and the government in Germany were quickly abandoned.

France's move in 1976 to a system of free price competition below the government-enforced "negotiated" price ceilings opened the way for greater price competition among products selling below those ceilings. To encourage this kind of downward price competition, the government of Raymond Barre undertook a number of projects to ensure that consumers had access to adequate information about product prices. In November 1977, it announced a four-month series of state-sponsored radio shows that would provide a forum for callers to report on their strategies for finding inexpensive products. The goal was to help consumers shop more wisely in order to put a check on abusive increases in prices. In the words of the newly appointed secretary of consumption: "Every idea helps us to better defend your budget."[9] The theme was repeated in 1979 when Economics Minister Michel Monory called on consumers to compare prices before buying in order to help hold down inflation.[10]

Consumer groups in France were enthusiastic supporters of price labeling and comparative price shopping, and they frequently mobilized their participants to visit stores in order to evaluate the adherence to the pricing regulations. They conducted regular price surveys. One study, conducted in Paris in June 1976, found that 28 percent of retailers and 30 percent of service providers failed to display the prices of their offerings. The worst offenders were concentrated in particular retail classes, including furniture stores (52 percent), florists (56 percent), and pharmacies (74 percent).[11] The scale of these price surveys (*relevés de prix*) could be enormous. In another survey conducted during the week of 20 November 1979, 110 local affiliates of the Federal Consumers' Union (Union fédérale des consommateurs, UFC) surveyed 27,735 stores in 160 cities in France. Mobilized under the slogan "Not seen, not bought" (*"Pas vu pas pris"*), they found that 38 percent of the stores visited were not displaying prices on their products.[12]

The French government itself soon became more heavily involved in providing consumers with product pricing information. Unsatisfied with the level of consumer awareness of product prices, in 1983 the Ministry of Consumption under the new Socialist government initiated a pilot project in the Nord-Pas de Calais region to offer consumers objective comparative information on product prices. Cooperating with the regional council on consumption (conseil régional de la consommation, CRC) in Lille, they established one hundred computer terminals on which product price information was made available to consumers. These local centers for price information (centres locaux de l'information prix, CLIP), which accounted for 60 percent of the Ministry of Consumption's yearly budget, were relatively well received.

9. Rosemonde Pujol, "Campagne d'information: "Acheter mieux—déposer moins," *Le Figaro*, 15 November 1977.

10. Luc Bihl, "Le contre-pouvoir des consommateurs," *Le Monde*, 5 December 1979.

11. "La publicité des prix a l'égard des consommateurs," *Note documentaire*, Direction générale de la concurrence et des prix, 4 June 1976.

12. "Une enquête de l'Union fédérale des consommateurs," *Le Monde*, 12 December 1979.

A survey conducted in 1986 by the CRC in Lille found that 85 percent of the population of the region knew of the program, compared with only 30 percent in 1984. Of those, 40 percent stated that they used the information for purchases (33.6 percent of the total population). Furthermore, 22 percent of the users reported shifting to products that were less expensive, and 18 percent reported shifting to retailers that were reported to be less expensive.[13] A survey of retailers found that 64 percent favored the program, 54 percent felt the price information was useful for their business, and 13 percent reported using CLIP information to set their own sales prices. Over half of the retailers felt that CLIP had an impact on their consumers, although only 34 percent reported that consumers used this information directly in their product choices.[14] Five new CLIP regions were included in France's five-year plan of 1984, with each of these sites offered a grant of 5 million francs from the federal government, to be matched by an equal contribution from the regional governments.[15]

The 1973 oil shock stimulated a similar collaboration in Germany between the government and consumer groups to raise public awareness about price, though this effort quickly faltered. In the summer of 1973, Germany's Social Democratic Party (SPD) launched a program for consumer education (*Verbraucheraufklärung*) with the goal of better informing citizens about product prices. The highlight of this new campaign was the "yellow dot protest" (*Aktion gelber Punkt*). The yellow dot referred to yellow stickers that were attached to the display windows of stores with particularly high prices. The project had been initiated by the publicity department of the SPD and carried out primarily by the SPD's Young Socialists group.[16] The program was modeled explicitly on the highly successful "red dot protests" (*Rote-Punkt-Aktionen*) of the late 1960s, in which leftist community organizations used red labels to protest price increases in local transportation. The memory of these *Rote-Punkt-Aktionen*, which led to one of the first large-scale consumer boycotts in postwar Germany, lent a radical tone to the SPD's new project.[17]

This attempt to create a politics of price in Germany was supported by labor but strongly opposed by business. Retailers felt particularly threatened by the SPD action and, in what was called the "greatest sign of retail solidarity ever," launched a counter-campaign against the government's program. Their posters read, "Retailers also oppose rising prices. We favor stability!"[18] The association of branded products criticized the *Aktion gelber Punkt* as "consumer politics in the mode of class conflict" ("*Verbraucherpolitik in Klassenkampfmanier*"). The top employers' association (Bundesvereinigung der Deutschen Arbeitgeberverbände, BDA) launched a

13. "CLIP de Lille," *Consommateurs actualités* 523 (17 October 1986), 16.

14. "CLIP: Impact sur les commerçants," *Consommateurs actualités* 538 (13 February 1987), 25.

15. "Le prix de l'information," *Consommateurs actualités* 517 (5 September 1986), 4.

16. Herbert Kremp, "Zielpunkt Unternehmer," *Die Welt*, 11 October 1973.

17. "Autofahrer gegen Ölkonzerne: Boykott letzte Waffe der Konsumenten," *Frankfurter Rundschau*, 24 July 1982.

18. Wolfgang H. Glöckner, "Aktion 'Gelber Punkt': Ins Rote verfälscht," *Vorwärts*, 18 October 1973.

campaign against the SPD program under the slogan "Yellow dot—red market—dead market" (*"Gelber Punkt—roter Markt—toter Markt"*), in which they claimed that the goal of the SPD was to dismantle the free market altogether: "The Yellow Dot [campaign] appears intended to move us away from the market economy, to 'deconstruct' it, to hollow it out, to plan it."[19] Characteristically, Germany's consumer associations did not participate in the SPD action.

Without active support from Germany's consumer groups and under withering criticism from industry associations, in the fall of 1973 the SPD began to pull away from politicizing price. In October, SPD leader Holger Börner assured the Chamber of Commerce and Industry (Deutscher Industrie- und Handelskammertag, DIHT), another industry group worried about the call to boycott, that the yellow dot protest was not an attack on the market system. Börner explained that the party had switched from focusing on wage formation as the cause of inflation because they felt that companies had increased prices more than was required by wage increases.[20] At the same time, Martin Grüner, the parliamentary state secretary for the Economics Ministry, emphasized that this would not be the beginning of price controls, which he described as incompatible with Germany's market economy. Grüner did, however, affirm the usefulness of protests that have the goal of informing consumers about price increases and alternative product choices.[21]

Setting Prices Right in France

France and Germany had a long history of restricting pricing practices, but the nature of their regulations were very different and tended to reflect their distinctive views about the economic role of prices. In France, where price restrictions were more aggressive, the government actively set prices for broad categories of goods. Authority for postwar government intervention in price-setting was grounded in ordinances 45–1483 and 45–1484 of June 1945, which were themselves restatements of the Code of Prices (*Code des prix*) established under the occupying government in October 1940.[22] These ordinances were unusual in that they placed absolute authority over prices in the hands of the French administration as well as full authority to deploy police or military forces to apply any price restrictions. In principle, the government could even enforce prices that were below production costs. Although the scope of administrative prerogative in France was uncommon, its use of price controls was by no means unusual. Sweden applied extensive price restrictions over much of the postwar period, as did the United States during the wage and price freeze imposed by the Nixon administration beginning in 1971.[23]

19. "SPD beschwichtigt Unternehmer," *Süddeutsche Zeitung,* 13 October 1973.

20. Ibid.

21. "Auch Verbraucher können Stabilitätsbeitrag leisten," *Süddeutsche Zeitung,* 9 October 1973.

22. Hervé Dumez and Alain Jeunemaître, *Diriger l'économie: L'état et les prix en France, 1936–1986* (Paris: Harmattan, 1989).

23. Lars Jonung, *The Political Economy of Price Controls: The Swedish Experience 1970–1985* (Brookfield, Vt.: Aldershot, 1990).

Price regulation in France began in earnest with the first burst of inflation in 1957, ending in 1986. During the intervening period, two major shifts in the nature of price regulation occurred, resulting in three distinct approaches to price control. In the first period, from 1957 to September 1974, price regulation imposed a minimal burden on producers. The prices of products already on the market could only be increased subject to direct approval from the Ministry of Economy and Finance's Office on Competition and Price (Direction de la concurrence et des prix, DCP). Any new products could be priced at the discretion of the producer and required no justification based on the actual costs of production. Producers of new products simply had to register their intended price lists with the government at least two weeks before actually putting their goods up for sale. This permissive stance toward new products was designed to promote innovation. It also had the unintended consequence of encouraging many companies to discontinue traditional product lines and reintroduce them under new names and with slight modifications in order to apply higher prices.

In 1974, under the pressure of 14 percent inflation, France sought to undo this "innovation loophole" by requiring that all new products be registered with the DCP with a justification for their proposed sales price. In order to limit bureaucratic slowdowns, the DCP had one month to respond. Any company that had heard nothing after one month was free to proceed with its proposed pricing. While this approach might have worked in an earlier period, 1970s saw an extraordinary growth in product kind and number. It became clear to price administrators that the burden of the new approach was overwhelming both companies and the government. The government simply could not evaluate enough proposals to have an overall impact on inflation.

December 1976 saw a final change made that reflected a growing interest in negotiated solutions to consumer protection.[24] According to the new scheme, producers could sign a "moderation agreement" (*engagement de modération*) consenting to price ceilings that had been previously negotiated between trade associations and the government. These ceilings were set based on sectoral growth rates determined by the DCP from production information provided by companies in the sector. The information used in setting price levels was evidently problematic; officials in the Office on Competition and Price reportedly watched German price levels closely.[25] In more concentrated sectors, companies were commonly able to negotiate price ceilings individually with the government.[26] Individual companies were still free to sell products above the negotiated ceilings, but they had to apply for special permission for the proposed prices with the DCP, as they had done before the 1976 reform. As an increasing number of sectors agreed to moderation agreements, the total

24. Reinhard Angelmar and Bernard Yon, "New Product Price Controls in France," *Journal of Consumer Policy* 2 / 1 (1978): 43–49.

25. French price-setting was prone to scandal. In one case, price-setters were accused of applying greater price restraint on products that they knew to be in the basket of goods surveyed for measuring consumer inflation.

26. Dumez and Jeunemaître, *Diriger l'économie,* 53–54.

volume of individually registered prices approved by the administration declined, from 137,000 in 1978 to 91,500 in 1979 and 61,300 in 1980.[27]

The French embrace of price control signaled a clear assertion of the popular interest over the interests of the business community. A series of public surveys on inflation conducted in the 1970s showed that support for price controls increased over time. In 1970, 27 percent of the population supported price controls as a means of protecting the value of the franc. Support rose to 35 percent in 1974, 47 percent in 1976, reaching a peak of 76 percent in 1982. France's largest business association, the Conseil national du patronat français (CNPF) had long called for the abolition of administered prices. They also opposed the negotiated ceilings introduced by the Barre government in 1976, which they felt merely gave government control of prices the spurious legitimacy of contractual consent.

France's consumer groups also opposed government price restrictions. The consumer group ORGECO first argued in 1971 that free competition rather than price restraint was the appropriate response to rising prices: "We insist at least that the conditions of free competition be saved, because they are, in the current state of things, the only guarantee of the consumer."[28] In their view, French companies were simply not price-competitive. A trade union survey conducted in 1969 had found that only 500 of the 8,000 companies they surveyed operating in France had what they felt were competitive prices. The rest were, in their words, "deplorably organized."[29] In 1976, ORGECO endorsed the plan to create negotiated ceilings on the grounds that it permitted limited competition below the negotiated level. But the group also stressed the need to attack the structural causes of inflation, which they felt meant establishing true competition in distribution and price formation.[30] Prices would be controlled not through any direct action of the French state but through greater consumer activism to raise awareness and sensitivity to prices.

Informative Pricing in Germany

Germany was unusual among the advanced industrial countries in not directly regulating product prices in response to the 1973 oil shock. It had traditionally granted producers extraordinary latitude to determine the retail price of their goods. The core of this tradition was resale price maintenance (*Preisbindung*), a practice that until 1973 allowed producers to stipulate in their distribution contracts the final sales price of branded goods. As resale price maintenance effectively eliminated price competition among retailers, it helped producers to establish and maintain a stable level of profitability, both for themselves and for their distributors. While in principal such vertical collusion fell under the scrutiny of the Federal Cartel Office (Bun-

27. "L'activité de la Direction générale de la concurrence et de la consommation en 1980," *Revue de la concurrence et de la consommation* 15 (1981): 4.

28. Jacques Dubois, "Reparlons des prix . . . ," *Information consommateur* 1 (1971): 3.

29. Editorial, *Information consommateur* 69/2 (1969): 2.

30. Jacques Dubois, "Le plan Barre et le consommation," *Information consommation OR-GE-CO* 18 (September–October 1976): 1.

deskartellamt, BKA), with whom companies were required to register resale price maintenance contracts, the practice was in fact rarely restricted.[31]

One of the early justifications for RPM was that uniform product prices helped to lower consumer search costs.[32] Increasingly, however, the practice of RPM was perceived to help keep costs artificially high. With the threat of price increases from the first oil shock, the Bundestag amended Germany's Antitrust Law (Gesetz gegen Wettbewerbsbeschränkungen, GWB) to prohibit resale price maintenance. The Ministry of Youth, Family, and Health particularly championed this move, arguing that retail competition would help to hold down prices for consumer products.[33]

In fact, Germany was late in coming to a trend already seen in other advanced industrial countries. The United States had restricted RPM in the Robinson-Patman Act of 1936, and Britain had taken similar action in 1964. In France, resale price maintenance was outlawed in 1954 in conjunction with the Pinay stabilization plan to hold down consumer and industry costs. French producers quickly found that they could effectively control resale prices, even without binding resale price agreements, through selective distribution practices. The "Fontanet circular" of March 1960 responded to this problem by prohibiting companies from taking punitive action, such as refusing distribution (*refus de vente*), against retailers wishing to offer discounts on their products. Enforcing vertical contractual freedom of this kind remained a mainstay of French competition policy.[34]

In contrast to France, the German government retained a variety of legal provisions that continued to assist companies in influencing the sales price of their goods in the absence of resale price maintenance. First, the 1973 amendment to the GWB did not explicitly prohibit the use of recommended prices (*unverbindliche Preisempfehlungen*), as unions and consumer groups had requested. German firms commonly use two kinds of recommended prices: those printed onto the product packaging itself (*Verbraucherpreisempfehlungen*), and those printed in a list for exclusive use by the retailer (*Händlerpreisempfehlungen*). While the prices printed on packaging could arguably help consumers to compare product prices for the same product among several retailers, unions and consumer organizations argued that prices presented in the form of lists never seen by consumers did not offer this benefit, and so instead had the effect of fostering price collusion.[35]

This concern was reinforced by producer reactions to the banning of resale price maintenance. Between 1973 and 1975, retailers reported that while the overall use of recommended prices remained nearly the same, the use of retailer price lists grew

31. Norbert Reich, "Neue Tendenzen des kartellrechtlichen Verbraucherschutzes in der BRD," *Zeitschrift für Verbraucherpolitik* 1 / 3 (1977): 236.

32. David Morris, "Competition Policy and the Consumer Interest," in *Economics of Consumer Protection*, ed. David Morris (London: Heinemann Educational Books, 1980), 177.

33. Katherina Focke, "Verbraucherpolitik in der Marktwirtschaft," *Bulletin des Presse- und Informationsamtes der Bundesregierung* 65 (30 May 1973), 643.

34. F. D. Boggis, "The European Economic Community," in *Resale Price Maintenance*, ed. Basil S. Yamey (London: Weidenfeld and Nicolson, 1966).

35. Verbraucherbeirat, *Jahresbericht* (1977).

from 22 to 37 percent of their total stock, while the use of recommended prices printed on the packaging fell from 30 to 14 percent. The shift was most dramatic for small shops (those with annual sales below 250,000 DM), for whom the use of re-tailer price lists nearly doubled, from 22 to 42 percent of their inventory, while con-sumer price recommendations fell by half, from 45 to 22 percent of inventory.[36] Unable to stipulate sales prices in their contracts, manufacturers appeared to move to less direct means of enforcing price levels. Germany's Competition Office, which tracked the use of recommended prices, all but recognized that retail list recom-mendations were tantamount to resale price maintenance.[37] But legal provisions for the restriction of effective resale price maintenance were interpreted by the BKA to the advantage of branded goods producers: "Protection of brands and distribution, not protection of the consumer, is . . . still the predominant criterion for interpret-ing GWB regulation."[38]

The debate over recommended prices highlighted how weak Germany's consumer organizations were. The AgV had long argued against both RPM and the practice of nonbinding price recommendations (*unverbindlichen Preisempfehlungen*) that replaced it. They were, however, unable to convince either the government or their own con-stituencies. The Economics Ministry's own consumer council (Beirat für Ver-braucher) had also proposed that recommended prices be forbidden in the Law on Unfair Competition, and that oversight on exclusion contracts be increased. Eco-nomics Minister Hans Friedrichs never adopted their position.[39] The Bundestag con-tended that recommended prices were consumer-friendly, since they did not exclude retail competition, gave consumers a comparison price, and amounted to an upper price limit on retailers.[40] Consumers, too, apparently found them useful. A 1973 sur-vey found that 87 percent of men and 82 percent of women favored recommended prices printed on packaging. Those who favored it felt that it helped them compare product prices and that it protected them against overreaching by retailers.[41] More-over, the leading association of German retailers, the Hauptverband des Deutschen Einzelhandels (HDE), argued that list recommendations, which were not made pub-lic, assisted retailers in calculating what prices they should charge.[42] The Bundestag, in a move to appease all parties, permitted recommended prices of both kinds.

Germany's permissive stance toward resale price maintenance was not the only

---

36. Erich Batzer, Erich Greipl, and Eugen Singer, *Handhabung und Wirkung der unverbindlichen Preisempfehlung* (Berlin: Duncker and Humblot, 1976), 121.

37. Bundeskartellamt, *Jahresbericht* (1975).

38. GWB § 18 and § 26 II; and Norbert Reich, "Der Schutz des Verbrauchers vor überhöhten Preisen und einseitigen Preiserhöhungen: Das GWB als Verbrauchergesetz," in *Verbraucher und Recht*, ed. Norbert Reich, Klaus Tonner, and Hartmut Wegener (Göttingen, Germany: Verlag Otto Schwartz, 1976), 73–74.

39. "Verbraucherpolitik nicht nur als 'Feuerwehr,'" *Süddeutsche Zeitung*, 13 March 1973.

40. Reich, "Neue Tendenzen," 227–43.

41. "Einstellung der Verbraucher zur Preisempfehlung," *Wirtschaft und Wettbewerb* (May 1973): 325.

42. The HDE also opposed the printing of recommended prices on packaging on the grounds that they restricted the freedom of retailers. Reich, "Neue Tendenzen," 237–41.

mechanism by which producers maintained control over the pricing of products. Other laws limited pricing practices in different ways. Typical of these was the Discount Law (Rabattgesetz), first enacted in 1933, which prohibited discounts or in-kind gifts of value greater than 5 percent of the cost of the product sold. The law did not prohibit sales on overstocked or seasonal goods—these were regulated by another restrictive pricing law, the Zugabeverordnung—but it did require that retailers sell goods for no less than 95 percent of their labeled value. Practices not permissible for German retailers under the Rabattgesetz included volume or loyalty discounts, sales inducements, coupons, and inflated price labeling.[43] The original goal of the law appears to have been to discourage the cooperative movement and repress immigrant shopkeepers who were willing to compete on narrow profit margins.[44] By the 1970s, however, the Rabattgesetz had also come to serve two useful purposes for producers. First, the Rabattgesetz made it easy for distributors to monitor the actual retail sales prices retailers were using. Second, producers could not use volume or loyalty discounts to reward their best customers—tactics that had helped retailers in other countries to consolidate their customer base, giving them greater power in negotiating contracts with producers.

Advocates of the Rabattgesetz argued that, in its absence, retailers would increase products' labeled prices so that they could offer consumers greater nominal discounts without affecting their profitability. This line of argument was apparently influential among consumer advocates as well. Even the leading consumer association, the AgV, which might normally be expected to oppose the restrictive Rabattgesetz, suggested that its elimination would result in a 20 to 30 percent increase in nominal prices. They noted that it helped consumers who might otherwise face price discrimination because they were less able or willing to haggle with sales staff for better prices.[45] In the words of Helmut Lenders, head of the AgV, elimination of the Rabattgesetz "would be totally impenetrable for the consumer."[46]

Why did the BKA acquiesce to what amounted to collusive practices, and why did the AgV actively support them? An important source of legitimacy for Germany's pricing policies derived from the "ordoliberal" tradition of German political economy, a view of market order that crystallized in the Freiburg School and formed the basis of Ludwig Erhard's post-occupation economic initiatives of 1957.[47] Broadly, the ordoliberal principle of competition embraced Schumpeterian rather than liberal market assumptions.[48] From this perspective, market regulations should be de-

43. Georg Klauer and Helmut Seydel, *Zugabeverordnung und Rabattgesetz Kommentar* (Munich: Franz Vahlen, 1993), 100–103.

44. Reuters News Service, *Western Europe*, 2 March 1994.

45. Olaf Sosnitza, *Wettbewerbsbeschränkungen durch die Rechtsprechung: Erscheinungsformen und Ursachen auf dem Gebiet des Lauterkeitsrecht* (Baden-Baden, Germany: Nomos, 1995), 144.

46. "Das wird für den Verbraucher völlig undurchsichtig." Wulf Petzoldt, "'Mondpreise' mit schwindelerregenden Rabatten," *Vorwärts* 13 (22 March 1984).

47. See François Souty, *La politique de la concurrence en Allemagne fédérale* (Paris: Presses universitaires de France, 1996), 115–20;

48. Manfred E. Streit, "Economic Order, Private Law, and Public Policy: The Freiburg School of Law and Economics in Perspective," *Journal of Institutional and Theoretical Economics* 148 (1992): 687–89.

ployed primarily to optimize economic transactions by balancing the power of market actors through increased transparency.[49] From an ordoliberal perspective, recommended prices and the Rabattgesetz worked together to promote prices that reflected the genuine costs of production. Although they tended to enforce prices proposed by producers, they avoided what from the "ordoliberal" perspective was the worst possible outcome: a situation in which manufacturers label product packaging with artificially elevated recommended prices (*Mondpreise*), permitting retailers to offer apparently attractive reductions from the manufacturer's price.[50]

Product Design Standards

In parallel with the regulation of product prices, politicians in both France and Germany began pushing for greater consumer participation in the actual product design process at the level of product standards. Germany did so by introducing consumer representatives into its technical standardization board, Deutsches Institut für Normung (DIN). France attempted to promote collective agreements between consumer associations and producer interest groups in which acceptable standards of quality and design would be negotiated. The difference in approaches was driven primarily by the way in which consumer interests had been organized in the two countries. In Germany, where standardization was centralized within the DIN, consumer representatives were able to participate in product standardization through the creation of a consumer advisory council within that organization. This kind of participation was possible in part due to the high level of technical competency among German consumer representatives, which allowed them to engage usefully in technical committee meetings for products of particular relevance to consumers. In France, by contrast, consumer organizations had pushed to be able to negotiate directly with the sectoral business groups and, later, with individual companies. This approach was necessary in part due to the weaker position of the French standardization board, AFNOR. The negotiation approach was also better suited to the capacities of consumer organizations in France, as their broad grassroots support enabled them to claim that they were negotiating legitimately on behalf of all consumers. After several years of experimentation, this negotiation strategy fell apart.

German Self-Regulation

On 8 October 1974, the German Standards Committee (Deutscher Normenausschuss, DNA) came to an agreement with the German Ministry of Economics to create a new consumer council (Verbraucherrat, VR) to represent consumer interests within the DNA.[51] This represented the outcome of a policy initiative announced

---

49. Souty, *La politique de la concurrence en Allemagne fédérale,* 110–15.
50. "Verbraucherpolitik nicht nur als 'Feuerwehr,'" *Süddeutsche Zeitung,* 13 March 1973.
51. The DNA was renamed DIN in 1974.

first in the government's First Consumer Report of 1971 and strongly supported by the AgV.[52] Germany's top trade association, the Bundesverband der Deutschen Industrie (BDI), opposed this "partnership in-house solution" to the problem of consumer access to standardization and probably would have blocked it.[53] However, the VR proposal was included as part of a larger negotiation with the government that the DNA could not turn down. At the end of 1973, the government approached the DNA with a proposal to receive significant federal funding in exchange for taking on duties that the government felt were central to the standardization process. The proposal would give the DNA, renamed the German Institute for Standardization (Deutsches Institut für Normung, DIN), a monopoly on technical standardization in Germany. According to the terms of this agreement, set out in DIN standard 820 governing the operations of the organization itself, consumers would participate in the newly created consumer council on an equal footing with producers.[54]

The consumer council had three goals: to oversee the standards process, to help select cases of interest to consumers for standardization, and to organize consumer representation on relevant DIN technical committees. The five members of the consumer council were selected, each for a term of three years, by the president of the DIN in consultation with the largest consumer association, AgV, and the Ministry of Economics. The work of the consumer council was seen largely as a success. Government support grew from 328,000 DM in 1975 to 451,000 DM in 1980, while the number of consumer representatives participating in DIN technical committees grew from 370 in 1976 to over 600 in 1980.[55] In 1982, 1,884 of 21,400 standards issued by DIN were found to be relevant to consumers according to consumer council criteria.[56] By 1989, the consumer council found about 2,400 of DIN's 25,700 standards to be relevant to consumers.[57] Consumer-relevant technical standards have consistently accounted for around 10 percent of all technical standards issued by DIN.

French Failure

Inaugurated in 1978, France's Raymond Barre pursued a different and, ultimately, far more tortuous strategy for involving consumers in the process of product de-

---

52. *Verbraucherbericht*, Bundestagsdrucksache VI/2724, 1971.

53. Christian Joerges, Josef Falke, Hans-Wolfgang Micklitz, and Gert Brüggemeier, *Die Sicherheit von Konsumgütern und die Entwicklung der Europäischen Gemeinschaft* (Baden-Baden, Germany: Nomos, 1989), 186.

54. In 1962 the DNA established a committee for product usefulness (Ausschuss Gebrauchstauglichkeit, AGt), on which consumer representatives held four seats, but their influence was small. The committee was eliminated after the formation of the VR.

55. Annemarie Bopp-Schmehl, Uwe Heibült, and Ulrich Kypke, *Technische Normung und Verbraucherinteressen im gesellschaftlichen Wandel* (Frankfurt: Haag and Herchen Verlag, 1984), 214.

56. Ibid., 216.

57. Joerges et al., *Die Sicherheit von Konsumgütern*, 187; and Jérôme Darigny, *Normalisation-certification-essais: Leur devenir, leurs enjeux industriels dans l'Europe du marché unique*, thesis, University of Paris I (Sorbonne), 1989, 16.

sign. Rather than trying to pursue the consumer interest through standardization, Minister of Economics René Monory called instead for consumer associations to negotiate product standards directly with producers. Seeking support, Monory charged the formerly neutral National Consumption Institute (INC) to support consumer associations in cultivating a "consumer counter-force to counterbalance the technical advantage of producers and the effects of advertising."[58] In the context of meetings organized by the CNPF, consumer representatives met with representatives of industry sectors to negotiate standards of quality and use that were felt to best suit consumer needs in a particular sector. While such partnerships were voluntary, companies that accepted negotiated standards could advertise this as a selling point. However, this inducement proved too weak, and by 1989 only forty-nine such voluntary accords had been signed between consumer associations and professional associations. Of these, 36 percent treated house construction, 20 percent used car sales, 18 percent small retailing, 8 percent furniture, and 6 percent dry cleaning.[59]

The government of François Mitterrand took a new approach to integrating consumers into product standardization. Rather than devolving state powers to sectoral agencies, Mitterrand's first minister of consumption, Catherine Lalumière, sought a legal contractual status for agreements negotiated directly between consumer groups and individual companies. In December 1982, Lalumière launched a program called "Contracts for the Improvement of Quality." Under this new legal form, products or services conforming to the norms established in negotiations between management and officially recognized consumer groups would be indicated with the "*Marque 'approuvé'*" and include a symbol with the letter A inscribed in a hexagon (the French commonly refer to their country as "the hexagon").[60] These "*approuvé*" agreements had a mixed reception among consumer groups. The Socialist and Communist consumer groups strongly favored them, and some companies even negotiated them through consumer groups affiliated with their own labor unions. Furthermore, because the agreements took the form of contracts that were legally binding, consumers could resort to the court system to hold companies to their agreed standards. This strategy of company-level negotiations was also favored by the CNPF, which was by 1982 becoming disillusioned with its national negotiations. "We are convinced that if the consumer debate has become conflictual," wrote the CNPF's Jean Levy, "it is because it has occurred at the national and multi-sectoral level. We want to bring the debate back to where the problems arise, at the level of sectors and companies, for it is there, and only there, that they can be solved."[61]

Not all consumer groups were happy with the new arrangement. The UFC re-

58. Gisèle Prevost, "Consommation: 'L'agressivité' de l'INC préoccupe de plus en plus le CNPF," *Les Échos*, 28 May 1979.

59. "Accords négociés entre associations de consommateurs et professionels," *INC Hebdo* 624 (3 February 1989), 14.

60. Jean Calais-Auloy, *Le droit de la consommation* (Paris: Editions Dalloz-Sirey, 1992), 49–50.

61. Gisèle Prevost, "Le CNPF ne veut pas d'un pouvoir consommateur dans l'entreprise," *Les Échos*, 19 February 1982.

mained critical of the *approuvé* program because they felt that it produced few results for consumers and had supplanted the more effective "Quality Certificates"
program attempted by the Ministry of Industry.[62] The Communist-affiliated consumer group INDECOSA-CGT complained that the government was not applying sufficient pressure on France's large nationalized companies to sign quality
agreements with consumer associations.[63] Nor was the system as successful as its
designers had hoped.[64] By 1985, only fifty-nine companies had signed quality contracts with consumer associations, most with a duration of only one to two years.[65]
Of these, thirty-three companies signed contracts to improve the quality of services;
twenty-six companies signed contracts that applied to a total of 305 different products. A survey in 1986, four years after the program began, showed that 16 percent
of the population recognized the *approuvé* certification.[66] While many judged the
individual agreements to have succeeded, it became increasingly clear that such
company-level negotiations could not provide an adequate consumer voice in product standardization. In hindsight, the system of negotiated quality contracts, indeed
France's entire experiment with negotiating product standards, appeared to have
been largely ineffectual.[67]

Meanwhile, AFNOR, France's official standardization body, remained a weak tool
for setting industry standards.[68] Companies were not required to adopt AFNOR
norms, although compliance earned them the right to post the "NF" symbol on their
products and packaging. Industry in general did not participate in the process of
standardization, and most small and medium-sized enterprises did not use AFNOR
standards.[69] While consumer groups were invited to sit on AFNOR's administrative council, they did not typically participate in actual standardization committees.
By the late 1980s, standardization had become an activity in which neither consumer
groups nor producer groups took great interest. The director general of AFNOR,
Bernard Vaucelle, lamented in 1989: "Standard setting has become too important an
activity to be left to professionals of standardization. It is a matter of strategy, of politics."[70]

In Germany, consumers were successfully integrated into the country's technical
standardization body. This occurred even though industry had initially opposed the

---

62. "Contrats d'amélioration de la qualité," *Consommateurs actualités* 501 (21 March 1986), 19.
63. "Contrats de qualité," *Consommateurs actualités* 498 (28 February 1986), 17.
64. Calais-Auloy, *Le droit de la consommation*, 49–50; and Didier Ferrier, *La protection des consommateurs* (Paris: Dalloz, 1996), 83.
65. "Contrats d'amélioration de la qualité," 17–19.
66. "Qualité: Les consommateurs veulent un label unique européen," *Consommateurs actualités*
604 (9 September 1988), 20.
67. Calais-Auloy, *Le droit de la consommation*, 49–50.
68. Jay Tate, "Varieties of Standardization," in Peter Hall and David Soskice, eds., *Varieties of
Capitalism* (Oxford: Oxford University Press, 2001), 457.
69. Darigny, *Normalisation-certification-essais*, 59.
70. "Les industriels doivent prendre la normalisation en main," *Consommateurs actualités* 579
(29 January 1988), 3.

move. In pricing policy, producers retained strong legal capacities to dictate prices for the consumer goods they sold, allowing them to resist price pressures from retailer competition. Together, these policies created a context in which consumer preferences for high-quality products could be accommodated. In France, nearly the opposite outcome emerged. Price politics were characterized by consumer mobilization and active government regulatory intervention. Active price setting ended in part because consumer representatives themselves argued that prices might be better controlled by informed consumers than by regulatory restraint. Industry standardization also became the focus of intensive consumer interest in the early 1980s. However, efforts to allow consumer groups to negotiate such standards directly with industry failed. The result was a set of policies that placed downward pressure on prices and failed to develop a workable set of technical standards adapted to the interests of consumers.

Why did price politics flourish in France but falter in Germany? Why were consumers successfully incorporated into standardization in Germany but not in France? Pricing and quality standards were old areas of regulation. National trajectories therefore depended in part on the institutional legacies with which the two countries entered the postwar period. In pricing policy, German's ordoliberal tradition focused on the critical information that prices could provide; France's emphasis on central planning and the legal admissibility of price fixing focused attention on issues of fair pricing. In standardization, German industry had organized strongly around industry-led standards; French industry had relied more heavily on direct interaction with the state. Still, these institutional heritages were not the sole force driving the differences we observe in France and Germany.

National differences also evolved out of the different strategies of consumer organizations in the two countries. In the realm of product standards, for example, German consumer groups were poorly organized but technically capable. Moreover, German producers were sufficiently organized within the framework of DIN to accept consumer input into standardization. In France, by contrast, organized consumers worked to negotiate with individual sectors and companies to help set product standards. But French producers were poorly organized. This meant that they were unable either to block this initiative or to propose more productive approaches to consumer participation in standardization. The result was a set of experiments that, when they failed, left the state to intervene on the consumers' behalf.

The cases of price and quality regulation illustrate the power of the new consumer citizenship to transform the logic of traditional areas of regulation. Similar changes occurred in other areas of industrial policy. Competition policy, for example, underwent a change in rationale during this period. Early postwar goals that focused on managing social conflict and protecting small-scale producers evolved into new priorities that focused on the goal of consumer welfare.[71] Trade policy, too, shifted in its public logic from the protection of domestic producers to the promotion of

71. Tony Freyer, *American Praxis: Antitrust and Global Capitalism in America, Japan, Europe, and Australia, 1930–2004* (Cambridge: Cambridge University Press, forthcoming).

consumer purchasing power. While this transformation has traditionally been understood as a shift in the balance of power among industrial sectors and factor endowments, it has also embodied a shift in the public logic of trade policy away from the interests of production and toward the interests of consumption.[72] Such policies fall outside the scope of this work. The findings of this research suggest that a closer look at the introduction of the consumer interest as a core logic of government policymaking can shed light on regulatory changes that have their roots in the period of consumer citizenship starting in the 1970s.

72. I. M. Destler and John S. Odell, *Anti-Protection: Changing Forces in United States Trade Politics* (Washington, D.C.: Institute for International Economics, 1987); Ronald Rogowski, *Commerce and Coalitions* (Princeton: Princeton University Press, 1989); and Kenneth F. Scheve and Matthew J. Slaughter, "What Determines Individual Trade Policy Preferences?" *Journal of International Economics* 54 (2001), 267–92.

CHAPTER EIGHT

The Consumer as Citizen

Consumers in advanced industrialized countries operate in a dense institutional environment. These institutions take the form of complex regulations covering product safety and quality standards, product liability and recall, truth in advertising and labeling, restrictions on retailing practice and consumer contract terms. Government agencies, ministry-level committees, and quasi-governmental consumer protection organizations collaborated to ensure that new policies took consumer protection into account. In France and Germany the new regulations and institutions emerged rapidly over the course of the 1970s and early 1980s. Understood as citizenship rights, these national consumer protection policies reflected a broad new consensus about the role and identity of the consumer in modern society.

This reorientation toward consumers displaced the boundary between the private and the public. Central to this transformation has been the role of consumer politics in setting the terms of production. Dimensions of product design and manufacturing that were previously set entirely by private industry have become increasingly subject to public inspection and regulation. Producers that in the immediate postwar period could dictate the terms on which their products were sold increasingly found their decisions dictated by the priorities and interests of consumers. Indeed, what we observe today as a deregulation of the business environment in advanced industrial countries might more accurately be understood as a transition away from regulation of the production sphere, including a progressive liberalization of labor and capital markets, toward comprehensive regulation of national consumption.

The institutional environment of consumption has also become highly differentiated across the advanced industrialized countries. From the common standards of producer sovereignty that pervaded the industrializing countries in the nineteenth century and the first two-thirds of the twentieth century, new and distinctive

161

national forms began to emerge. Each of the advanced industrialized nations now has its own legal standard of manufacturer liability for product-related damage. These range from near immunity in the cases of Germany and Austria to almost full consumer indemnity in the United States and France. Similarly, product labeling standards have diverged, with distinctive national labeling requirements imposing significant burdens on producers targeting multiple domestic markets. Across a broad range of consumer product regulation—including product safety standards, product recall, truth in advertising, consumer contracts, pricing practices, technical standards, and even consumer access to justice—the advanced industrial countries have pursued multiple and overlapping approaches. In the French and German cases, how governments regulated the consumer sphere was dictated by a struggle between the organized interests of producers and consumers over the social and economic identity of the modern consumer. The outcome of this struggle defined the nature of modern consumer citizenship in those countries.

The struggle itself depended on the organizational capacities of producers and consumers to secure their preferred policy models. This interaction between organized interests and organizing ideas provides insight into the ways in which economic actors help to set policy even during periods of dramatic regulatory discontinuity. Policy innovation does not suspend the politics of interest representation; it engages these interests in a second-order contest over competing ideas about the proper organization of society.

Policy Models and Product Market Strategy

Consumer protection policies in France and Germany followed different policy models. The German model of increased consumer information and the French model of increased producer responsibility for product-related risk have both succeeded in addressing the problems of market failure arising from information and risk asymmetries. Yet these different models are not neutral with respect to product choice, either for the consuming public or for producing companies. Each model works to eliminate market failure, but each also generates a different competitive dynamic in the consumer marketplace. In general, solutions of the kind adopted in Germany that focus on consumer information favor a competition for high-quality production and gradualist innovation. Conversely, solutions of the kind adopted in France (and in the United States) that focus on allocating product-related risk to producers favor a competition for lower-quality production and radical forms of innovation.

One way to interpret the impact on consumer choice is in terms of the hidden and visible qualities of products. Hidden qualities include aspects such as internal engineering, safety features, and extensive laboratory testing. These are qualities of the product that the consumer cannot assess by simple inspection without specialized knowledge. By contrast, visible qualities are those that all consumers naturally evaluate as they purchase, including product traits such as aesthetics, taste, and feel. Different kinds of products naturally incorporate different proportions of visible and hidden qualities. Traditional products such as clothing and leather goods all have a high level of visible qualities and a relatively low level of hidden qualities. Other products such as pharmaceuticals and sophisticated "black-box" equipment have a high level of hidden qualities and a relatively low level of visible qualities. All products lie somewhere in the space that defines their degree of hidden and visible qualities.

The information model of consumer protection relies on formal institutions—labeling, accurate advertising, quality standards, comparative test results, contractual clarity, consumer advice centers—that reveal to consumers some of the hidden qualities of products. Among those hidden qualities lie aspects of the product that are relevant to consumer safety. Hidden qualities also include product features such as durability, design, engineering, company experience, and workmanship. Thus, in the information model, information about consumer safety comes with related information about other aspects of products that provide consumers with a broad insight into their hidden qualities. Moreover, because consumers in the information model face a relatively high burden of risk from product-related failure, they have an incentive to seek out this information and to take it into account as they make their purchasing decisions. Consumers in the information model thus protect themselves against product risk by purchasing higher-quality goods. The higher price they pay can be interpreted as a form of insurance against unsafe products. Producers in this market therefore develop capacities and designs that allow them to compete for a high level of the hidden product qualities that consumers prefer.

By contrast, the protection model relies on formal institutions—strict product liability, class actions, product recalls, rigorous general product safety and policing policies—that protect consumers by assigning product-related risk to producers. It achieves a high level of consumer safety by allocating both product risk and product information to the producer. Producers in this model absorb the full cost of product-related risk, which they pool and pass on to consumers in the form of a price premium on their products. To take an extreme example, it is estimated that 95 percent of the cost of children's vaccines pays for liability insurance and legal fees.[1] The vaccine producer collects this risk premium, then divides it in some efficient way between new product safety measures and liability insurance.

The findings from this research help to explain recent trends in consumer sentiment in France and Germany. Through a series of surveys focused on consumer issues, Eurobarometer tracked French and German consumer orientations toward product risk and information during the 1990s. On the one hand, these surveys confirm that German consumers are more preoccupied than their French counterparts with accurate product information. Asked about problems facing consumers, 35 per-

---

1. Richard J. Mahoney and Stephen E. Littlejohn, "Innovation on Trial: Punitive Damages versus New Products," *Science* 246 (December 1989): 1397.

cent of Germans pointed to a lack of information about product features, compared to 23.5 percent of French.[2] Asked why they went to consumer organizations, 44.8 percent of Germans reported that they sought product information, compared to the 25.7 percent who sought legal advice. In France the trend was reversed: 23.5 percent of consumers sought product information, while 54 percent went for legal advice.[3]

On the other hand, German consumers also seem more preoccupied than their French counterparts with product-related risk. Asked about a typical group of consumer products, roughly the same percentage of French consumers (72 percent) reported feeling that they were safe as did German consumers (69 percent). Yet when asked separately how concerned they were about the safety of each of these products, 78 percent of German consumers reported feeling concern, compared to only 38 percent of French consumers. This result suggests that French consumers generally approach products as if they are safe. In Germany, surprisingly, consumers actually expressed greater concern about those products they perceived to be *safer*. For example, 81 percent of Germans felt that toys were generally safe, yet 88 percent also reported being concerned about the safety of toys. This seemingly odd attitude appears to support the view that German consumers take on a personal burden of ensuring that the products they buy are safe.[4]

These differences in consumer sentiment also have implications for product choice. The protection approach employed in France, for example, creates incentives for both consumers and producers to favor goods of lower quality. For consumers, the protection strategy means that products that are more expensive are not necessarily safer. This is true because consumers cannot know whether each additional unit of product price reflects better safety and design or simply the additional cost premium from insurance against product failures. In other words, the consumer in the protection model is unable to distinguish between higher prices that reflect the cost of better hidden qualities and higher prices that reflect higher product risk.[5] Without information that would allow them to distinguish between a quality premium and a risk premium, the consumer will ration demand for higher-priced goods.

For the producer, the protection strategy means that consumers have little incentive to inform themselves about their products. Consumers facing a low regulatory and legal burden of risk simply don't have a strong motivation to learn. As a consequence, these consumers also have a low recognition of hidden product qualities. Conversely, producers facing a high burden of product risk have strong incentives to ensure that the products they sell are safe. In this way the protection model

2. Anna Melich, "Images of Germany, Consumer Issues, Electronic Information, and Fair Trade Practices," *Eurobarometer* 47.0 (January–February 1997): 156.

3. INRA, "Europeans and Consumer Associations," *Eurobarometer* 51.1 (1999), 97.

4. Melich, "Images of Germany."

5. The situation is analogous to loan rationing. See Joseph E. Stiglitz and Andrew Weiss, "Credit Rationing in Markets with Imperfect Information," *American Economic Review* 71/3 (June 1981): 393–410.

leads to producer investment in consumer safety but without incentives to improve other hidden qualities of products, such as design or durability, since their consumers are not informed to recognize these improvements. Producers in the protection model therefore invest heavily in safety measures but minimize investment in other hidden qualities such as engineering and durability.

Market rules governing the context in which consumers shop may influence producer decisions not only about product quality but also about product innovation. In markets governed by the information model, consumers and producers are likely to emphasize gradual kinds of innovation to existing products. Producers have strong market incentives to invest in innovations that improve the hidden qualities of existing products, since they know that consumers recognize and favor this kind of quality emphasis. For example, the factor that has contributed to the success of the German automobile industry is not just the skill of German engineers but also the knowledge and quality emphasis of Germany's consuming public. This quality emphasis also comes with a down side. Concerned about safety, German consumers face new kinds of products with strong skepticism. It is a mistake to attribute this to some cultural inclination; it is a perfectly logical product of Germany's market rules. German consumers protect themselves in the marketplace through accurate information that allows them to purchase high-quality goods. However, for radically new kinds of products reliable information may not be available. Faced with this kind of uncertainty, German consumers may simply avoid dramatically innovative products. For German industry, the conservative nature of domestic demand makes this sort of innovation a bad business strategy.

If the information strategy favors a gradual approach to product innovation, the protection strategy may induce radical product innovation. Entirely new kinds of products typically carry greater uncertainty and correspondingly higher levels of risk than conventional products. They may not work as well as expected and may, in some cases, turn out to be harmful. In the protection model, the consumer enjoys—at least in principle—the same high level of protection against risk from all kinds of products. Thus, the consumer in the protection model is not strongly deterred by the potential higher risk of radically new kinds of products. From the consumer's perspective, the risk is the same. Indeed, the consumer in the protection model may actually be attracted to radically new kinds of products. New kinds of products differ from existing products in ways that are immediately visible to any consumer. Thus, recognizing radically new products does not require detailed knowledge of their hidden qualities. In other words, because consumers in the protection model do not have a high level of information about the hidden qualities of products (or a strong risk-driven incentive to secure this kind of information), they have a comparative advantage in products with visible qualities. This creates a competitive dynamic that favors not only radically new kinds of products, for which the innovation is immediately apparent to the consumer, but also certain very traditional kinds of products, whose qualities are apparent to all.

This finding suggests a potential tension with the role that supply-side institutions—labor markets, capital markets, and systems of corporate governance—have been understood to play in shaping producers' product-market strategies. If both supply-side and demand-side institutions tend to favor the same product market strategies, then these institutions may reinforce each other. This has been the case in Germany, where the highly coordinated supply-side institutions tend to favor the production of high-quality products—precisely the kinds of products emphasized by consumers who have inexpensive access to accurate product information. In Germany's case, of course, the alignment was far from accidental. The country's relatively weak consumer movement permitted industry to advocate their own preferred approach to consumer protection.

France's coordinated supply-side institutions at one time favored quality production.[6] Beginning in the early 1980s, however, these increasingly confronted a consumer protection regime that promoted lower quality and radical innovation. This left French producers in a difficult strategic situation. They could either continue to rely on coordinated supply-side institutions but risk that their products would go unsold; or they could follow the logic of consumer demand, but in the process undermine the very labor-market and capital-market institutions that had been the basis of their earlier success. This dynamic, in which the incentives of supply-side and demand-side institutions in France became misaligned, may have been a contributing factor in France's plunge into economic liberalization in the 1980s and 1990s.

Evaluating Alternative Explanations

Political scientists who have considered consumer policy have tended to approach the issue tangentially. They have observed consumer protection primarily as it relates to other policy debates.[7] Researchers focused on international trade have noted the impact that distinctive national consumer protection policies can play in global competition.[8] The European Union's ban on hormone-treated beef and restrictions on the use of genetically modified organisms have raised concerns about consumer protections as nontariff barriers to trade.[9] And researchers focused on European in-

6. Andrew Shonfield notes that France in the immediate postwar period excelled in quality production. Many manufacturers who produce primarily for the government still maintain this tradition of quality production. Andrew Shonfield, *Modern Capitalism: The Changing Balance of Public and Private Power* (Oxford: Oxford University Press, 1965), ch. 5.

7. Recent studies of the Japanese consumer movement are an exception. See Steven K. Vogel, "When Interests Are Not Preferences: The Cautionary Tale of Japanese Consumers," *Comparative Politics* 31/2 (1999): 187–207; and Patricia L. MacLachlan, *Consumer Politics in Postwar Japan* (New York: Columbia University Press, 2002).

8. David Vogel, *Trading Up: Consumer and Environmental Regulation in a Global Economy* (Cambridge, Massachusetts: Harvard University Press, 1995), 150; and Dale Murphy, *The Structure of Regulatory Competition: Corporations and Public Policies in a Global Economy* (Oxford: Oxford University Press, 2004).

9. Grace Skogstad, "Legitimacy and/or Policy Effectiveness? Network Governance and GMO Regulation in the European Union," *Journal of European Public Policy* 10/3 (June 2003): 334; and David Vogel, "The Hare and the Tortoise Revisited: The New Politics of Consumer and

tegration have noted the challenge that distinctive national consumer regulations pose for policymakers working to draft common market rules with Europe.[10] While these accounts have provided valuable analyses of the impact of distinctive national consumer protection regimes, they have been less attentive to the sources of national diversity. To the extent that they have addressed the causes of consumer protection, three kinds of explanations have been proposed.

The first and most common of these explanations points to the role of industry itself in creating consumer policies that protect domestic producers. In this view, consumer protection *is* protectionism. This *productionist* view is grounded in the assumption that concentrated producer interests must necessarily trump diffuse consumer interests in the policy marketplace.[11] This productionist view is partly correct. Once in place, consumer protection policies do appear to create constituencies among the producers that they tend to favor. Historically, however, producer interests were not the only voice in setting national consumer protection policies. The accounts of consumer protection in France and Germany show that industry opposed most new consumer protections. Only once regulation appeared inevitable did producer groups step forward to help shape regulatory outcomes. Yet even then business interests frequently failed to shape policy. French producers ended up with an approach to consumer protection—one one based on aggressive government intervention in the economy—that had initially been their least favored approach. In Germany, where industry seems to have enjoyed a greater ability to influence consumer regulation, the state nonetheless stepped in to impose regulations in the areas of misleading advertising and consumer contracts that were far stricter than what business desired. Business interests did influence national consumer policy, but so did the interests of organized consumers.

A second explanation of national consumer protection policies finds its roots in the enlightened regulatory acts of entrepreneurial politicians and bureaucrats.[12] According to this *liberal* hypothesis, entrepreneurial regulators step in on behalf of aggrieved consumers. Their goal may be to capture political advantage, to secure bureaucratic independence, or to act on a conviction about the consumer's plight.[13]

Environmental Regulation in Europe," *British Journal of Political Science* 33/4 (October 2003): 557–80.

10. Mark Pollack, "Representing Diffuse Interests in EC Policy-making," *Journal of European Public Policy* 4/4 (December 1997); Michelle P. Egan, *Constructing a European Market: Standards, Regulation, and Governance* (Oxford: Oxford University Press, 2001); Paulette Kurzer, *Markets and Moral Regulation: Cultural Change in the European Union* (Cambridge: Cambridge University Press, 2001); and Wade Jacoby, *The Enlargement of the European Union and NATO: Ordering from the Menu in Central Europe* (Cambridge: Cambridge University Press, 2004).

11. George J. Stigler, *The Citizen and the State: Essays on Regulation* (Chicago: University of Chicago Press, 1975); and Sam Peltzman, "Toward a More General Theory of Regulation," *Journal of Law and Economics* 19 (August 1976): 211–40.

12. Sykes, *Product Standards.*

13. James Q. Wilson, *Bureaucracy: What Government Agencies Do and Why They Do It* (New York: Basic Books, 1989); and James Q. Wilson, "The Politics of Regulation," in *The Politics of Regulation,* ed. James Q. Wilson (New York: Basic Books, 1980), 357–94.

But once they decide to act, these policy entrepreneurs survey regulatory options and then select among known policy solutions in an economically optimal way.[14] In the liberal view of policy formation, we should tend to observe policy convergence around successful regulatory options. Moreover, policymaking should be dictated by elite problem-solving combined with extensive borrowing.

The liberal explanation offers only limited insights into the process of consumer protection in France and Germany. While government legislators and bureaucrats did play a role in promoting government policies towards consumers, they did not do so in a vacuum. They instead relied on organized consumer groups to advocate relevant consumer interests and to serve as a counterweight to industry. Both French and German governments supported independent consumer groups precisely so that they could play this balancing role. While technocrats surveyed the consumer protection strategies adopted in other countries, they tailored their own approaches— often through a messy process of trial and error—to their domestic constituencies. The very fact of systematic divergence in France and Germany suggests the weakness of the liberal account.

The most striking failures of the liberal account came in those areas of consumer regulation that were both obscure and complex. Policy analysts have noted that regulatory discretion is greatest in cases of low issue salience (that is, low public visibility) and high task complexity.[15] Although arguably all areas of consumer protection fall into this category, few had lower salience or higher complexity than consumer contract regulation. Because consumer contracts had never before been regulated, policymakers were also working with a blank slate. If any policy area was going to give technical experts wide latitude, this was it. But the reality was very different. Policymakers within the French and German economics ministries were never able to escape the pressures of consumer and producer interests. In Germany, the Bundestag ended up negotiating acceptable terms for consumer contracts under intensive scrutiny from industry and consumer representatives. Even in France, where regulatory autonomy is commonly thought to be high, policymakers were unable to shape the regulatory environment to their own goals. Administrative efforts to ban specific kinds of contract terms repeatedly failed. National regulators were not entirely powerless, but they lacked the capability and legitimacy to dictate their own solutions to the new challenge. They ended up delegating this responsibility, first to negotiations arranged between consumers and producers and then, with the failure of negotiations, to the French legal system. Despite the high complexity and low salience of the issues involved in consumer contracts, government regulators had insufficient autonomy to design their own solutions.

A third, *cultural,* explanation emphasizes the ways in which past regulatory experiences and institutional legacies conditioned domestic responses to the challenge

14. Hugh Heclo, *Modern Social Politics in Britain and Sweden: From Relief to Income Maintenance* (New Haven: Yale University Press, 1974).

15. Wilson, "The Politics of Regulation"; William T. Gormley, "Regulatory Issue-Networks in a Federal System," *Polity* 18 (1985–86): 595–620.

of consumer regulation.[16] This cultural view draws on the lessons of research on institutional adaptation suggesting that new areas of regulatory policy are addressed through familiar regulatory strategies and institutional configurations.[17] Researchers who study the institutional bases of risk perception in particular have found that persistent structural features of society may dictate the kinds of risks that become publicly and politically salient.[18] If this view is correct, we should find strong continuity in national policy over time, with past institutional configurations constraining future policy options.

There is surprisingly little evidence that national cultural and institutional traditions were important to the regulation of consumption. First, national traditions of popular protest appear to offer little explanatory power in the case of consumer mobilization. While Germany has been noted for strong citizen movements, consumerism did not follow the track of popular mobilization that characterized issues such as the protests for environmental safeguards or against nuclear proliferation. In France, by contrast, consumer groups mobilized actively in a country traditionally characterized by weak civic engagement. One of the challenges in understanding French and German consumer policies is to explain why consumers organized in unexpected ways given the associational traditions in which they emerged.

Second, the case of consumer protection highlights the creative ways in which competing societal interest groups were able to draw on overlapping national regulatory traditions to legitimate often opposing views. The indeterminacy of national traditions was particularly striking in France. On first inspection, the interventionist *protection* model that eventually emerged in France appears to be a direct extension of France's strong administrative state. It hardly seems surprising that the French state should step in to regulate the consumer market in the face of new consumer grievances and dangerous product failures. What is surprising is how contingent this outcome seems to have been. Before France's statist tradition was invoked, consumer advocates experimented extensively with negotiated solutions, ones that drew on a different French intellectual tradition with roots in associational liberalism.[19] In the negotiation approach, consumers were portrayed as analogous

16. Jacqueline Poelmans, *L'Europe et les consommateurs* (Brussels: Editions Labor, 1978); Roberta Sassetilli, *Power Balance in the Consumption Sphere: Reconsidering Consumer Protection Organisations* (Florence: European University Institute Working Paper, 1995); Vogel, "When Interests Are Not Preferences"; Paulette Kurzer, *Markets and Moral Regulation: Cultural Change in the European Union* (Cambridge: Cambridge University Press, 2001); and David Vogel and Jabril Bensedrine, "Comparing Risk Regulation in the United States and France: Asbestos, Aids, and Genetically Modified Agriculture," *French Politics, Culture and Society* 20 / 1 (Spring 2002), 26.

17. Peter A. Hall, "The Case of Economic Policymaking in Britain," *Comparative Politics* (April 1993).

18. Mary Douglas and Aaron Wildavsky, *Risk and Culture: An Essay on the Selection of Technical and Environmental Dangers* (Berkeley: University of California Press, 1982); and Ulrich Beck, *Risk Society: Towards a New Modernity*, trans. Mark Ritter (London: Sage Publications, 1992), 24.

19. Jonah D. Levy, *Tocqueville's Revenge: State, Society, and Economy in Contemporary France* (Cambridge: Harvard University Press, 1999).

to workers, with the right to negotiate agreements with producers directly. That this experiment eventually failed does not necessarily mean that it could not have succeeded under somewhat different historical circumstances. France's consumer protection experience suggests that the ways in which national regulatory traditions are perpetuated may be more complicated than is often assumed in institutional analysis that emphasizes path dependency. Rather than imposing specific policy models on government regulators, national institutional traditions may emerge as the repeated outcome of iterated policy experiments that follow similar patterns of experimentation, evaluation, and adoption.

One final explanation for national consumer protection policies must be considered. Do these perhaps simply reflect the partisan orientation of the governments that enacted the consumer protection legislation? It seems plausible that right-wing governments would tend to support business interests while left-wing governments would support consumers. But the French and German cases give no indication of partisan influence. In Germany, consumer protection policies initiated under Social Democratic control in the 1970s were actively supported under the Christian Democrats in the 1980s. Surveys conducted by German consumer groups in 1969 and 1976 found no appreciable difference in the consumer policy priorities of the two major parties.[20] In France, where major shifts in policy did occur, these shifts did not coincide with changes in government leadership. France's move to a negotiation strategy of consumer protection occurred in 1978, in the middle of the presidency of Valéry Giscard d'Estaing. The subsequent move to a protection strategy occurred in 1983, again deep into the presidency of François Mitterrand. It appears that consumer politics aligned poorly with traditional partisan issues, leaving the major political parties unsure of what positions they should endorse.

Each of these alternative theories fails to explain important elements of the emergence of consumer protection in France and Germany. Each also overlooks the specific politics of consumption. As the history of consumer protection movements in France and Germany makes clear, the installation of consumer protections was a highly contentious process. Consumer groups took to the streets for boycotts and rallies; producers lobbied the government and filed lawsuits against consumer groups; government agencies struggled to define the consumer interest and to understand their role in defending it; judges reinterpreted old laws in new and surprising ways. A historically authentic account of the rise of consumer capitalism must confront the rich and often contentious texture of this transformation.

One implication of this analysis is that the politics of consumer protection is likely to differ significantly from that of environmental politics. The difference is in part conceptual. Environmental concerns focus on public goods that, because of free rider problems, are underprovided by private actors. These public goods include clean air, stable climate, and species diversity. Consumer concerns focus instead on

---

20. See "Verbraucherpolitik muß verstärkt werden," *Verbraucherpolitische Korrespondenz* 27 (15 September 1969), 2; "Die Vorstellungen der Parteien zur Verbraucherpolitik," *Verbraucherpolitische Korrespondenz* 39 (28 September 1976), 7.

private contractual issues that face no direct free rider challenge. These private goods include the safety of purchased products and protection against fraud. One of the puzzles of consumer protection is the application of public resources to secure goods that could in principle be privately contracted for. Moreover, where environmentalist concerns have typically embodied postmaterialist values, consumer concerns have normally been explicitly materialist. This difference in emphasis means that the priorities of the two groups often conflict. To the extent that environmental protections raise production costs or limit access to environmentally unfriendly products, for example, these may antagonize consumers who do not also share an environmentalist outlook. Conversely, environmentalists with strong ecological views may oppose the very premise of modern consumer capitalism. Research projects that combine the two policies—grouping them under the common framework of government protections of diffuse interests, or in the context of regulatory competition among regions—risk missing important differences in the dynamics of policy formation.[21]

Historically, consumer and environmental movements emerged separately, and with different organizations, memberships, and motivations. The difference is evident when the consumer movement is compared to the environmental movement in France and Germany. Since the early 1970s, surveys have consistently found a higher degree both of citizen mobilization and of radicalism in the German environmental movement than in its French counterpart.[22] On a standardized index of mobilization from 1975 to 1989, for example, one set of researchers coded Germany an 11 and France a 2 (Switzerland, the highest-ranked, was a 16).[23] In surveys conducted during the 1980s, 31 percent of Germans described themselves as environmental activists, compared to only 13 percent of French.[24] Dieter Rucht, an expert on West European environmental movements, characterizes French grass-roots environmental groups as "very weak" and their West German counterparts as "very strong."[25] The German environmental movement, in other words, looks remarkably

21. See, for example, Pollack, "Representing Diffuse Interests"; Vogel, "The Hare and the Tortoise Revisited"; Murphy, *The Structure of Regulatory Competition.*

22. Dieter Rucht, "Impact of Environmental Movements in Western Societies," in *How Social Movements Matter,* ed. Marco Giugni, Doug McAdam, and Charles Tilly (Minneapolis: University of Minnesota Press, 1999), 216.

23. Hanspeter Kriesi, Ruud Koopmans, Jan Willem Duyvendak, and Marco Giugni, *New Social Movements in Western Europe* (London: University College London Press, 1995).

24. Robert Rohrschneider concurs with this view. He writes: "The environmental movement is very strong in Germany . . . and weaker in France." Robert Rohrschneider, "The Roots of Public Opinion toward New Social Movements: An Empirical Test of Competing Theories," *American Journal of Political Science* 34/1 (February 1990): 8. See also Dieter Fuchs and Dieter Rucht, "Support for New Social Movements in Five Western European Countries," in *A New Europe? Social Change and Political Transformation,* ed. Chris Rootes and Howard Davis (London: University College London Press: 1994).

25. Dieter Rucht, "The Impact of National Contexts on Social Movement Structures: A Cross-Movement and Cross-National Comparison," in *Comparative Perspectives on Social Movements,* ed. Doug McAdam, John D. McCarthy, and Mayer N. Zald (Cambridge: Cambridge University Press, 1996), 197–98.

similar to the French consumer movement and vice versa. This suggests that different political dynamics are at work in the two policy areas.

In certain cases, consumer and environmental concerns have coincided. In France, consumer group evaluations of the quality of French beaches in the 1970s led them to focus on the environmental damage of the 1978 Amoco-Cadiz oil spill off the coast of Brittany.[26] More recently, concerns about genetically modified organisms have bridged consumer concerns about food safety and environmental concerns about their likely impact on the genetic makeup of other plants and animals. In France, where GMOs emerged primarily as a food safety issue, policymakers and the public favored a strict regulation of "Frankenfoods." In Germany, where GMOs were the focus primarily of environmental concerns, regulators have pushed for a less stringent EU response.[27] The difference was played out within the European Union, where responsibility for GMOs was transferred in the late 1990s from the consumer protection dossier to the directorate general on the environment.[28] This dual nature of the GMO debate has created an interesting regulatory dynamic. While different national interpretations of GMO risk helped to generate broad support for EU regulation, they also made it more difficult to come to agreement on a unified regulatory framework.[29]

Consumer Protection and Globalization

Since the 1970s, consumer markets in the advanced industrial countries have experienced two apparently opposing trends: liberalization in the interest of greater competition and trade and regulation in the interest of consumer protection. The two trends share a common goal of improving consumer welfare, yet they exist in tension. Consumer protections raise nontariff barriers to trade; free trade confronts consumers with potentially dangerous products and business practices from less regulated markets abroad. The result has been a difficult tradeoff in which policymakers have had to balance the costs and benefits of greater liberalization and greater protection. In France and Germany, this balancing act took place as a contest of ideas about the nature of the consumer interest in modern society. Although the solutions they found were different, each drew a deep legitimacy from the political contest out of which it was forged.

This double movement of consumer markets—combining liberalization and pro-

26. François Daujam, *Information et pouvoir des consommateurs: Le rôle de l'Union fédérale des consommateurs,* doctoral thesis, University of Toulouse, 29 April 1980, 32–33.

27. Grace Skogstad, "Legitimacy and / or Policy Effectiveness?" 336; and Sheila Jasanoff, "Product, Process, or Program: Three Cultures and the Regulation of Biotechnology," in *Resistance to New Technology,* ed. Martin Bauer (Cambridge University Press, 1995), 323.

28. Herbert Gottweis, "Regulating Genetic Engineering in the European Union: A Post-structuralist Perspective," in *The Transformation of Governance in the European Union,* ed. Rainer Eising and Beate Kohler-Koch (London: Routledge, 1999).

29. Julia Black, "Regulation as Facilitation: Negotiating the Genetic Revolution," *Modern Law Review* 61 / 5 (1998): 650.

tective regulation—has also posed challenges for international institutions. The European Union and the World Trade Organization, for example, are primarily charged with promoting trade. In doing so they confront issues of consumer protection for which they originally had little or no specific political mandate. This makes consumer protection policy both a potential opportunity and a potential risk. To the extent that international institutions can be seen to protect what are perceived as basic rights to consumer safety, they may draw greater legitimacy to the purposes of their organizations. Yet their formal goals of promoting free trade mean that they must promote the same solutions for different countries—a move that risks undermining the legitimacy of the international institutions in countries whose standards of protection must be reduced. This book has focused on domestic policies. Lessons from the history of national consumer protection initiatives may also help to clarify the challenges that these international institutions face.

The founding document of the European Community (EC), the 1957 Treaty of Rome, makes no mention of the consumer. Indeed, early actions to create a common market served to mobilize consumers in the member states. Efforts to develop a standard for European jams squared off French consumers of lumpy jam against Dutch advocates of smooth jams.[30] German consumers opposed a "Euro-Chocolate" standard on the grounds that it would weaken Germany's chocolate quality by allowing chemical extraction of cocoa butter from cocoa beans.[31] French and German consumer groups took aim at the common agricultural policy, which they felt came at the expense of European consumers. A series of protracted debates over "euro-bread," "euro-beer," and other "euro-" products finally led national leaders to call for a formal consumer representation within the EC at the Paris Summit in 1972.

This move launched a decade of great expectations in European consumer protection. The European Office of Consumer Unions (Bureau européen des unions de consommateurs, BEUC) was founded in 1972. The following year, the European Commission created the Consumers' Consultative Committee to consult on new consumer initiatives. In 1975, the commission issued its first preliminary program on consumer protection and information policy. A second program followed in 1981. These programs elaborated specific new rights for consumers: safety, protection of economic interests, redress, information, and representation.[32] Over the course of the 1970s, the Committee of Ministers adopted draft directives that would give substance to these rights. These included texts on misleading advertising (1972), door-to-door sales (1973), unfair clauses in contracts (1976), post-sale service (1978), consumer representation in standardization bodies (1979), consumer education and information (1971 and 1979), protection and defense of consumer collective interests (1978), consumer legal assistance (1981), and consumer access to justice

30. Michelle Egan, *Constructing a European Market* (Oxford: Oxford University Press, 2001), 74–77.

31. "Brusseler Schokolade für uns ungenießbar!" *Verbraucherpolitische Korrespondenz* 8 (15 March 1967), 8.

32. Hans-Wolfgang Micklitz and Stephen Weatherill, "Consumer Policy in the European Community: Before and After Maastricht," *Journal of Consumer Policy* 16 (1993): 293.

(1981).[33] Most of these draft initiatives paralleled domestic policy efforts existing in the individual member states to address the same problems. The EC proposals pursued a strategy of "positive harmonization," embracing solutions that would impose some of the strongest policy solutions on all member states. Depending on the area of policy, this approach drew opposition from almost every member state. Britain, for example, argued that the proposed advertising directive would undermine its own system of self-regulation.[34] The product liability text embraced a strict standard of liability, one that was approved by France but strongly opposed by Germany.[35] Conversely, the text on unfair clauses in contracts embraced a list of prohibited clauses that was approved by Germany but opposed by France. Because the Treaty of Rome required unanimous support for directives, none of these early consumer protection initiatives were ratified. In 1981, Richard Lawson wrote starkly: "Few would deny that the Community has altogether failed to make the progress [in consumer protection] anticipated in 1975."[36]

Ironically, it was only once the very different domestic French and German consumer protection strategies had been fully implemented that EC initiatives began to see success. The 1980s saw an apparent turnaround in the EC's initiative on consumer protection. Directives that had failed in the 1970s were redrafted and passed during the 1980s and early 1990s. These included directives on misleading advertising (1984), liability for defective products (1985), doorstep selling (1985), consumer credit (1987, amended 1990), toy safety (1988), general product safety (1992), and unfair contract terms (1993).[37] The introduction of qualified majority voting with the Single Europe Act in 1987 facilitated the process for later legislation. The success of the earlier directives, however, reflected a new strategy of policy approximation that might be called "ambiguous harmonization." While few of the obstacles to policy harmonization that had come to light in the 1970s had been overcome, the new texts were carefully written to gloss over contentious issues. The new product liability directive called for strict liability but offered exemptions for the uncertainties of product development (the "development defense") and for agricultural products. The directive on unfair contract terms included a "provisional grey list" (modeled on the German approach) of illicit contract terms, but member states

33. Thierry M. Bourgoignie, "Consumer Law and the European Community: Issues and Prospects," in *Integration through Law: Europe and the American Federal Experience,* ed. Thierry Bourgoignie and David Trubek (Berlin: Walter de Gruyter, 1987), 95; and *Protection du consommateur* (Strasbourg, France: Conseil de l'Europe, 1979).

34. Richard Lawson, "Consumer Protection: A World Perspective," in *Consumer Legislation* (Paris: International Chamber of Commerce and Industry, 1981), 51–52.

35. Anita Bernstein, "L'Harmonie Dissonante: Strict Products Liability Attempted in the European Community," *Virginia Journal of International Law* 31 (Summer 1991): 676.

36. Lawson was not alone in his assessment. Thierry Bourgoignie, one of Europe's top legal scholars on consumer protection, wrote several years later: "the record of EC actions as they affect consumers . . . is quite negative." Lawson, "Consumer Protection," 51; and Bourgoignie, "Consumer Law," 97.

37. This is only a small sample of consumer legislative activity of the commission during this period. Micklitz and Weatherill, "Consumer Policy," 291.

could decide whether or not to enforce these.[38] Ambiguity surrounded the very identity of the consumer. Germany had adopted strategies on consumer protection that did not formally distinguish between consumers as end-users and other kinds of economic actors, such as small traders. French policy explicitly identified consumers as nonprofessional end users. In most cases, EU directives simply did not define who the consumer was.

In some important respects, the "ambiguous harmonization" approach was a success. It broke the logjam of consumer protection within the EU. It established a common minimum standard of protection that made consumer protection a part of the *acquis communautaire*. It initiated a debate at the European level over basic issues of consumer protection. It also posed challenges for member states that had already implemented domestic strategies of consumer protection. Some of these challenges were technical. The conceptual framing of issues in EU directives often matched poorly with their domestic treatment. Directives were therefore frequently implemented in domestic legislation without any attempt to reconcile them with previous legislation. Moreover, important aspects of national consumer protection had been elaborated through judge-made law, and the new directives typically did not address these provisions. Perhaps most surprisingly, national legislators were extremely hesitant to lower the level of consumer protection offered by their own domestic provisions in the interest of greater market integration. France resisted implementing the product liability for fifteen years, for example, because both consumer *and* producer groups opposed the lower level of liability that the European solution provided.[39] For Germany, which implemented the directive in 1990, the impact has been uncertain at best. Klaus Tonner writes: "The outcome of the new act is that product liability legislation is even more complicated than before, and the legal situation of people who suffered damages from hazardous products has hardly been improved."[40]

In the 1970s, attempts to pursue market integration through common EC standards of consumer protection failed over objections of individual states. The principle of mutual recognition espoused in the 1979 *Cassis de Dijon* case came as a formal recognition of this failure.[41] But by embracing diverse national approaches,

---

38. "Les clauses abusives et la présentation des contrats dans la loi no. 95–96 du 1er février 1995," *Recueil Dalloz Sirey* 14 (1995): 99–108.

39. "La responsabilité du fait des produits," *Consommateurs actualités* 528 (30 July 1988), 9–12; and Dominique Rambure, "Le nouveau droit de la résponsabilité du fait des produits défectueux," *CNPF Patronat* 497 (January–February 1988): 75.

40. Klaus Tonner, "The European Influence on German Consumer Law," *Journal of Consumer Policy* 17/1 (1994): 46. See also Pierre Legrand, "European Legal Systems Are Not Converging," *International and Comparative Law Quarterly* (1996).

41. The German firm Rewe, planning to import cassis de Dijon, found that French cassis did not have a sufficiently high alcohol content (10–20 percent instead of over 32 percent) to meet German product standards. The ECJ decided in Rewe's favor, arguing that (1) less alcohol is not more dangerous, and (2) the relevant information was on the label. Régine Loosli, "Entre cassis et pommes: Libre circulation des produits et protection des consommateurs," *Consommateurs actualité* 270 (9 January 1981), 9.

Cassis de Dijon raised concerns—especially among countries with high protection standards—over a potential regulatory race to the bottom.[42] In the following decade, during the 1980s and early 1990s, member states accepted ambiguous directives in order to further market integration and to set a common baseline for all member states. These efforts incorporated consumer protection into the common market project but without attempting to elaborate entirely new consumer rights at the EC level.[43]

Europe today appears to be in a third stage of consumer protection. Since the mid-1990s, European Union policymakers have once again begun trying to pursue consumer protection as a distinct goal of the EU. This approach has three components. First, the Maastricht Treaty added, for the first time, an explicit reference to consumer protection to the Treaty of the European Union. Article 129(a) formalizes a strategy of "minimum harmonization." Under this provision, member states always enjoy the right to enforce stronger standards than those embraced by community legislation. Article 153 of the Amsterdam Treaty further called for consumer protection to be incorporated into new community policies. Second, the EU has created a series of new institutions to promote consumer protection at the community level. These include a Directorate General for Health and Consumer Protection (DG XXIV–1995), the European Medicines Agency (EMEA–1995), the European Consumer Voice in Standardization (ANEC–1995), the Transatlantic Consumer Dialogue (1998), the European Food Safety Authority (EFSA–2002), and the European Consumer Consultative Group (2003). Third, the EU has begun to provide funds to support national consumer groups, setting aside 72 million Euros to support these groups from 2004 to 2007.[44]

The goal of this new approach has been to earn legitimacy for EU-level consumer policies by creating the context for policy discourse among consumers within the EU itself. Recent product concerns—bovine spongiform encephalopathy (BSE), hormone-treated beef, genetically modified organisms (GMOs), toys treated with phthalates—have helped to focus attention on these new institutions. In most cases, they have provided an opportunity for the EU to define a pro-consumer agenda that does not directly conflict with existing domestic consumer protection policies. This new activism, one that in many cases has pushed EU regulatory standards beyond those developed in the United States, has the potential to increase the legitimacy of the European project.[45] By advocating new consumer protections as basic rights, the EU can reinforce its own legitimacy in the absence of greater democratic accountability.

But the opportunity also comes with risks. The challenge for the EU is that most

---

42. Loosli, "Entre cassis et pommes," 14; and Pierre Marleix, "Que peuvent espérer en 1981 les consommateurs?" *Les cahiers de l'AFOC* (May 1981): 34.

43. The Council Directive of 1986 on consumer protection emphasized consumer access and market choice. It no longer mentioned the consumer rights that had dominated EC consumer policy statements in the previous decade. Micklitz and Weatherill, "Consumer Policy," 294.

44. *Official Journal of the European Union* 5/3 (9 January 2004).

45. Vogel, "The Hare and the Tortoise Revisited."

of the consumer protections are still implemented and enforced at the domestic level, in the framework of the domestic responses to consumer protection that emerged in the 1970s and 1980s. Even the new accession countries, ones with little institutional legacy in consumer protection, appear to be incorporating EU consumer policies that depend in different ways on their domestic institutional contexts.[46] Because these national policies are closely tied to distinctive ideas of consumer citizenship, further efforts to harmonize national practice risk undermining, rather than bolstering, the EU's newly won legitimacy among consumers. A set of decisions by the European Court of Justice in 2002 highlighted this risk. In three cases bearing on product liability, the court found that strict domestic rules governing product liability in Spain, France, and Greece were inconsistent with the less stringent terms of the EU product liability directive.[47] In an unusual move, one that offered a strong endorsement of member state prerogative, the Council of Ministers chastised the court for its narrow interpretation and proposed to amend the directive to permit more stringent national treatment.[48] The challenge for the EU will be to get this balance right: working toward market integration while also continuing to accept a reasonable degree of divergence among national market rules.

The challenge is not limited to the European Union. With the proliferation of free-trade agreements, distinctive national consumer protection policies are likely to come under increasing scrutiny by international institutions. In February 1998, for example, the Dispute Settlement Body of the World Trade Organization found that the European Union's ban on hormone-treated beef was not grounded in sufficient scientific risk assessment.[49] In July 1999, Canada and the United States responded by imposing elevated tariffs on a selection of EU products. The EU ban on the use of hormones in beef had its roots in domestic disputes between consumers and beef producers that had emerged twenty years earlier in 1979. At the time, the France consumer association UFC had called for a boycott of all hormone-treated veal products.[50] This was quickly echoed by a similar consumer boycott in Germany.[51] In October 1980, the French agriculture ministry and a set of French consumer groups came to agreement on a "veal charter" that banned hormone use and advocated periodic testing, animal tracking, and a provision for seizing lots of veal

46. Jacoby, *The Enlargement of the European Union and NATO.*

47. *Victoria González Sánchez v. Medicina Asturiana SA* (C-192/25), *Commission v. France* (C-52/00), and *Commission v. Greece* (C-154/00), 25 April 2002.

48. Because the Product Liability Directive was ratified before the introduction of Chapter 129(a) in the Maastricht Treaty, the court found that more stringent national policies were inconsistent with the directive, which does not itself include a minimum-harmonization provision. Christophe U. Schmidt, "Co-ordination problems between European and national private law," draft, EUI, 7.

49. Their finding was based on the provision in the Sanitary and Phytosanitary (SPS) Agreement setting a scientific basis for acceptable consumer protections.

50. Rosemonde Pujol, "Boycott ou dissuasion?" *Le Figaro,* 18–19 May 1985.

51. "Autofahrer gegen Ölkonzerne: Boykott letzte Waffe der Konsumenten," *Frankfurter Rundschau,* 24 July 1982.

that showed signs of hormone use.[52] The French charter became the basis for the 1981 European decision to stop both hormone-beef production and imports.[53]

Issues of consumer protection are invariably complex. They bring together highly technical scientific inquiry with the diffuse interests of the consuming public. The regulation of consumer markets in the 1970s and 1980s teaches us that such issues are often contentious. The challenge for international institutions, both the EU and the WTO, is to recognize the legitimacy of the consumer protection policies that have emerged from this contentious process. The benefits of economic liberalization are based on the continued protection of consumers against the risks that accompany free commerce. This means that successful international institutions can build their legitimacy only by finding a balance between their primary goal of free markets and the legacy of consumer rights that different countries have elaborated to promote a confident consumer culture.

Consumer protection today remains primarily national. These national consumer protection regimes have earned a high level of legitimacy through the process of political contestation out of which they emerged. They are understood by citizens to respond to genuine consumer interests. A domestic polity that has erected elaborate institutions to ensure product safety will not easily cast these aside for somewhat lower prices for products from abroad. The benefits of safety, measured by the standards that emerged in each individual country, must be weighed fairly against the benefits of lower prices and greater competition. This does not mean that national divergence must persist. But greater openness comes with costs, and such costs must ultimately be accounted.

52. *Les Échos*, 8 October 1980, 8.
53. For a more detailed account, see Tim Josling, Donna Roberts, and Ayesha Hassan, "The Beef-Hormone Dispute and its Implications for Trade Policy" (http://iis-db.stanford.edu/pubs/11379/HORMrev.pdf).

INDEX

Page numbers with an *f* indicate figures; those with a *t*
indicate tables; those with an *n* indicate footnotes.

179

Cornell Studies in Political Economy

The Nordic States and European Unity by Christine Ingebritsen

The Paradox of Continental Production: National Investment Policies in North America by Barbara Jenkins

The Government of Money: Monetarism in Germany and the United States by Peter A. Johnson

A World of Regions: Asia and Europe in the American Imperium by Peter J. Katzenstein

Corporatism and Change: Austria, Switzerland, and the Politics of Industry by Peter J. Katzenstein

Cultural Norms and National Security: Police and Military in Postwar Japan by Peter J. Katzenstein

Small States in World Markets: Industrial Policy in Europe by Peter J. Katzenstein

Industry and Politics in West Germany: Toward the Third Republic edited by Peter J. Katzenstein

Beyond Japan: The Dynamics of East Asian Regionalism edited by Peter J. Katzenstein and Takashi Shiraishi

Monetary Orders: Ambiguous Economics, Ubiquitous Politics edited by Jonathan Kirshner

Norms in International Relations: The Struggle against Apartheid by Audie Jeanne Klotz

International Regimes edited by Stephen D. Krasner

Disparaged Success: Labor Politics in Postwar Japan by Ikuo Kume

Business and Banking: Political Change and Economic Integration in Western Europe by Paulette Kurzer

Power, Protection, and Free Trade: International Sources of U.S. Commercial Strategy, 1887–1939 by David A. Lake

Money Rules: The New Politics of Finance in Britain and Japan by Henry Laurence

Why Syria Goes to War: Thirty Years of Confrontation by Fred H. Lawson

The Rules of Play: National Identity and the Shaping of Japanese Leisure by David Leheny

Remaking the Italian Economy by Richard M. Locke

France after Hegemony: International Change and Financial Reform by Michael Loriaux

The Power of Institutions: Political Architecture and Governance by Andrew MacIntyre

Economic Containment: CoCom and the Politics of East-West Trade by Michael Mastanduno

Business and the State in Developing Countries edited by Sylvia Maxfield and Ben Ross Schneider

The Currency of Ideas: Monetary Politics in the European Union by Kathleen R. McNamara

The Choice for Europe: Social Purpose and State Power from Messina to Maastricht by Andrew Moravcsik

At Home Abroad: Identity and Power in American Foreign Policy by Henry R. Nau

Collective Action in East Asia: How Ruling Parties Shape Industrial Policy by Gregory W. Noble

Mercantile States and the World Oil Cartel, 1900–1939 by Gregory P. Nowell

Negotiating the World Economy by John S. Odell

Opening Financial Markets: Banking Politics on the Pacific Rim by Louis W. Pauly

Who Elected the Bankers? Surveillance and Control in the World Economy by Louis W. Pauly

Regime Shift: Comparative Dynamics of the Japanese Political Economy by T. J. Pempel

Remapping Asia: The Emergence of Regional Connectedness edited by T. J. Pempel

Remapping East Asia: The Construction of a Region edited by T. J. Pempel

The Politics of the Asian Economic Crisis edited by T. J. Pempel

The Limits of Social Democracy: Investment Politics in Sweden by Jonas Pontusson

The Fruits of Fascism: Postwar Prosperity in Historical Perspective by Simon Reich

The Business of the Japanese State: Energy Markets in Comparative and Historical Perspective by Richard J. Samuels

"Rich Nation, Strong Army": National Security and the Technological Transformation of Japan by Richard J. Samuels

Crisis and Choice in European Social Democracy by Fritz W. Scharpf, translated by Ruth Crowley and Fred Thompson

Europeanization of Central and Eastern Europe edited by Frank Schimmelfennig and Ulrich Sedelmeier